WHAT EVERYONE NEEDS TO KNOW ABOUT ISLAM

SECOND EDITION

WHAT EVERYONE NEEDS TO KNOW ABOUT ISLAM

SECOND EDITION

JOHN L. ESPOSITO

OXFORD
UNIVERSITY PRESS

Oxford University Press, Inc., publishes works that further
Oxford University's objective of excellence
in research, scholarship, and education.

Oxford   New York
Auckland   Cape Town   Dar es Salaam   Hong Kong   Karachi
Kuala Lumpur   Madrid   Melbourne   Mexico City   Nairobi
New Delhi   Shanghai   Taipei   Toronto

With offices in
Argentina   Austria   Brazil   Chile   Czech Republic   France   Greece
Guatemala   Hungary   Italy   Japan   Poland   Portugal   Singapore
South Korea   Switzerland   Thailand   Turkey   Ukraine   Vietnam

Copyright © 2011 by Oxford University Press, Inc.

Published by Oxford University Press, Inc.
198 Madison Avenue, New York, NY 10016

www.oup.com

Oxford is a registered trademark of Oxford University Press

Library of Congress Cataloging-in-Publication Data
Esposito, John L.
What everyone needs to know about Islam / John L. Esposito. — 2nd ed.
p.   cm.
Includes index.
ISBN 978-0-19-979413-3 (hardcover) — ISBN 978-0-19-979423-2 (ebook)
1. Islam--Essence, genius, nature.   I. Title.
BP163.E85 2011
297—dc22   2010044252

1 3 5 7 9 8 6 4 2

Printed in the United States of America
on acid-free paper

For Jean,
Who Makes All Things Possible

CONTENTS

PREFACE   xiii
ACKNOWLEDGMENTS   xvii

General Information   3

Why do we need to know about Islam?   3
Are all Muslims the same?   3
How many Muslims are there, and where do they live?   4

Faith   5

What do Muslims believe?   5
Why do Muslims say they are descended from Abraham?   6
How did Islam originate?   7
What is the Muslim scripture?   9
Why is Arabic so important in Islam?   10
What role does Muhammad play in Muslim life?   11
Was Muhammad a prophet like the prophets in the Bible?   12
Why is so much known about Muhammad's life?   12
Why do Muslims object to images of Muhammad?   14
Did Muhammad have multiple wives?   15

What do Muslims believe about a worldwide Muslim community
(ummah)?   16

What are the core beliefs and practices that unite all Muslims?   18

What do Muslims do on the pilgrimage to Mecca?   22

What is the Kaaba?   23

What is the significance of Mecca?   24

How do Muslims pray?   25

Do Muslims believe in angels?   27

How do Muslims view the Day of Judgment?   28

Do Muslims believe in heaven and hell?   29

What are Muslim women promised in the afterlife?   31

Do Muslims believe in saints?   31

Do Muslims believe in sin and repentance?   32

What do Muslims believe about Mary and Jesus?   33

Do Muslims have a Sabbath like Jews and Christians?   35

Do Muslims have a weekly worship service?   35

Do Muslims have religious holidays or holy days?   36

Does Islam have a clergy?   37

What is a mosque?   38

What is an Islamic center?   40

What is a madrasa?   40

Are there any divisions in Islam?   42

What is the difference between Sunni and Shii Muslims?   48

What are the divisions among Shii Muslims?   51

Who is the Aga Khan?   52

What is Wahhabi Islam?   53

What is Salafi Islam?   55

Is there a difference between Muslims and Black Muslims?   57

Who are the Sufis?   61

Who are these Islamic fundamentalists?   63

Is Islam medieval and against change?   65

Is Islam compatible with modernization?   67

Are there any modern Muslim thinkers or reformers?   68

Islam and Other Religions   72

Do Muslims believe Islam is the only true religion?   72

What about Muslim religious intolerance?   73

How is Islam similar to Christianity and Judaism?   76

How do Muslims view Judaism? Christianity?   77

Why do Muslims persecute Christians in Muslim countries?   78

Haven't Jews and Christians always been enemies of Islam?   81

Who won the Crusades?   87

Are Muslims involved in interfaith dialogue?   90

Customs and Culture   95

Why does Islam separate men and women?   95

Are women second-class citizens in Islam?   97

What do Muslims say about women's rights?   101

What kinds of roles did women play in early Islam?   104

Why do Muslim women wear veils and long garments?   105

Why do Muslim men wear turbans or caps?   109

Why do Muslim men wear beards?   109

Does Islam require circumcision?   110

Is the practice of Muslim arranged marriages changing?   111

Can Muslim men have more than one wife?   112

Can Muslims marry non-Muslims?   113

What does Islam have to say about domestic violence?   114

How does Islam treat divorce?   116

Why are Muslims reluctant to shake hands?   118

How do Muslims feel about pets, or petting animals?   118

What is Islam's attitude toward alcohol and pork?   119

Why are Muslims against dancing?   121

Why are some Muslims opposed to music?   122

What is Muslim hip-hop?   123

How do Muslims greet each other, and why?   127

Why do Muslims say "Peace be upon him?" What does PBUH mean?   128

How does Islam handle burial and cremation?   128

What does Islam say about the environment?   129

Violence and Terrorism   133

What is jihad?   133

Is there a global jihad today?   134

Is Islam a primary cause and driver of terrorism?   137

How can Islam be used to justify terrorism, hijacking, and hostage taking?   140

Does Islam permit suicide bombers?   142

Why are Muslims so violent?   145

Who are the "moderate" Muslims?   147

Why haven't Muslims denounced terrorism?   148

Do Muslims have a martyrdom complex?   151

Why do they hate us?   153

Why was Salman Rushdie condemned to death?   155

Society, Politics, and Economy   158

What is Islamic law?   158

Do Muslims today want Shariah law?   160

Will Muslims impose Shariah in the West?   162

What is the role of a fatwa?   166

What does Islamic law say about marriage, divorce, and inheritance?   167

What does Islam say about homosexuality?	173
What does Islam say about abortion?	173
What does Islam say about birth control?	174
How does Islam respond to stem cell research?	174
What does Islam say about slavery?	175
Is honor killing sanctioned by Islam?	176
How does Islam view female genital mutilation?	177
Why are Islamic punishments for crimes so harsh?	178
Why don't Muslims practice a separation of church and state?	180
Why does religion play such a big role in Muslim politics?	182
What is Islamism?	185
Why do Muslims reject secularism?	187
Why is Jerusalem so important to Muslims?	188
Is Islam compatible with democracy?	190
Are Muslims in America more loyal to the Quran or the Constitution?	191
Why aren't Muslim countries more democratic?	192
Does Islam reject Western capitalism?	193
What does Islam say about poverty and social justice?	194
Are Muslim Americans engaged in community service?	197
What is Islamic finance and banking?	199
Are there Muslim televangelists-preachers?	202
What role does the Internet play in Islam today?	207
What are the major obstacles to Islamic reform?	210
Is there a clash of civilizations?	212
What contributions have Muslims made to world civilizations?	214

Muslims in the West

	221
Who are the Muslims of America?	221
What kinds of problems do Muslims face in America?	224
Who and where are the Muslims of Europe?	228

What kinds of problems do Muslims in Europe face?   *231*

What is Islamophobia?   *234*

GLOSSARY   **241**

SUGGESTIONS FOR FURTHER READING   **251**

INDEX   **257**

PREFACE

What Everyone Needs to Know about Islam grew out of my experiences after the tragedy of 9/11. Like many of my colleagues, I was bombarded with questions about Islam and Muslims. While some questions centered on the attacks against the World Trade Center and the Pentagon, many were the same queries that have arisen time and again over the years in media interviews, government and corporate briefings, and presentations at universities and civic organizations: Why is Islam so violent? Does the Quran approve terrorism and suicide bombing? Is Islam compatible with modernity? Why do Muslims persecute Jews and Christians?

Reflecting on 9/11 and these persistent questions, I realized how much has changed and how much remains the same. Islam is the second-largest of the world's religions globally as well as in Europe, and it is the third-largest religion in America. Yet many in the West continued and still today continue to function within an enormous information vacuum, the same one I myself suffered from over thirty years ago. When I first encountered Islam in graduate school, I was astonished to discover that there was another Abrahamic faith. We had always talked about the Judeo-Christian connection, but never the Judeo-Christian-Islamic tradition. Why? If Muslims recognize and revere many of the major patriarchs and prophets of Judaism and Christianity (including

Abraham, Moses, and Jesus) and God's revealed books, the Torah and the Message (Gospels) of Jesus, why had I not been aware of this after all my years of liberal arts and theological training?

Learning about Islam gave me a new perspective, a new way of understanding history, from the Crusades and European colonialism to American and Soviet neocolonialism. Thus not only religion but also history, politics, and civilization, classical and modern, came alive for me. Today, however, many are still relying on media stereotypes, seeing Islam through distorted lenses that focus on terrorists, religious extremists, and oppressed women. The actions of a radicalized minority become equated with the faith of the mainstream majority. And yet Muslims are now an integral part of the religious landscape of America and Europe; they are increasingly our fellow citizens, neighbors, and colleagues.

Of course, many more introductions to Islam exist today than thirty years ago. I myself wrote *Islam: The Straight Path* and other books and articles that I have drawn upon in compiling this book. But many people today have specific questions and are looking for quick, brief, and direct answers, ones not easily found in historical and religious histories. *What Everyone Needs to Know About Islam* is meant to meet that need. Its primary purpose is to communicate what Muslims believe and why they do what they do. The book is not designed to be read from cover to cover; readers can look for answers to specific questions of interest to them. Because each question and answer is self-contained (it does not presume previous knowledge or that one has read previous answers), some material will appear in more than one answer.

Many of the questions, which have come from people in very diverse audiences, reflect a predisposition to believe that there is something profoundly wrong with Islam and Muslims. This underlying belief can result in the unconscious application of a double standard, approaching Islam differently than we would Judaism or Christianity when discussing how religion relates to extremism, militancy, violence, and terrorism. While we accept historical development in our own faiths with respect to pluralism, human rights, the status of women, and democratization, there is often a presumption that change is impossible in Islam.

I have had the good fortune to study, observe, and teach several religions, in particular Christianity and Islam as well as Judaism, Hinduism, and Buddhism. All these faiths have given meaning to and transformed the lives of millions of people throughout history. Regrettably, all also have had their dark side; religions that preach compassion, justice, and peace have been used—or abused—by extremists and militants. All are challenged in our modern and postmodern world to embrace a pluralism that balances affirmation of the truth of their faith with a respect for the truth to be found in others. For religion should be about righteousness, not self-righteousness.

Regrettably, the legacy of 9/11, continued terrorist attacks, and fears of growing radicalization have resulted in a sharp increase in Islamophobia (discrimination against Muslims because of their faith or race), hate speech, and violence. Politicians, far-right political commentators, hard-line Christian Zionist ministers, and a proliferation of anti-Muslim hate blogs have exploited the situation. They blur the distinction made by Presidents George W. Bush and Barack Obama and many other Americans between, on the one hand, Islam and the vast majority of Muslims and, on the other, a dangerous fraction of the world's Muslims. This latter group, like Jewish, Christian, Hindu, and other religious extremists, hijack religion to legitimate their acts of terror.

The encounter between the West and the Muslim world, between American and European Muslims and the Judeo-Christian and secular traditions of America and Europe, is not a clash of two separate and antithetical worlds. Jews, Christians, and Muslims are children of Abraham, part of a

Judeo-Christian-Islamic tradition. The world of Islam is global; its capitals and communities are not only Cairo, Damascus, Mecca, Jerusalem, Istanbul, Islamabad, Kuala Lumpur, and Jakarta but also London, Paris, Marseilles, Bonn, New York, Detroit, and Washington. Our common future demands a new, more inclusive sense of pluralism and tolerance built upon mutual understanding and respect. If we are ever to achieve such mutual understanding, an essential part of the package must be knowledge of what Islam teaches and what Muslims believe about Islam as well as what we believe about them.

ACKNOWLEDGMENTS

There are so many people to whom I am indebted for assistance with the first and now second edition. John Voll and Tamara Sonn are colleagues with whom I have collaborated closely on many projects and who can always be counted on for information, review, and feedback. Dalia Mogahed is executive director of Gallup's Muslims Studies Program and Gallup World Polls, which provide the most comprehensive and systematic polling of the Muslim world and have enabled us to listen to the voices of Muslims globally on critical issues. Much of that data is discussed in our co-authored book *Who Speaks for Islam? What a Billion Muslims Really Think*.

I have been fortunate to have a wonderful group of Georgetown graduate students as researchers at different stages of this project. Melanie Trexler was invaluable in research and proofing, always ready and quick to respond. Hadia Mubarak provided help at the end of the project.

Oxford University Press has long been my main publisher, and with good reason. I have been privileged to work with many first-class professionals. None has been more important than Cynthia Read, a gifted and remarkable editor as well as a good friend, with whom I have worked for almost thirty years. She has never ceased to be a source of encouragement and critical feedback and is a major reason why I have been an Oxford author all these years. I am fortunate to again have the pleasure of working with India Cooper as copy editor and Joellyn Ausanka as production editor, both consummate professionals.

Georgetown University and the Center for Muslim-Christian Understanding (now the Prince Alwaleed bin Talal Center for Muslim-Christian Understanding), which I helped create and direct, have been my academic home since 1993. The passing of Hasib Sabbagh, the man who envisioned the creation of the center and was our first major donor, was a great loss. Our current and future existence and work are now assured by a generous endowment from Prince Alwaleed bin Talal's Kingdom Foundation. I am especially indebted to the ongoing friendship and support of Georgetown's president, John J. Degioia. I am truly fortunate to have an extraordinary administrative team that enables the center and me "to run often and on time"! Alexa Poletto, associate director and our key administrative officer; Denisse Bonilla-Chaoui, executive assistant; Adam Holmes, program coordinator; and Mona Mogahed are outstanding professionals and friends. They are a seamless team without whom my colleagues and I could not function, let alone be as active, visible, and effective.

Whatever I may have accomplished or achieved in life is due in large part to the presence and influence of my family. My parents, John and Mary Esposito, provided the most loving and supportive environment, in which they motivated and inspired "their boys" to care about family, society, and education and to value values. My brothers, Lou and Rick, have carried on their legacy. Jean Esposito, wife, life partner, and best friend, during our forty-five years of marriage has always managed to balance her life, career, projects, and me and made all our life's experiences far richer than I could ever have imagined. She is my best editor and critic; without her encouragement, persistence, and research assistance I would never have finished my dissertation, let alone the many writing projects since that time. My journey in Islamic studies and religion and international affairs has been both my profession and vocation; my experiences with so many Muslims across the world have enriched my life immeasurably.

Washington, D.C.

September 2010

WHAT EVERYONE NEEDS TO KNOW ABOUT ISLAM

SECOND EDITION

GENERAL INFORMATION

Why do we need to know about Islam?

- Islam is the second-largest religion in the world (after Christianity) and will soon be the second-largest religion in America.
- Muslims are and increasingly will be our neighbors, colleagues at work, and fellow citizens.
- Although Islam is similar in many ways to Judaism and Christianity, most Americans and Europeans think of Muslims as strange, foreign, and frightening, inevitably linked to headline terrorist events. This state of affairs needs to change—and *can* change with better information and deeper understanding.
- We must put an end to Islamophobia and the spiral of fear, hatred, and violence, spawned by ignorance, that no longer only afflicts other countries but has come home to America.

Are all Muslims the same?

Since we are more familiar with Christianity, we know without thinking that there is great diversity in Christianity. Christianity expresses itself in many forms and contexts. There are different Christian churches or sects (from Baptists to Unitarians, Roman Catholics to Greek and Russian Orthodox), existing in different cultures (North American, Middle Eastern, European, Asian, and African). The result is a diversity of beliefs and practices within what we call Christianity. So too in Islam, although Muslims maintain that there is one divinely revealed and mandated Islam, there are many Muslim interpretations of Islam. There are two major branches, Sunni (85 percent of the world's Muslims) and Shii (15 percent). Within them are diverse schools of theology and law. In addition, Islam has a rich mystical tradition that includes many Sufi orders or brotherhoods. Islam represents a basic unity of belief within a rich cultural diversity. Islamic practice expresses itself in different ways within a vast array of cultures that extend from North Africa to Southeast Asia as well as Europe and America. (See pages 42–61 for more specific questions on this topic.)

How many Muslims are there, and where do they live?

Muslims represent the majority population in fifty-seven countries worldwide, including Indonesia, Bangladesh, Pakistan, Egypt, Iraq, and Nigeria. In addition, significant Muslim populations can be found in India, China, the Central Asian Republics, and Russia, as well as in Europe and America. Contrary to popular assumption, the majority of Muslims are not Arab. In fact only 20 percent of the world's 1.5 billion Muslims originate from Arab countries. The largest Muslim communities are to be found in Indonesia, Pakistan, Bangladesh, and India.

In recent decades, Islam has gone from being invisible in America and Europe to being a prominent feature in the religious landscape. Muslims represent a broad spectrum of racial and ethnic groups. The racial and ethnic diversity of Islam is represented in America by two broad Muslim groups: indigenous and immigrant. In America, in addition to indigenous African American Muslims (35 percent), prominent immigrant ethnic groups include Arabs, Pakistanis, Afghanis, Africans, Albanians, Bangladeshis, Bosnians, Indians, Iranians, Malaysians, Indonesians, and Turks.

FAITH

What do Muslims believe?

Like Jews and Christians, Muslims are monotheists. They believe in one God: the creator, sustainer, ruler, and judge of the universe. Muslims believe in prophets, not just the Prophet Muhammad but the prophets of the Hebrew Bible, including Abraham and Moses, and of the New Testament, Jesus and John the Baptist. They also believe in angels, heaven, hell, and the Day of Judgment. Islam acknowledges that God's revelation was received in the Torah, the Psalms, the Gospels, and the Quran: "We sent Jesus the son of Mary, confirming the Torah that had come before him: We sent him the Gospel in which is guidance and light, and confirmation of the Torah that had come before him, a guidance and an admonition to those who fear God" (Quran 5:46). Thus Muslims view Jews and Christians as "People of the Book," a community of believers who received revelations, through prophets, in the form of scriptures or revealed books from God.

As Christians view their revelation as both fulfilling and completing the revelation of the Old Testament, Muslims believe that the Prophet Muhammad received the final and complete revelation from God through the angel Gabriel to correct human error that had made its way into the scriptures and belief systems of Judaism and Christianity. Therefore,

Muslims believe that Islam is not a new religion with a new scripture. Far from being the youngest of the major monotheistic world religions, from a Muslim point of view Islam is the oldest because it represents the original, as well as the final, revelation of the God of Abraham, Moses, Jesus, and Muhammad. "He established for you the same religion as that which He established for Noah, that which We have sent to you as inspiration through Abraham, Moses, and Jesus, namely that you should remain steadfast in religion and make no divisions within it" (Quran 42:13).

Why do Muslims say they are descended from Abraham?

Muslims see themselves, along with Jews and Christians, as children of Abraham, belonging to different branches of the same religious family. The Quran and the Old Testament both tell the story of Abraham, Sarah, and Hagar, Sarah's Egyptian servant. While Jews and Christians are descended from Abraham and his wife Sarah through their son Isaac, Muslims trace their religious roots back to Abraham through Ismail, his firstborn son by Hagar.

According to both Hebrew and Muslim scriptures, when after many years Sarah did not conceive a child, she urged Abraham to sleep with her maidservant, Hagar, so that he might have an heir. The child who was the result of that union was a boy named Ismail. After Ismail's birth, Sarah too finally became pregnant and gave birth to Isaac. She then became jealous of Ismail, who as firstborn would be the prime inheritor and overshadow her own son Isaac. So she pressured Abraham to send Hagar and Ismail away. Abraham reluctantly let Hagar and her son go, because God promised that God would make Ismail the father of a great nation. Islamic sources say that Hagar and Ismail ended up in the vicinity of Mecca in Arabia, and both scriptures say that they nearly died but were saved by a spring that miraculously gushed from the desert.

The Quran and Muslim tradition tell a rich story about how father and son were reunited. This reunion gave rise to two of the most visible symbols of Islam. According to Islamic sources, Abraham learned that Hagar and Ismail were alive and found them living near present-day Mecca. After hearing of Hagar's harrowing experiences in the desert and the story of the miracle that saved them, Abraham and Ismail rebuilt the Kaaba, which Muslims believe Adam originally built, as a temple to the one true God. It is for this reason that Muslims across the globe turn in the direction of the Kaaba when they pray, as a unifying act of worship of the one true God. Today the Kaaba is considered the most sacred place in the Muslim world. Its distinctive cube shape with its black covering is one of the most familiar symbols in Islam. (See page 23, "What is the Kaaba?") Muslim scripture also tells that Abraham established the rites of the sacred pilgrimage to Mecca, many of which recreate Hagar's experiences there. The pilgrimage attracts over two million people annually and is another striking symbol of the faith. (See page 22, "What do Muslims do on the pilgrimage to Mecca?")

There is one significant difference between the biblical and Islamic accounts of the Abraham story. Contrary to the biblical tradition (Genesis 22:1–2), most Islamic scholars designate Ismail rather than Isaac as the intended victim in the story of Abraham's willingness to sacrifice his son at God's command (Quran 37:99–113).

How did Islam originate?

Like Judaism and Christianity, Islam originated in the Middle East. It was not a totally new monotheistic religion that sprang up in isolation. Belief in one God, monotheism, had been flourishing for many centuries. Knowledge of Judaism, Christianity, and Zoroastrianism had been brought to Mecca in Arabia by foreign caravan trade as well as through the travels and contacts of Meccan traders throughout the Middle

East. Moreover, Christian, Zoroastrian, and Jewish tribes lived in Arabia.

In the sixth century, Mecca was emerging as a new commercial center with vast new wealth but also with a growing division between rich and poor, challenging the traditional system of Arab tribal values and social security. This was the social environment in which the Prophet Muhammad preached the message of the Quran, which formed the basis for the religion we know as Islam, calling all to return to the worship of the one true God and a socially just society.

Muslims believe that God sent revelations first to Moses (as found in the Hebrew scriptures, the Torah), then to Jesus (the Gospels), and finally to Muhammad (through the Islamic scripture, the Quran). Muhammad is not considered the founder of the new religion of Islam. Like the biblical prophets who came before him, he was a religious reformer. Muhammad said that he did not bring a new message from a new God but called people back to the one true God and to a way of life they had forgotten or deviated from.

Because it is not a new revelation, the Quran contains many references to stories and figures in the Old and New Testaments, including Adam and Eve, Abraham and Moses, David and Solomon, and Jesus and Mary. Islam and worship of Allah—the Arabic word for God, meaning literally "the God"—was a return in the midst of a polytheistic society to the forgotten past, to the faith of the first monotheist, Abraham.

To Muhammad, most of his contemporaries in Mecca, with its tribal polytheism, lived in ignorance of the one true God and His will as revealed to the prophets Adam, Abraham, Moses, and Jesus. The revelations Muhammad received led him to believe that Jews and Christians over time had distorted God's original message to Moses and later to Jesus. Thus Muslims saw the Torah and the Gospels as a combination of original revelation and later human additions, such as the elevation of Jesus from a prophet to the Son of God.

The revelations Muhammad received were calls to religious and social reform. They emphasized social justice (concern for the rights of women, widows, and orphans), corrected distortions to God's revelations in Judaism and Christianity, and warned that many had strayed from the message of God and the prophets. They called upon all to return to what the Quran refers to as the straight path of Islam or the path of God, revealed one final time to Muhammad, the last or "seal" of the prophets.

What is the Muslim scripture?

Quran (sometimes written *Koran*) means "recitation" in Arabic. The Quran is the Muslim scripture. Muslims believe it contains the revelations received by the Prophet Muhammad from God through the angel Gabriel. Muhammad, who was illiterate, functioned as God's intermediary; he was told to "recite" the revelation he received. For Muslims, Muhammad was neither the author nor editor of the Quran. Therefore, the Quran is the eternal, literal word of God, preserved in the original Arabic language. Over a period of twenty-three years, from Muhammad's fortieth year until his death in 632, the Quran's 114 chapters (called *surahs*) were revealed to him.

Muslims believe that the Quran was initially preserved in oral and written form during the lifetime of the Prophet. The entire text was finally collected in an official standardized version some fifteen or twenty years after his death. The Quran is approximately four-fifths the size of the New Testament. Its chapters were assembled according to length, beginning with the longest chapter and ending with the shortest, not edited or organized thematically. This format has proved frustrating to many non-Muslims, who find the text disjointed or disorganized from their point of view. However, it enables a believer to simply open the text at random and start reciting at the beginning of any paragraph, since each represents a lesson to be learned and reflected upon.

Recitation of the Quran is central to a Muslim's life; many Muslims memorize the Quran in its entirety. Recitation reinforces what Muslims see as the miracle of hearing the actual word of God expressed by the human voice. There are many examples throughout history of those who were drawn and converted to Islam upon hearing the Quran recited. Muslims recite passages from the Quran that are included in their five daily prayers; musical and poetic recitations of Quranic verses serve as an introduction to every community event, from weddings and funerals to lectures and business dinners. Quran recitations are performed before stadiums of devout and enthusiastic Muslims in numbers resembling those of American or European audiences at an opera or a concert. Many Muslims experience deep aesthetic pleasure from listening to the rich, resonant, rhyming prose, with its repetitions and subtle inflections.

Why is Arabic so important in Islam?

Muslims believe that the Quran, as well as the Torah and the Gospels, is based on a tablet written in Arabic that exists in heaven with God. They believe that the teachings of these scriptures, revealed at different times in history, originate from this source. The Quran, recited by Muhammad as it was revealed to him by the angel Gabriel, and later recorded in Arabic, is thus believed to be the direct word of God. All Muslims, regardless of their native language, memorize and recite the Quran in Arabic, the language in which it was revealed, whether they fully understand this language or not. So too, all over the world, regardless of their local language, when Muslims pray they do so in Arabic. Until modern times, the Quran was printed in Arabic only. Even now, in translations, which more correctly are viewed by Muslims as "interpretations," the Arabic text is often printed alongside.

The oral recitation of the Quran has remained a powerful source of inspiration to the present day. Chanting of the Quran in Arabic is an art form, and Quran reciters and their performances are held in esteem, comparable to that of opera stars in the West. Recordings of the Quran are enjoyed for their aesthetic as well as their religious value. Walking in the streets of a Muslim country, a visitor is bound to hear the Quran being recited on radios, televisions, or cassette tapes in shops or passing taxis. Crowds fill stadiums and auditoriums throughout the Islamic world for public Quran recitation contests. Memorization of the entire Quran brings great prestige as well as merit.

What role does Muhammad play in Muslim life?

During his lifetime and throughout the following centuries, the Prophet Muhammad has been the ideal model for Muslims to follow as they strive to do God's will. Islam places great emphasis upon action—exhorting Muslims to strive, to make an effort, to do their best. Some Muslims say that Muhammad is the "living Quran," the witness whose words and behavior reveal God's will. In contrast to the frequently spiritualized Christian view of Jesus, Muslims look upon Muhammad as both a prophet and a very human figure, one with great political as well as spiritual insights. Thus Muslims look to Muhammad's example for guidance in all aspects of life: how to treat friends as well as enemies, what to eat and drink, how to mourn and celebrate. The importance given to Muhammad's example is a variation on a tradition that originated with pre-Islamic Arabian tribes who preserved their ideals and norms in what was called their *sunnah* (trodden path). These were the tribal customs, the traditions handed down from previous generations by word and example. Muhammad reformed these practices, and as a result his Sunnah (his words and deeds) became the norm for Muslim community life.

Muhammad's life translated the guidance revealed in the Quran into action; he lived the revelation, giving concrete form to the laws that God revealed for the various conditions of ordinary human life. For Islam, no aspect of life is outside the realm of religion. Muslims' observations or remembrances of what the Prophet said and did were passed on orally and in writing through "traditions" (*hadith*). The hadith deal with all aspects of Muhammad's life: the intensely personal and public, social, and political. Thus, for example, when Muslims pray or make the pilgrimage to Mecca, they try to pray as the Prophet prayed, without adding to or subtracting from the way Muhammad is said to have worshipped. This is not to imply that Muslims worship Muhammad in any way. Rather, traditions of the Prophet provide guidance regarding personal hygiene, dress, eating, spousal treatment, diplomacy, and warfare. The detailed records of Muhammad's actions in war and peace, his interactions with family, friends, and foes, his judgments in good and bad times, and his decisions when under siege and when victorious recall and reinforce for Muslims what it takes to follow the word of God.

Was Muhammad a prophet like the prophets in the Bible?

In Islam the concept of prophecy is broader than in Judaism and Christianity. Muslims distinguish between "prophets" and "messengers," to whom God gives a message for a community in book form. Unlike prophets, God's messengers are assured success by God. While all messengers are prophets, not all prophets are messengers. Prophets bring a specific message to a particular group of people. The word *prophet* is applied to Abraham, Noah, Joseph, and John the Baptist as well as nonbiblical prophets of Arabia like Hud and Salih. Messengers, on the other hand, bring a universal message to all peoples. The title *Messenger* is limited to the prophets Moses, Jesus, and Muhammad, whose revelations were preserved in scriptural form.

Why is so much known about Muhammad's life?

Muslims believe that Muhammad not only received God's final revelation to humankind but also perfectly lived out the revelation he received. Thus he is sometimes referred to as the "living Quran." Muhammad was and is the model of the Muslim ideal to be emulated by all believers. While Muhammad was alive, people could go directly to him to request his advice or opinion about any topic. When Muhammad died, the Muslim community lost its direct channel of revelation.

Because Muslims believe that Muhammad's words and actions serve as a living example of the meaning of the Quran, the early Muslim community was anxious to preserve as many memories of his words and actions as possible. Narrative stories about the Prophet's example (Sunnah), known as the *hadith* (traditions) of the Prophet, record many aspects of Muhammad's life, including religious belief and ritual, eating, dress, personal hygiene, marriage, treatment of spouses, diplomacy, and warfare. These detailed records of Muhammad's actions in war and peace, his interactions with family, friends, and foes, his judgments in good and bad times, and his decisions when under siege and when victorious recall and reinforce for Muslims what it takes to follow the word of God. Excluded from imitation is anything Muhammad did in his specific capacity as Prophet.

The hadith were collected over a period of several hundred years. In many cases, there are several hadith that deal with the same situation, since many people were typically present when Muhammad was answering questions from the Muslim community. Although there are many hadith collections, two in particular, those compiled by Muslim Ibn al-Hajjaj and Ismail al-Bukhari, enjoy special authoritative status in Sunni Islam.

Early on, given the proliferation of traditions of the Prophet, questions quickly arose about the authenticity of the hadith; as a result, a special science of hadith criticism was developed in order to authenticate them. The most important method of hadith authentication was through verification of the chain of transmitters. Most began with the format that so-and-so told so-and-so that she or he heard from so-and-so, tracing the line of transmitters (*isnad*) back to either Muhammad himself or one of his Companions who had reported that Muhammad said or did something. Great care was taken to determine the honesty of the various transmitters and whether they could possibly have known the person from whom they received the hadith. If the chain of transmitters could be proven possible, then the hadith was accepted as authentic.

A second method of hadith criticism focused on the content of the hadith rather than just the chain of transmitters. Those who examined the content (*matn*) attempted to verify that the hadith was consistent with both the Quran and other hadith on a similar topic. In cases where two hadith conflict, religious scholars use the Quran as the final authority with respect to content, regardless of who the transmitter was.

Although some modern scholars, both non-Muslims and Muslims, have raised questions about the authenticity of the hadith, the majority of Muslims continue to consider the hadith as scripture and cite them as evidence of God's commands about a particular topic. Equally important, whether or not they came directly from Muhammad, the traditions of the Prophet provide a rich religious and social history, a substantial record of how the Prophet of Islam has been and continues to be regarded by the Muslim community, and insight into the issues and debates within early Islamic history.

Why do Muslims object to images of Muhammad?

Islam, like Judaism and Christianity, strictly prohibits idolatry; worshipping anything (other gods, persons, religious images) but the one true God is a major sin. Neither the Quran nor the *hadith* (Prophetic traditions) explicitly ban depictions of Muhammad, but the hadith do prohibit images of any living being. As a result, many Muslims today argue that the visual depiction of the Prophet (and other prophets such as Moses and Jesus), whether positive or negative, should not be allowed.

Muslims have treated the prohibitions against images in various ways throughout history. The absence of figures (technically known as aniconism) became characteristic of Islamic religious art, and can be seen in the common practice of decorating mosques and manuscripts with Arabic calligraphy, tile work, and intricate geometric, vegetal, and floral designs.

However, at some times and in some places, particularly in lands now stretching from Turkey to India, Muslims did make images of the Prophet to use in illustrating stories about his life and deeds. In some cases he was shown veiled, but in others his features are visible. All these pictures were intended only to illustrate stories, never to be worshipped. Yet the fear of idolatry has often been so great that for many Muslims today the making of such images has been forbidden.

This belief has been taken to extremes. In 2001 the Taliban in Afghanistan dynamited the ancient Buddhas of Bamyan, which date back two thousand years, because they were believed to be un-Islamic and idolatrous. The world community, including many prominent Muslims, denounced the destruction.

Did Muhammad have multiple wives?

During the prime of his life, Muhammad had one wife, Khadija, for twenty-four years, until her death when he was forty-nine. Much is recorded about Muhammad's relationship with Khadija, who served as his closest confidante and comforter and strongest supporter. They had six children, two sons who died in infancy and four daughters.

After Khadija's death Muhammad started to contract other marriages, all but one of them to widows. As was customary for Arab chiefs, some of these marriages were arranged to cement political alliances. Others were marriages to wives of his Companions who had fallen in combat, women who were in need of protection. Remarriage for widows was difficult in a society that placed a high value on a bride's virginity. However, talk of the political and social motives behind many of Muhammad's marriages should not obscure the fact that Muhammad was attracted to and enjoyed the company of women as friends as well as spouses. His life reflects the Islamic outlook on marriage and sexuality, found in both revelation and Prophetic traditions, which emphasizes the importance of family and views sex as a gift from God to be enjoyed within the bonds of marriage.

What do Muslims believe about a worldwide Muslim community (ummah)?

Muslims believe that they are members of a worldwide Muslim community, known as the *ummah*, united by a religious bond that transcends tribal, ethnic, and national identities. This belief is based upon Quran 2:143, which declares that God created the Muslim ummah to serve as witnesses of God's guidance to the nations.

Islam was revealed in a time and place in which tribal loyalty was considered a person's most important identification. The individual's status was based upon membership in a particular tribe. Islam declared the absolute equality of all believers. The primary identity of the Muslim was as a Muslim, rather than as a member of a tribe, ethnicity, or gender. This radical egalitarianism shattered the importance of tribal identities and fostered the belief that Muslims should always defend and protect other Muslims. Quran 9:71 says: "The believers, men and women, are protectors of one another. They enjoin what is just and forbid what is evil. They observe regular prayers, regularly give alms, and obey God and His Messenger [i.e., Muhammad]. On them will God pour His mercy, for God is exalted in power, wise."

Ummah is often used to refer to the essential unity of all Muslims, despite their diverse geographical and cultural settings. The traditions of the Prophet (*hadith*) speak of the ummah as the spiritual, nonterritorial community of Muslims that is distinguished and united by the shared beliefs of its members. This concept became particularly important during the nineteenth-century era of European colonialism and the rise of nationalism. Islamic resistance movements called for the defense of the ummah against European intrusions throughout the Islamic world. The Ottoman Empire also appealed to the unity of the ummah as a way of reinvigorating Islamic solidarity. Nationalists, although trying to unite their countries on the basis of national loyalty, did not challenge the authority of the concept of the ummah and in fact used it as the basis for calling for political unity. Although nationalists since the 1960s have called for a separation of national and religious identities, Islamists continue to support the notion of membership in the ummah as the primary identity for all Muslims, rather than ethnic, linguistic, or geographic identities. Contemporary Muslims still believe in the ummah as a social identity, despite the secularization of public life and contemporary emphasis on national political identities.

Muslims have been commanded to protect each other and to consider their identities as Muslims to be more important than any other identities they might have. They refer to their membership in the Muslim ummah as the reason for their concern for Muslims throughout the world. Causes that have received broad attention from the worldwide Muslim community include the Afghan struggle against Soviet occupation from 1979 to 1989, ethnic cleansing of Bosnian Muslims in 1994 and of Kosovar Albanian Muslims in 1997, and the ongoing plight of the Palestinians, as well as conflicts and occupations in Iraq, Kashmir, and Chechnya. Muslims have also been active in fund-raising to assist victims of natural disasters in the Muslim world, such as earthquakes and floods in Turkey, Pakistan, and Afghanistan.

What are the core beliefs and practices that unite all Muslims?

Amidst the rich diversity of interpretations and experiences in Islam, there are certain core beliefs and observances. The five core beliefs—the oneness of God *(tawhid)*, prophets, scriptures, angels, and Day of Judgment—are complemented by five required observances, which the Quran prescribes that all practicing Muslims accept and follow. These "Pillars of Islam" represent the core and common denominator that unites all Muslims and distinguishes Islam from other religions. Following the Pillars of Islam requires dedication of your mind, emotions, body, time, energies, and possessions. Meeting the obligations required by the Pillars reinforces an ongoing presence of God in Muslims' lives and reminds them of their membership in a single worldwide community of believers.

1. The first Pillar of Islam is called the *declaration of faith*. A Muslim is one who bears witness, who testifies that "there is no god but God [Allah] and Muhammad is the messenger of God." This declaration is known as the *shahada* (witness, testimony). Allah is the Arabic name for God, just as Yahweh is the Hebrew name for God used in the Old Testament. To become a Muslim, one need only make this simple proclamation.

The first part of this proclamation affirms Islam's absolute monotheism, the uncompromising belief in the oneness or unity of God, as well as the doctrine that association of anything else with God is idolatry and the one unforgivable sin. As we see in Quran 4:48: "God does not forgive anyone for associating something with Him, while He does forgive whomever He wishes to for anything else. Anyone who gives God associates [partners] has invented an awful sin." This helps us to understand the Islamic belief that Islam's revelation is intended to correct such departures from the "straight path" as the Christian concept of the Trinity and veneration of the Virgin Mary in Catholicism.

The second part of the confession of faith asserts that Muhammad is not only a prophet but also a messenger of God, a higher role also played by Moses and Jesus before him. For Muslims, Muhammad is the vehicle for the last and final revelation. In accepting Muhammad as the "seal of the prophets," they believe that his prophecy confirms and completes all of the revealed messages, beginning with Adam's. In addition, somewhat like Jesus Christ, Muhammad serves as the preeminent role model through his life example. The believer's effort to follow Muhammad's example reflects the emphasis of Islam on practice and action. In this regard Islam is more like Judaism, with its emphasis upon the law, than Christianity, which gives greater importance to the importance of doctrines or dogma. This practical orientation of Islam is reflected in the remaining four Pillars of Islam.

2. The second Pillar of Islam is *prayer* (*salat*). Muslims pray (or, perhaps more correctly, worship) five times throughout the day: at daybreak, noon, midafternoon, sunset, and evening. Although the times for prayer and the ritual actions were not specified in the Quran, Muhammad established them.

In many Muslim countries, reminders to pray, or "calls to prayer" (*adhan*), echo out across the rooftops. Aided by a megaphone, from high atop a mosque's minaret, the muezzin calls out:

God is most great [Allahu Akbar], God is most great, God is most great, God is most great, I witness that there is no god but God [Allah]; I witness that there is no god but God. I witness that Muhammad is the messenger of God. I witness that Muhammad is the messenger of God. Come to prayer; come to prayer! Come to prosperity; come to prosperity! God is most great. God is most great. There is no god but God.

These reminders throughout the day help to keep believers mindful of God in the midst of everyday concerns about work and family with all their attractions and distractions. It strengthens the conscience, reaffirms total dependence on God, and puts worldly concerns within the perspective of death, the Last Judgment, and the afterlife.

The prayers consist of recitations from the Quran in Arabic and glorification of God. These are accompanied by a sequence of movements: standing, bowing, kneeling, touching the ground with one's forehead, and sitting. Both the recitations and accompanying movements express submission, humility, and adoration of God. Muslims can pray in any clean environment, alone or together, in a mosque or at home, at work or on the road, indoors or out. It is considered preferable and more meritorious to pray with others, if possible, as one body united in the worship of God, demonstrating discipline, brotherhood, equality, and solidarity.

As they prepare to pray, Muslims face Mecca, the holy city that houses the Kaaba (see page 23, "What is the Kaaba?"). Each act of worship begins with the declaration that "God is most great" ("Allahu Akbar") and is followed by fixed prayers that include the opening verse of the Quran.

At the end of the prayer, the *shahada* (declaration of faith) is again recited, and the "peace greeting"—"Peace be upon all of you and the mercy and blessings of God"—is repeated twice.

3. The third Pillar of Islam is called the *zakat*, which means "purification." Like prayer, which is both an individual and communal responsibility, zakat expresses a Muslim's worship of and thanksgiving to God by supporting the poor. It requires an annual contribution of 2.5 percent of an individual's wealth and assets, not merely a percentage of annual income. In Islam, the true owner of things is not man but God. People are given their wealth as a trust from God. Therefore, zakat is not viewed as "charity"; it is an obligation for those who have received

their wealth from God to respond to the needs of less fortunate members of the community. The Quran (9:60) as well as Islamic law stipulates that alms are to be used to support the poor, orphans, and widows, to free slaves and debtors, and to support those working in the "cause of God" (e.g., construction of mosques, religious schools, and hospitals, etc.). Zakat, which developed fourteen hundred years ago, functions as a form of social security in a Muslim society. In Shii Islam, in addition to the zakat, which is not limited to 2.5 percent, believers pay a religious tax (*khums*) on their income to a religious leader. This is used to support the poor and needy.

4. The fourth Pillar of Islam, the *Fast of Ramadan,* occurs once each year during the month of Ramadan, the ninth month of the Islamic calendar and the month in which the first revelation of the Quran came to Muhammad. During this month-long fast, every Muslim whose health permits must abstain from dawn to sunset from food, drink, and sexual activity. Fasting is a practice common to many religions, sometimes undertaken as penance, sometimes to free us from undue focus on physical needs and appetites. In Islam the discipline of the Ramadan fast is intended to stimulate reflection on human frailty and dependence upon God, focus on spiritual goals and values, and identification with and response to the less fortunate.

At dusk the fast is broken with a light meal popularly referred to as breakfast. Families and friends share a special late evening meal together, often including special foods and sweets served only at this time of the year. Many go to the mosque for the evening prayer, followed by special prayers recited only during Ramadan. Some will recite the entire Quran (one-thirtieth each night of the month) as a special act of piety, and public recitations of the Quran or Sufi chanting can be heard throughout the evening. Families rise before sunrise to take their first meal of the day, which must sustain them until sunset.

Near the end of Ramadan (the twenty-seventh day) Muslims commemorate the "Night of Power" when Muhammad first received God's revelation. The month of Ramadan ends with one of the two major Islamic celebrations, the Feast of the Breaking of the Fast, called Eid al-Fitr, which resembles Christmas in its spirit of joyfulness, special celebrations, and gift giving.

5. The fifth Pillar is the *pilgrimage*, or *hajj*, to Mecca in Saudi Arabia. At least once in his or her lifetime, every adult Muslim who is physically and financially able is required to make the sacrifice of time, possessions, status, and normal comforts necessary to make this pilgrimage, becoming a pilgrim totally at God's service. The pilgrimage season follows Ramadan. Every year over two million believers, representing a tremendous diversity of cultures and languages, travel from all over the world to the holy city of Mecca to form one community living their faith. In addition to the hajj there is a devotional ritual that is referred to as the "lesser pilgrimage." It is called the *umrah* (visitation) and involves visiting the holy sites at other times of the year. Many who are on pilgrimage also perform the umrah rituals before, during, or after the hajj. However, performing the umrah does not fulfill the hajj obligation.

What do Muslims do on the pilgrimage to Mecca?

Those who participate in the pilgrimage wear simple garments. Men wear two seamless white cloths, and women wear an outfit that entirely covers the body, except the face and hands. These coverings symbolize purity as well as the unity and equality of all believers. Men and women worship together; there is no separation of the sexes.

As the pilgrims approach Mecca they shout, "I am here, O Lord, I am here!" When they enter Mecca their first obligation is to go to the Kaaba, which is located inside the compound of the Grand Mosque. (See next question.) The crowds of pilgrims move counterclockwise around the Kaaba seven times. This circumambulation, like prayer, symbolizes the believer's entry into the divine presence.

In the days that follow, pilgrims participate in a variety of ritual actions and ceremonies symbolizing key religious events. They walk and sometimes run along a quarter-mile corridor of the Grand Mosque seven times to commemorate Hagar's frantic search in the desert for water for her son Ismail. This rite, in great contrast to the circumambulation of the Kaaba, which centers on spiritual contact with God, symbolizes humankind's ongoing effort, movement, and struggle through life, expressing a believer's persistence in life's struggle for survival. The pilgrims drink water from the well, called Zamzam (meaning "bubbling"), which is located within the Grand Mosque, where Muslims believe God provided water for Hagar and Ismail. They assemble for a day at Arafat, a vast, empty plain, in commemoration of the final pilgrimage of Muhammad, who delivered his farewell sermon to his people from the Mount of Mercy, a hill in the middle of the plain. They symbolically reject the devil, the source of all evil, by throwing stones at three pillars that stand at the site where Satan met Abraham and Ismail and tempted them to disobey God when Abraham was preparing to sacrifice his son in obedience to God's command.

What is the Kaaba?

The Kaaba is seen as the most sacred space in the Muslim world, the site to which hundreds of millions of Muslims throughout the world turn each day when they pray.

Located inside the compound of the Grand Mosque at Mecca, the Kaaba (literally, "cube") is a cube-shaped structure known as the House of God. It contains the sacred Black Stone, a meteorite that Muslims believe was placed by Abraham and Ismail in a corner of the Kaaba, a symbol of

God's covenant with Abraham and Ismail and by extension with the Muslim community itself. The Kaaba is approximately forty-five feet high and thirty-three by fifty feet wide and is draped with a woven black cloth embellished with Quranic verses embroidered in gold.

The Kaaba is considered the first house of worship of the one God, originally built by Adam and replicating the heavenly House of God, which contains the divine throne that is circumambulated by the angels. This heavenly ritual is reenacted during the *hajj* by pilgrims, who circumambulate the Kaaba seven times. This symbolizes their entry into the divine presence. Muslims believe that Adam's Kaaba was destroyed by the neglect of believers and the flood, and according to the Quran (2:127) Abraham and his son Ismail rebuilt the holy house. However, by the time of Muhammad the Kaaba was under the control of the Quraysh of Mecca, who used it as a shrine for the tribal gods and idols of Arabia. The Quraysh held an annual pilgrimage to the Kaaba and a fair that attracted pilgrims from all over Arabia.

Muslim tradition tells us that one of the first things Muhammad did when he returned from exile and triumphantly entered Mecca was to cleanse the Kaaba of its 360 idols and restore the "religion of Abraham," the worship of the one true God.

What is the significance of Mecca?

Mecca, in Saudi Arabia, is the birthplace of the Prophet Muhammad and the most sacred location in the Islamic world. It is the site of the Grand Mosque, which houses the Kaaba. (See previous question.) Millions of Muslims travel there each year from all over the world to perform the *hajj*. Mecca is seen as housing the spiritual center of the earth. Many Muslims believe that the actions of worship in Mecca, such as the circumambulation of the Kaaba (see page 22,

"What do Muslims do on the pilgrimage to Mecca?"), are duplicated in heaven at the Throne of God. Mecca, like Medina, is closed to non-Muslims.

How do Muslims pray?

Prayer, one of the Five Pillars of Islam, is central in the life of a Muslim. Here are some highlights:

Five times each day, hundreds of millions of Muslims face Mecca (holiest city of Islam, birthplace of Muhammad, and site of the Kaaba, or House of God) to pray—at daybreak, noontime, midafternoon, sunset, and evening. These five obligatory prayers have to be performed in Arabic, regardless of the native tongue of the worshipper. Each part of the prayer has its function within this daily ritual and is designed to combine meditation, devotion, moral elevation, and physical exercise. Prayers can be performed individually or in congregation.

The actions and words a Muslim uses during the prayer demonstrate his or her ultimate submission to God. This process combines faith and practice, putting into action what is expressed in the First Pillar of Islam, in which Muslims proclaim their belief in the one God and in Muhammad as God's messenger.

Preparing to meet and address the Lord, Muslims perform a ritual ablution, or cleansing, to ensure that they are in a state of spiritual and physical purity. First, they cleanse their minds and hearts from worldly thoughts and concerns, concentrating on God and the blessings he has given them. Second, they wash hands and face, arms up to the elbow, and feet, then say, "I bear witness that there is no god but God; He has no partner; and I bear witness that Muhammad is His servant and messenger." This purification process is as spiritual as it is physical, as can be seen in the fact that sand can be used if water is not available. The objective is for the mind and body to be clean as Muslims approach or put themselves in the presence of God.

The movements Muslims perform while praying, individually or in groups, reflect past customs used when entering the presence of great kings or rulers: raising our hands in greeting, bowing, and finally prostrating ourselves before this great power. Worshippers begin by raising their hands and proclaiming God's greatness ("Allahu Akbar"—God is most great). Then, folding their hands over stomach or chest or leaving them at their sides, they stand upright and recite what has been described as the essential message of the Quran, the opening discourse:

> Praise be to God, Lord of the Worlds; the Beneficent, the Merciful; Master of the Day of Judgment. You alone do we worship and from you alone do we seek aid. Show us the Straight Way, the way of those upon whom You have bestowed Your grace, not of those who have earned Your wrath or who go astray. (Quran 1:2–6)

After reciting another (this time self-selected) verse from the Quran, Muslims bow and proclaim, "Glory to God in the Highest," three times. Returning to an upright position, they say, "God hears the one who praises Him" and "Our Lord, all praise belongs to you!"

The next phase of worship involves what is commonly called "prostration" in English, although it does not involve lying down at full length. The position Muslims take represents an expression of ultimate submission. Before beginning the act of prostration, Muslims first repeat, "Allahu Akbar" (God is most great). Then they fall to their knees, placing hands flat on the ground and bringing their foreheads down between their hands to touch the ground. While in this bowing position, Muslims recite three times, "Glory to the Lord Most High!" After this, they stand up and repeat the entire cycle of prayer.

Prayer includes sitting on the heels and reciting a formula known as "the witnessing" because it contains the declaration of Muslim faith. The witnessing is followed by asking God's blessings for the first and last of God's Prophets, Abraham and Muhammad.

Finally, prayer is ended with an invocation of peace (*salam*). Worshippers turn their heads right and left and say, "May the peace, mercy, and blessings of Allah be upon you." Although this invocation is addressed to fellow believers on the right and left, some Muslims also believe they are addressing their guardian angels, who remain over their shoulders as they pray. After completing the obligatory prayers, Muslims can privately petition (*dua*) God regarding their individual needs. There are recommended prayer texts in Arabic for such individual needs and problems, but in these prayers the worshipper can also address God in his or her own native language and own words.

When Islam first appeared in the Middle East, it was common practice in the Byzantine and Sasanian empires to prostrate oneself before the Byzantine emperor (a Christian) and the Shah of Persia (a Zoroastrian), since these rulers were both king and high priest. However, Muslims historically were especially adamant in refusing to prostrate themselves before anyone or anything but Allah. In the mid-seventh century the T'ang Dynasty of China recorded that a delegation of Arab and Persian visitors refused to prostrate themselves in front of the emperor, whom the Chinese believed to be the "Son of Heaven."

In modern times we can still find examples of prostration in other religions. To the present day Anglican and Catholic clergy prostrate themselves before the altar at the beginning of the Good Friday liturgy, and so do the ordinands in the rite of ordination. Members of some Catholic monastic orders regularly prostrate themselves instead of genuflecting before the Eucharist on the altar.

Do Muslims believe in angels?

Like Jews and Christians, Muslims believe that angels are a part of God's creation. Angels act as God's agents and serve

Him by protecting humans, relaying His messages, or performing a variety of other functions. For example, the angel Gabriel brought divine revelation to Muhammad; the angel Michael provides sustenance for human bodies and knowledge to human minds; the angel Israfil (Raphael, in the Judeo-Christian tradition) will sound the trumpet at the Final Judgment.

According to Islamic tradition, angels are created from light. Unlike humans, they do not have free will. They are absolutely obedient to God's commands and are engaged everlastingly in worship and service to Him. Many Muslims believe that two angels attend each human being, recording all of his or her words and actions up until the moment of death. They will present this account on the Day of Judgment.

How do Muslims view the Day of Judgment?

The Last Day, or Judgment Day, is one of the main themes of the Quran. It includes the destruction of the world and all creatures, resurrection of the body, and judgment, reward (heaven), and punishment (hell) for all creatures. On the Day of Judgment, or Day of Resurrection, a cataclysmic cosmic event that will occur at a time known only to God, all will be raised from the dead.

Signs of the Last Day are foretold in many prophetic traditions. They include the appearance of the Great Deceiver—al-Dajjal—(who will spread corruption and evil in this earth), the Return of the Mahdi (Muslim messianic figure), and the Second Coming of Jesus. Muslims are divided over the coming of a Mahdi. Some believe that the Mahdi will appear to bring justice and truth to all before the Day of Resurrection. Other Muslims believe that Jesus' second coming will fulfill that role, citing those Quranic commentators who believe verse 43:61 refers to the resurrection of Jesus: "And he/it (Jesus) shall be a Sign (for the coming of) the Hour (of Judgment):

therefore have no doubt about the (Hour), but follow ye Me: this is a Straight Way" (43:61). They reinforce this interpretation by noting that Jesus is specifically mentioned in the preceding verses. The Second Coming of Jesus is definitively established in the prophetic traditions: Jesus will kill al-Dajjal, establish justice, and reign over the world for forty years as an upright and just ruler. On the Judgment Day all the dead will be resurrected, body and soul. God will gather people together "as if they had stayed [in their tombs] only one hour of the day" (10:45). According to some traditions, the Prophet Muhammad will be the first to rise and arrive at the place of assembly.

Do Muslims believe in heaven and hell?

Muslims believe that heaven or hell, eternal reward or punishment, depends on whether human beings follow the will of God and act with justice and mercy toward others during their lifetime. The Quran frequently emphasizes the ultimate moral responsibility and accountability of each believer.

God will judge each person by the standards brought by the person's community's prophets and scripture, using the record of each person's actions throughout his or her life that are recorded in the Book of Deeds: "Then those whose balance of good deeds is heavy will attain salvation, but those whose balance is light will have lost their souls and abide in Hell forever" (Quran 23:102–3).

The Quran's vision of the afterlife is both spiritual and physical. Bodies and souls will be joined, and the pleasures of heavenly gardens of bliss and the pain of hellfire will be experienced fully. The Garden of Paradise is a heavenly mansion of peace and bliss with flowing rivers, beautiful gardens, and cool drink from a shining stream. Quranic descriptions of heavenly bliss are life-affirming, emphasizing the beauty of creation and enjoyment of its pleasures within the limits set by God:

> Those who believe and do righteous deeds, they are the
> best of creatures. Their reward is with their Lord:
> Gardens of Paradise beneath which rivers flow. They
> will dwell therein forever, God well-pleased with them
> and they with Him. This is for those who hold their
> Lord in awe. (98:7–8)

Later traditions elaborated on the joys of paradise and the
role of *houris*, or beautiful companions. The Quran makes no
reference to a sexual role for the houris, a word sometimes
translated as "virgins." Many Quranic commentators and
most Muslims understand houris as virgins but only in the
sense of pure or purified souls.

Hell is a place of endless pain, suffering, torment, and
despair, with roaring flames, fierce boiling waters, and
scorching wind. The destiny of the damned, their punishment,
is a just punishment, the result of human choice:

> Verily, the sinners will be in the punishment of Hell, to
> remain therein. It will not be lightened for them and
> they will be overwhelmed in despair. And we shall not
> be unjust to them, but it is they who have been unjust to
> themselves. (43:74–76)

The Quran's comprehensive and integrated view of life
contrasts with Christianity's tendency to compartmentalize
life into the sacred and profane, body and soul, sensual and
spiritual. In contrast to the "spiritual" images of a more
sedate, celibate, and blissful paradise that predominate in
Christian visions of heaven, the Quran does not draw a distinction between enjoying the joys of beatific vision and those
of the fruits of creation.

In modern times, conservative and fundamentalist writers
and religious leaders continue to appeal to literalist interpretations of the afterlife. But most contemporary Muslim

commentary emphasizes the importance of moral responsibility and accountability in this life and its direct connection to divine justice with eternal reward and punishment without getting into explicit, concrete descriptions of the afterlife.

What are Muslim women promised in the afterlife?

The Quran makes no gender distinction as to the reward or punishment of the afterlife. Gender is irrelevant as a criterion of judgment; faith and deeds are the ultimate determiners of one's status in the afterlife: "If any do deeds of righteousness, be they male or female—and have faith, they will enter Heaven, and not the least injustice will be done to them" (4:124) and "Verily, the noblest of you in the sight of God is the one who is most deeply conscious of Him" (49:13).

Both men and women will be rewarded with pure spouses and with gardens beneath which rivers flow (see verses 2:25, 3:15, and 4:57). For example, verse 4:57 reads, "But those who believe and do deeds of righteousness, We shall soon admit to Gardens, with rivers flowing beneath, their eternal home: Therein shall they have companions pure and holy: We shall admit them to shades, cool and ever deepening." In all three verses, the term *azwaj* (companions) indicates that both male and female believers will be rewarded with pure spouses in heaven.

Classical Quranic commentaries regard the *houris* as heavenly spouses. Nonetheless, the Quran also makes specific reference to one's earthly spouses. It promises to rejoin believers with their parents, spouses, and children who were among the righteous: "Gardens of perpetual bliss, which they shall enter together with the righteous from among their parents, their spouses, and their offspring..." (13:23; see also 36:56 and 43:70).

Do Muslims believe in saints?

Saint in Arabic is somewhat equivalent to the Arabic word *wali*, which means "friend, helper, or patron." There is no mention of saints in the Quran, which emphasizes that God alone is the wali of believers and there is no helper but Him. In fact, the Quran warns against "intercession," seeking help from anyone but God. Therefore, some Muslims oppose the concept of sainthood as un-Islamic. They say that such beliefs and practices violate monotheism by potentially treating saints as if they are equal to God. Others, however, believe that there can be intercession with God's permission and that some receive a special favor from God allowing them to intercede for others. Certain saints are known for providing intercessions for particular causes: helping women to bear children, solving domestic problems, curing illnesses, or avoiding certain disasters.

The Christian and Islamic concepts of sainthood differ in a number of ways. Sainthood in Islam is not determined by Catholicism's method of canonization but rather by a less formal process of acclamation. The majority of popular saints are Sufi. (Sufis are the mystics of Islam; see page 61, "Who are the Sufis?") The tombs of Sufi saints are often the object of pilgrimage and a focal point for festivals and processions celebrating a saint's birth or death. Other Sufi saints are more remembered for their wise sayings, virtues, and miracles. A significant number of popular, Sufi, and legendary saints are women.

Do Muslims believe in sin and repentance?

Sin is a violation of God's will or commands, the deliberate misuse of the freedom that has been given to human beings. The Quran speaks of two kinds of sins, major and minor (4:31, 53:31–32). Among the most serious offenses is idolatry, associating other gods, or anything else, with the one true God. The term *idolatry* (or *shirk*) has been dynamic throughout history. In modern times it has been applied in diverse ways to any action that places anything above God, from superstition to greed to power, personal or political. Other major sins are murder and illicit sexual acts.

Sin in the Quran and Islamic tradition comprises both individual and collective sin, the behavior of a community or nation. In modern times, Quranic concerns with the welfare of society have led many Muslim religious leaders and scholars to label political and social injustice and oppression as great transgressions, sins that must be resisted and fought.

If sin is a violation of God's commands, departing from the straight path of Islam, to repent is to turn toward God, literally to return *(tawbah)* to God, who is compassionate and forgiving, after falling into sin or error. Repentance is a major theme, mentioned over seventy times in the Quran, and the title of an entire chapter (Surah 9). Repentance in Islam is a personal, moral, individual act of remorse. It is an informal act that does not require a formal act of confession or atonement, as in some forms of Christianity. In cases where the sin has violated the rights of others, restitution is required. If the sin does not infringe on others' rights but involves an offense against God, then penitence, remorse, and making a resolution to abstain from the sin in the future are sufficient.

In modern times, just as the notion of sin has been applied not only to the acts of individuals but to those of a group or community, so too repentance has not only an individual but also a social dimension, and requires publicly acknowledging the transgression, such as political oppression or social injustice.

What do Muslims believe about Mary and Jesus?

Mary, the mother of Jesus, is a prominent figure in Islam and the only woman mentioned by name in the Quran. The Quran upholds Mary as one of the four perfect examples of womanhood (66:12). An entire chapter, Surah 19, is dedicated to her and her history. Mary is mentioned more times in the Quran than in the entire New Testament, and more biographical information about her is contained in the Quran than in the New Testament.

The Quranic account of Mary includes the pregnancy of her mother Anna, Mary's birth, the annunciations of the coming births of John the Baptist and Jesus, and affirmation of the virgin conception and birth of Jesus: "[Remember] her who preserved her chastity, into whom We breathed a life from Us, and made her and her son a token for mankind" (21:91). The Quran teaches that Mary is to be revered because she completely submitted herself to God's will, even though it meant that her own family would accuse her of unchastity when it was discovered that she was pregnant (19:16–21). The Quran also records Jesus as an infant verbally defending Mary's innocence (19:27–34).

Jesus is an important figure in the Quran. No one can be a Muslim unless he or she believes in the prophethood of Jesus. Like Christians, Muslims believe in the virgin conception of Jesus by God's Spirit. The Quran also records some of Jesus' miracles, including giving sight to the blind, healing lepers, raising the dead, and breathing life into clay birds (5:110). This last miracle is not recorded in the canonical New Testament but does appear in the noncanonical Gospel of Thomas. The Quran also reports Jesus' proclamation of the need to worship God as the only God and his own status as a witness to God (5:116–17).

Muslim and Christian beliefs about Jesus differ in two areas. First, although Muslims believe in the virgin conception and birth of Jesus through an act of God's Spirit, they do not believe that Jesus is the Son of God. They believe that he is one of the long line of righteous prophets and second only to Muhammad in importance (Quran 6:83–87). For Muslims, the Christian doctrine of the Trinity represents a form of polytheism, affirming belief in three gods rather than one God alone (Quran 4:171, 5:17, 5:72–77).

Second, Muslims do not believe in the crucifixion and resurrection of Jesus (Quran 4:157–58). They believe that, although it appeared that Jesus was crucified, instead God took Jesus to Himself in a manner similar to what happened to Elijah (Quran 3:55, 4:157–589). Muslims do not believe in the Christian doctrine of Original Sin, so there is no theological need for the all-atoning sacrifice of Jesus through his crucifixion and resurrection. Muslims further believe that each of us will be held accountable before God for our own actions and thus responsible for our own salvation. Therefore, we will not be able to rely upon anyone else, not even Jesus or Muhammad, to save us from our sins.

Do Muslims have a Sabbath like Jews and Christians?

Friday is the Muslim day of congregational worship. It was not traditionally considered a day of rest, but in some Muslim countries today Friday has replaced the Sunday holiday, which was instituted by colonial powers and therefore often seen as a Western, Christian legacy.

In both Muslim and Western countries, congregational prayer (*juma*) in a mosque takes place at noon on Friday. Many Muslims in America arrange to use their lunch hour or request a flexible work schedule (coming to work earlier or staying later) in order to attend their hour-long Friday services. (See next question.) Those who cannot do so go to their mosque or Islamic center on Sunday for congregational prayer, religious education classes, and socializing.

Do Muslims have a weekly worship service?

Muslims gather at a mosque on Friday for the noon congregational prayer (*juma*). Together Muslims of different ages, ethnic groups, and social status stand side by side in straight rows facing the niche in the wall (*mihrab*) that indicates the direction (*qibla*) of the holy city of Mecca. Men and women worship in separate groups, women behind the men—for reasons of modesty, because prostrations are part of the prayer ritual. Traditionally only men were required to attend the Friday congregational prayer. Increasingly today, however, women attend the service in large numbers. An *imam* (leader) stands in front of the congregation to lead Friday prayers.

A special feature of the Friday prayer is a sermon (*khutba*), often delivered from a wooden pulpit (*minbar*) modeled on the platform used by Muhammad when he gave sermons to his community. The preacher begins by reciting a verse from the Quran and then gives a short talk addressing the affairs and problems of the community, often combining religious advice on social or political issues with commentary based on the Quran's message. Although in mosques with a permanent staff the imam will usually deliver the sermon, any member of the congregation can do so.

Do Muslims have religious holidays or holy days?

Muslims celebrate two great Islamic holidays. The first is Eid al-Fitr, the Feast of the Breaking of the Fast of Ramadan, a celebration that extends for three days. The second holiday is the greater of the two. It occurs two and a half months after the first and lasts for four days. This is the Eid al-Adha, the Feast of Sacrifice, which marks the annual completion of the pilgrimage to Mecca (*hajj*). These holidays represent a religious obligation for Muslims as well as a social celebration.

In America, Eid prayers are observed in every community where Muslims reside, and gatherings to celebrate the holidays are common. In 2001 the U.S. Post Office issued a stamp to commemorate the Eid al-Fitr. Many Muslim children stay home from school to celebrate these festivals, and in some areas school authorities recognize the Eids as holidays for Muslim youth, as they recognize the Jewish holidays of Rosh Hashanah and Yom Kippur.

Traditionally both Eids are occasions for exchanging visits with relatives and friends. As at Christmas celebrations, gifts of money or new clothes are given to children, and special sweets and other foods are served to family and guests.

In many contexts other religious holidays are celebrated, such as the birthday of the Prophet Muhammad and, in Shii Islam, the birthdays of Ali and the Imams. Shii annually commemorate the "passion" of Hussein during a ten-day period of remembering, ritually reenacting, and mourning the last stand of the Imam Hussein and his followers against the army of the caliph. (See page 48, "What is the difference between Sunni and Shii Muslims?")

Does Islam have a clergy?

Islam does not have an ordained clergy or representatives of a church hierarchy in the way that Christianity does. Any Muslim can lead the prayer or officiate at a wedding or burial. In fact, however, historically certain functions came to be filled by a class that took on distinctive forms of dress and authority that are clergy-like. A variety of roles have come to be played by religious scholars and leaders.

In early Islam, pious Muslims from many walks of life also led prayer or became scholars of the Quran and Islamic sciences, but over time many turned these activities into a profession. Every mosque has an *imam*, respected in the community, the one who "stands in front" to lead the prayer and delivers the Friday sermon. In smaller congregations, various members take turns in performing this role. Larger communities have a full-time imam, the chief official who performs the many functions that a priest or rabbi might perform: leading a ritual prayer, administering the mosque or Islamic center or school as well as community activities, visiting the sick, and instructing young people preparing to marry, etc.

Scholars of the Quran, Islamic law, and theology (who are called *ulama*, meaning "the learned") came to represent a permanent class of religious scholars often distinguished in society by their form of dress. They claimed a primary role as the protectors and authoritative interpreters of Islam. Many titles exist for Islamic religious scholars, reflecting their functions in interpreting Islam, some in theology, others in law. Among the ulama, *mujtahid* is a special title for one who is qualified to interpret Islamic law (using *ijtihad*, or independent reasoning). A *mufti* is a specialist in Islamic law competent to deliver a *fatwa*, a legal interpretation or judgment. In Sufism (Islamic mysticism), a Sufi master (*pir*) functions as spiritual leader of his followers.

In Sunni Islam, many governments have created the position of Grand Mufti, or senior religious leader. In Shii Islam (the Twelver, or Ithna Ashari, sect), a hierarchy of religious leaders evolved, at whose apex were Grand Ayatollahs.

In modern times, Islamic reformers include not only the ulama but also educated laity who combine a knowledge of Islam and modern sciences. Today the laity shares with the ulama the role of interpreters of Islam.

What is a mosque?

The word *mosque* comes from the Arabic word *masjid* (place for ritual prostration). The Prophet Muhammad's mosque in Medina, the first Muslim place of worship, functioned as a gathering place for worship, meditation, and learning. Unlike churches or synagogues with their rows of benches or pews, the mosque's main prayer area is a large open space, the expansive floors adorned with oriental carpets. An important feature of the prayer area is the *mihrab*, an ornamental arched niche set into the wall, which indicates the direction of Mecca (which Muslims always face when praying). Next to the mihrab is the *minbar*, a raised wooden platform (similar to a pulpit) modeled after the one that the Prophet Muhammad ascended to give his sermons to the community. The prayer leader delivers his sermon from the steps of the minbar. Because of the need for cleansing prior to prayer, most mosques have a spot set aside for performing ablutions away from the main prayer area.

The mosque, as the sacred space for individual and congregational worship, has social and intellectual significance for Muslims. Mosques have served as places for prayer, meditation, and learning as well as focal points for the religious and the social life of the Muslim community throughout its history. A mosque's atmosphere is one of tranquility and reflection but also of relaxation. When visiting a mosque, one is as likely to see people chatting quietly or napping on the carpets as praying and reading the Quran.

Historically, wherever Muslims have settled in sufficient numbers, one of their first efforts has been to erect a mosque. In twenty-first-century America, where Islam will soon be the second-largest religion, mosque construction has increased exponentially. Over 2,100 mosques and/or Islamic centers, large and small, located throughout the United States in small towns and villages as well as in major cities, are currently serving a diverse American Muslim community. Many of these mosques incorporate and reflect the diversity of Muslims in America. The membership of others, however, is drawn along ethnic or racial lines. The same phenomenon has been seen in other faiths. For example, years ago one could find two Catholic churches with separate schools, one Irish and one Italian- or French-speaking, across the street from each other. In some places more mosques than might be needed to serve the Muslim population have been created to accommodate such differences. In some cities and towns one can identify separate Arab, South Asian, Turkish, and African American mosques.

Mosques have served a multiplicity of functions all over the world. Beyond their use for individual worship and Friday congregational prayer, they are often the site of Quranic recitations and retreats, especially during Ramadan. They are used as centers for the collection and distribution of *zakat* (charitable contributions). Many pilgrims visit their local mosques when they depart for and return from the *hajj* (pilgrimage to Mecca) and *umrah* (minor pilgrimage). The dead are placed before the mihrab for funerary prayers. Mosques are sometimes the nucleus of an Islamic center housing activities for a multigenerational, multiethnic Islamic community. (See next question.) Marriages and business agreements are often contracted in the mosque, and education takes place in various forms. In times of crisis, worshippers gather for mutual support and to receive guidance from religious leaders.

What is an Islamic center?

An Islamic center is similar to the Christian and Jewish community centers that have become an integral part of many churches and synagogues in America and around the world. For Muslims, while it has a prayer room, much of the center is used for other activities: educational programs and seminars, social gatherings, community celebrations, religious classes, and sports events. In America, many of these community activities take place on Sunday, when Muslims are free from weekday work obligations. The Islamic center may be a building that stands alone or is part of a mosque complex.

The diverse offerings of some American mosques and centers might include youth sports activities, social services such as job and computer training or job placement, and programs featuring political candidates. Internationally, mosques and Islamic centers have also provided the social services that some governments have failed to offer their citizens.

What is a madrasa?

The term *madrasa* means "a place where learning or studying occurs." Historically, madrasas were institutions of higher learning, similar to the universities that began as institutions of the Church in the Western world. While in some countries *madrasa* refers to both religious and secular schools, today the term is most often used to describe Islamic schools, including major Islamic universities and seminaries as well as primary and secondary Islamic schools such as Indonesia's *pesantren*s, residential schools long noted for their espousal of "moderate Islam," which make up 20 to 25 percent of Indonesia's educational system.

Defining madrasas became a contentious issue after 9/11 and during the 2008 presidential campaigns. In the Western media some political leaders and commentators have equated madrasas with terrorist training grounds indoctrinating young militants with a "jihadist" and anti-American worldview. Barack Obama's opponents made use of this association with radicalism when they repeatedly referred to an Indonesian primary school that Obama had attended as a "madrasa."

Despite the radicalization of some madrasas in recent years, they have a long history in the Muslim world as mainstream educational institutions. The *New York Times* published a correction after equating the word *madrasa* with a radical Islamic school: "An article...that said Senator Barack Obama had attended an Islamic school or madrassa in Indonesia as a child referred imprecisely to madrassas. While some teach a radical version of Islam, most historically have not."

Historically, the core curriculum of madrasas included the study of Arabic language and syntax, the Quran, Quranic interpretation (*tafsir*), *hadith* (tradition), and Muslim history. With the advent of European colonialism and the introduction of Western curricula, many madrasas across the Muslim world began to change, often combining religious and secular education. This trend continued post-independence (after World War II), when the introduction of modern Western-influenced educational reforms resulted in a split between secular and religious schools. These networks of more secular schools and universities eroded the traditional authority of the *ulama* (religious scholars) and their dominant role in education and law. In most Muslim countries, modern secular educational systems were privileged over traditional religious schools, whose diplomas came to have a more limited value in society. State-controlled education further reduced the ulama-madrasa system as ministries of religious affairs took control of many religious institutions and social welfare programs (influencing appointments, salaries of teachers and preachers, and in some countries the content of sermons).

Madrasas came to be associated with religious extremism and terrorism after the Afghan-Soviet war in the 1990s and especially after the 9/11 attacks and the rise of the Taliban, who were students or graduates of madrasas. The role of certain madrasas in producing the Taliban and the growth of militant madrasas in Afghanistan and Pakistan, often supported by wealthy businessmen and Saudi- or Gulf-sponsored organizations, sparked deep concerns about so-called jihadi madrasas with their extremist brand of Islam and its "jihadi" culture. As a result, all madrasas rather than a radical minority, especially in Pakistan, were indiscriminately associated with militancy. The Yale Center for the Study of Globalization reported this bias in American newspaper coverage of Pakistan: "When articles mentioned 'madrassas,' readers were led to infer that all schools so-named are anti-American, anti-Western, pro-terrorist centers having less to do with teaching basic literacy and more to do with political indoctrination."

Madrasas remain an important educational institution in many, though not all, Muslim countries. Most are not radicalized. While in some countries they provide an excellent education in both religious and nonreligious subjects, in many more they are in need of substantial reform in their Islamic and non-Islamic curriculum.

Are there any divisions in Islam?

As a world religion, Islam is practiced in diverse cultures in Africa, the Middle East, Asia, Europe, and America.

Differences in religious and cultural practices are therefore wide-ranging. Although there are no denominations in Islam such as exist in the Christian faith (Roman Catholic, Methodist, Episcopalian, Lutheran, etc.), like all faiths, Islam has developed divisions, sects, and schools of thought over various issues. While all Muslims share certain beliefs and practices, such as belief in God, the Quran, Muhammad, and the Five Pillars of Islam, divisions have arisen over questions of political and religious leadership, theology, interpretations of Islamic law, and responses to modernity and the West.

The division of opinion about political and religious leadership after the death of Muhammad led to the division of Muslims into two major branches—Sunni (85 percent of all Muslims) and Shii (15 percent). (See next question.) In addition, a small but significant radical minority known as the Kharijites should be mentioned. Although they have never won large numbers of followers, their unique theological position continues to influence political and religious debate up to the present day.

Sunni Muslims believe that because Muhammad did not designate a successor, the best or most qualified person should be either selected or elected as leader (*caliph*). Because the Quran declared Muhammad to be the last of the prophets, this caliph was to succeed Muhammad as the political leader only. Sunni believe that the caliph should serve as the protector of the faith, but he does not enjoy any special religious status or inspiration.

Shii, by contrast, believe that succession to the leadership of the Muslim community should be hereditary, passed down to Muhammad's male descendants (descended from Muhammad's daughter Fatima and her husband Ali), who are known as Imams. Imams are to serve as both religious and political leaders. Shii believe that the Imam is religiously inspired, sinless, and the interpreter of God's will as contained in Islamic law, but not a prophet. Shii consider the sayings, deeds, and writings of their Imams to be authoritative religious texts, in addition to the Quran and Sunnah. Shii further split into three main divisions as a result of disagreement over the number of Imams who succeeded Muhammad. (See page 51, "What are the divisions among Shii Muslims?")

The Kharijites (from *kharaja*, to go out or exit) began as followers of the caliph Ali, but they broke away from him because they believed him to be guilty of compromising God's will when he agreed to arbitrate rather than continue to fight a long-drawn-out war against a rebellious general. After separating from Ali (whom they eventually assassinated), the Kharijites established a separate community designed to be a "true" charismatic society strictly following the Quran and Sunnah of the Prophet Muhammad. The Kharijite world was separated neatly into believers and nonbelievers, Muslims (followers of God) and non-Muslims (enemies of God). These enemies could include other Muslims who did not accept the uncompromising Kharijite point of view. Sinners were to be excommunicated and were subject to death unless they repented. Therefore, a caliph or ruler could only hold office as long as he was sinless. If he fell from this state, he was outside the protection of law and must be deposed or killed.

This mentality influenced the famous medieval theologian and legal scholar Ibn Taymiyya (d. 1328) and has been replicated in modern times by Islamic Jihad, the group that assassinated Egypt's President Anwar Sadat, as well as by Osama bin Laden and other extremists who call for the overthrow of "un-Islamic" Muslim rulers.

Differences of opinion about political and religious leadership have led Sunni and Shii to hold very different visions of sacred history. Sunni experienced a glorious and victorious history under the Four Rightly Guided Caliphs and the expansion and development of Muslim empires under the Umayyad and Abbasid dynasties. Sunni can thus claim a golden age in which they were a great world power and civilization, which they see as evidence of God's guidance and the truth of the mission of Islam. Shii, on the other hand, struggled unsuccessfully during the same time period against Sunni rule in the attempt to restore the imamate they believed God had appointed. Therefore, Shii see in this time period the illegitimate usurpation of power by the Sunni at the expense of creating a just society. Shii historical memory emphasizes the suffering and oppression of the righteous, the need to protest against injustice, and the requirement that Muslims be willing to sacrifice everything, including their lives, in the struggle with the overwhelming forces of evil (Satan) in order to restore God's righteous rule.

Divisions of opinion also exist with respect to theological questions. One historical example is the question of whether a ruler judged guilty of a grave (mortal) sin should still be considered legitimate or should be overthrown and killed. Most Sunni theologians and jurists taught that the preservation of social order was more important than the character of the ruler. They also taught that only God on Judgment Day is capable of judging sinners and determining whether or not they are faithful and deserving of paradise. Therefore, Sunni concluded that the ruler should remain in power since subjects could not judge the ruler. Ibn Taymiyya was the one major theologian and jurist who rejected this position and taught instead that a sinful ruler should and must be overthrown.

Ibn Taymiyya's ire was directed at the Mongols. Despite their conversion to Islam, they continued to follow the Yasa code of laws of Genghis Khan instead of the Islamic law (*shariah*). For Ibn Taymiyya this made them no better than the polytheists of the pre-Islamic period. He issued a *fatwa* (formal legal opinion) that labeled them as unbelievers (*kafirs*) who were thus excommunicated (*takfir*). This fatwa established a precedent: despite their claim to be Muslims, their failure to implement Shariah rendered the Mongols apostates and hence the lawful object of jihad. Muslim citizens thus had the right, indeed the duty, to revolt against them, to wage jihad.

Ibn Taymiyya's opinions remain relevant today because they have inspired the militancy and religious worldview of organizations like Osama bin Laden's al-Qaeda network.

Other examples of divisions over theological questions include arguments over whether the Quran was created or uncreated and whether it should be interpreted literally or metaphorically and allegorically. Historically, Muslims have also debated the question of free will versus predestination. That is, do human beings have their own agency to choose their actions, or are all actions predetermined by an omniscient God? What are the implications of such beliefs for human responsibility and justice?

Islamic law provides one of the clearest and most important examples of diversity of opinions. Islamic law developed in response to the concrete realities of daily life. Since the heart of Islam and being a Muslim is submission to God's will, the primary question for believers was "What should I do and how?" During the Umayyad Empire (661–750), rulers set up a rudimentary legal system based upon the Quran, the Sunnah, and local customs and traditions. However, many pious Muslims became concerned about the influence of rulers on the development of the law. They wanted to anchor Islamic law more firmly to its revealed sources and make it less vulnerable to manipulation by rulers and their appointed judges.

Over the next two centuries, Muslims in the major cities of Medina, Mecca, Kufa, Basra, and Damascus sought to discover and delineate God's will and law through the science of jurisprudence. Although each city produced a distinctive interpretation of the law, all shared a general legal tradition. The earliest scholars of Islamic law were neither lawyers nor judges nor students of a specific university. They were men who combined professions such as trade with the study of Islamic texts. These loosely connected scholars tended to gather around or associate with major personalities. Their schools of thought came to be referred to as law schools.

While many law schools existed, only a few endured and were recognized as authoritative. Today, there are four major Sunni law schools (Hanafi, Hanbali, Maliki, and Shafii) and two major Shii schools (Jafari and Zaydis). The Hanafi came to predominate in the Arab world and South Asia; the Maliki in North, Central, and West Africa; the Shafii in East Africa and Southeast Asia; and the Hanbali in Saudi Arabia. Muslims are free to follow any law school but usually select the one that predominates in the area in which they are born or live.

Perhaps nowhere are the differences in Islam more visible than in the responses to modernity. Since the nineteenth century, Muslims have struggled with the relationship of their religious tradition developed in premodern times to the new demands (religious, political, economic, and social) of the modern world. The issues are not only about Islam's accommodation to change but also about the relationship of Islam to the West, since much of modern change is associated with Western ideas, institutions, and values. Muslim responses to issues of reform and modernization have spanned the spectrum from secularists and Islamic modernists to religious conservatives or traditionalists, "fundamentalists," and Islamic reformists.

Modern secularists are Western oriented and advocate a separation between religion and the rest of society, including politics. They believe that religion is and should be strictly a private matter. Islamic modernists believe that Islam and modernity, particularly science and technology, are compatible, so that Islam should inform public life without necessarily dominating it. The other groups are more "Islamically" oriented but have different opinions as to the role Islam should play in public life. Conservatives, or traditionalists, emphasize the authority of the past and tend to call for a reimplementation of Islamic laws and norms as they existed in that past. "Fundamentalists" emphasize going back to the earliest period and teachings of Islam, believing that the Islamic tradition needs to be purified of popular, cultural, and Western beliefs and practices that have "corrupted" Islam. However, the term *fundamentalist* is applied to such a broad spectrum of Islamic movements and actors that, in the end, it includes both those who simply want to reintroduce or restore their pure and puritanical vision of a romanticized past and others who advocate modern reforms that are rooted in Islamic principles and values. There are a significant number of Islamic reformers, intellectuals, and religious leaders who also emphasize the critical need for an Islamic reformation, a wide-ranging program of reinterpretation (*ijtihad*) and reform urging fresh approaches to Quranic interpretation as well as to issues of gender, human rights, democratization, and legal reform.

What is the difference between Sunni and Shii Muslims?

Sunni and Shii Muslims represent the two largest institutional divisions within the Muslim community. Today, Sunni constitute approximately 85 percent of Muslims and Shii make up 15 percent. The Shii have significant numbers in Iran, Iraq, Bahrain, and Lebanon. The differences that led to the formation of these two groups centered on disagreements about who should be the successor to the Prophet Muhammad.

In the early Muslim community, Muhammad provided immediate and authoritative answers. Muhammad's death in 632 was a traumatic event for the Muslim community, marking not only the end of direct, personal contact with and guidance from the Prophet but also the end of direct revelation from God. The Companions of the Prophet moved quickly to steady and reassure community members. Abu Bakr, the man whom Muhammad had appointed to lead the Friday communal prayer in his absence, announced the death of the Prophet in this way: "Muslims! If any of you has worshipped Muhammad, let me tell you that Muhammad is dead. But if you worship God, then know that God is living and will never die!"

The majority of Muslims, who came to be called Sunni, or followers of the Sunnah (example) of the Prophet, believed that Muhammad had died without establishing a system for selecting a successor or designating a replacement. After an initial period of uncertainty, the elders or leaders of Medina selected Abu Bakr to be the *caliph* (successor, deputy). An early convert who had been Muhammad's close companion and trusted adviser as well as his father-in-law, Abu Bakr was respected for his sagacity and piety. Thus Sunni Muslims adopted the belief that leadership should pass to the most qualified person, not through hereditary succession.

As caliph, Abu Bakr became the political and military leader of the community. Although he was not a prophet—the Quran had declared Muhammad to be the last of the prophets—the caliph had religious prestige as head of the community of believers (*ummah*). This was symbolized in later history by the caliph's right to lead the Friday prayer and the inclusion of the caliph's name in the community's prayers.

A minority of the Muslim community, the Shii, or Party of Ali, opposed the selection of Abu Bakr as caliph, believing that succession should be hereditary. Since Muhammad had no sons who survived infancy, this minority believed that succession should pass through Muhammad's daughter Fatima and that her husband Ali, Muhammad's first cousin and closest living male relative, should be the leader (called Imam) of the Islamic community. Shii took strong exception to the fact that Ali was passed over for the position of caliph three times, finally gaining his rightful place after thirty-five years only to be assassinated a few short years later. To make matters worse, Ali's charismatic son Hussein, who had been persuaded to lead a rebellion against the caliph Yazid, was overwhelmed and massacred along with his small band of followers.

Muslims point out that the differences between Sunni and Shii do not have to do with dogma but rather are political, having to do with the qualifications for the head of the Muslim community. Their shared beliefs and practices notwithstanding, however, they also developed different views about the meaning of history.

Historically, Sunni have almost always ruled over Shii. Because Shii existed as an oppressed and disinherited minority, they understood history to be a test of the righteous community's perseverance in the struggle to restore God's rule on earth. Realization of a just social order led by their Imam became the dream of Shii throughout the centuries. While Sunni history looked to the glorious and victorious history of the Four Rightly Guided Caliphs and then the development of imperial Islam under the Umayyads, Abbasids, and Ottomans, Shii history was the theater for the struggle of the oppressed and disinherited. Thus, while Sunni can claim a golden age when they were a great world power and civilization, which they believe is evidence of God's favor upon them and a historic validation of Muslim beliefs, Shii see in these same developments the illegitimate usurpation of power by Sunni rulers at the expense of a just society. Shii view history more as a paradigm of the suffering, disinheritance, and oppression of a righteous minority community who must constantly struggle to restore God's rule on earth under His divinely appointed Imam.

In the twentieth century, Shii history was reinterpreted as a paradigm providing inspiration and mobilization to actively fight against injustice, rather than passively accept it. This reinterpretation has had the most significant impact among the Shii in Lebanon, who struggled to achieve greater social, educational, and economic opportunities during the 1970s and 1980s, and in Iran, where the Shah was equated with Yazid, and Ayatollah Khomeini and his followers with Hussein, during the Islamic revolution of 1978–79. Thus the victory of the Islamic revolution was declared the victory of the righteous against illegitimate usurpers of power.

What are the divisions among Shii Muslims?

Shii Islam developed three main divisions, stemming from disagreement over the number of Imams who succeeded Muhammad: the Zaydis (also called the Fivers) recognized five Imams, the Ismailis (also called the Seveners) recognized seven, and the Ithna Ashari (also called the Twelvers) recognized twelve.

The Zaydis split with the other Shii by recognizing Hussein's grandson Zayd as the fifth Imam. They believed that any descendant of Ali who was willing to assert his claim to the imamate publicly and fight for it could become Imam. The Zaydis were the first Shii group to achieve independence. They founded a dynasty in Tabaristan on the Caspian Sea in 864. Another Zaydi imamate state was founded in Yemen in 893 and lasted until 1963.

The split between the Ismailis (Seveners) and Ithna Ashari (Twelvers) occurred in the eighth century over the question of who succeeded the sixth Imam, Jafar al-Sadiq (d. 765). The Ismailis recognize seven Imams, ending with Jafar al-Sadiq's son Ismail, who was designated to become the seventh Imam. Ismail predeceased his father and left no son. The Ismailis formed a revolutionary movement against the Sunni caliphate and established the Fatimid Dynasty, whose empire stretched from Egypt and North Africa to the Sind province of India between the tenth and twelfth centuries.

The Nizari Ismailis were particularly vehement in their violent opposition to Sunni Abbasid rule. Their tactics of violence and terror earned them the epithet of the Assassins. One of the ironies of history is that a Nizari leader who fled to India established a line of Imams known by the honorific title of Aga Khan and created a nonviolent mainstream form of Shii Islam that now has prosperous communities in Canada, Britain, East Africa, and South Asia. The current Harvard-educated Aga Khan oversees the cultural and spiritual lives of his followers, in addition to looking after the educational, social, and commercial institutions of the community.

The third and most populous Shii group, the Ithna Ashari (Twelvers), recognized twelve legitimate successors to Muhammad. Today, they are a majority in Iran, Iraq, and Bahrain. The twelfth Imam, Muhammad al-Muntazar (Muhammad the Awaited One), "disappeared" in 874 as a child, leaving no sons. This created a major dilemma for the line of succession. Shii theology resolved this dilemma with the doctrine of the Hidden Imam, which declares that the twelfth Imam did not die but rather "disappeared" and is in hiding (or in "occultation") for an unspecified period of time. This messianic figure is expected to return as the divinely guided Mahdi at the end of time to vindicate his followers, restore his faithful community, and usher in a perfect Islamic society of justice and truth. In the interim, religious experts or *mujtahids* (those capable of independently interpreting Islamic law) guide the Shii community. In contrast to the majority Muslim experience, Twelver Shiism developed a clerical hierarchy at whose apex are religious leaders acknowledged by their followers as *ayatollahs* (signs of God) because of their reputation for knowledge and piety.

Who is the Aga Khan?

During the time of Hasan Ali Shah (d. 1881), the religious leader, or Imam, of the Nizaris (the largest branch of the Ismaili followers in Shii Islam) inherited the title of Aga Khan. Ismailis believe that the present Imam, Prince Karim al-Husseini, Aga Khan IV (1936–), is the forty-ninth hereditary Imam, descended directly from the first Shii Imam, Ali and his wife Fatima, the Prophet Muhammad's daughter.

Born in Geneva, the Aga Khan spent his early childhood in Kenya. He was schooled in Switzerland, and in 1959 he earned a degree in Islamic history from Harvard University. While still at Harvard, he became the spiritual leader of the fifteen million members of the worldwide Ismaili community in 1957.

The Aga Khan's fifty-three-year leadership has been known for its emphasis on the spiritual as well as the material. He expresses the belief that he has a mandate, as Imam, to improve the quality of life for the world community. His interests center on eliminating global poverty, advancing women, promoting Islamic art, architecture, and culture, and fostering pluralistic values in society.

The Aga Khan has created major philanthropic institutions to achieve his goals. He is founder and chair of the Aga Khan Development Network, one of the largest in the world, employing a staff of seventy thousand who coordinate the social and economic development work of over two hundred agencies and institutions and operate in thirty-five of the poorest countries in the world, especially in Asia and Africa. They focus on the environment, health, education, architecture, culture, microfinance, rural development, disaster reduction, private-sector enterprise promotion, and historic-cities revitalization projects.

What is Wahhabi Islam?

Until recently, most Westerners had never heard of Wahhabi Islam, but we have now repeatedly heard this term applied to Osama bin Laden and Saudi Arabia. There are many interpretations of Islam, many schools of theology and law. Among the most ultraconservative is Wahhabi Islam, the official form of Islam in Saudi Arabia.

The Wahhabi movement takes its name from Muhammad Ibn Abd al-Wahhab (1703–1791), a scholar of Islamic law and theology in Mecca and Medina. Disillusioned by the decline and moral laxity of his society, Abd al-Wahhab denounced many popular beliefs and practices as un-Islamic idolatry and a return to the paganism of pre-Islamic Arabia. He rejected blind imitation or following (*taqlid*) of past scholarship. He regarded the medieval law of the *ulama* (religious scholars) as fallible and, at times, unwarranted innovations (*bida*) or heresy. Abd al-Wahhab called for a fresh interpretation of Islam that returned to the "fundamentals" of Islam, the Quran and the Sunnah (example) of the Prophet Muhammad.

Muhammad Ibn Abd al-Wahhab joined with Muhammad Ibn Saud, a local tribal chief, to form a religious-political movement. Ibn Saud used Wahhabism to legitimate his jihad to subdue and unite the tribes of Arabia, converting them to this puritanical version of Islam. Like the Kharijites, Wahhabi theology saw the world in white and black categories— Muslim and non-Muslim, belief and unbelief, the realm of Islam and that of warfare. They regarded all Muslims who did not agree with them as unbelievers to be subdued (that is, fought and killed) in the name of Islam. Central to Muhammad Ibn Abd al-Wahhab's theology was the doctrine of God's unity (*tawhid*), an absolute monotheism reflected in the Wahhabis' self-designation as "Unitarians"—those who uphold the unity of God.

In imitation of Muhammad's destruction of the pantheon of pre-Islamic tribal gods in Mecca's sacred shrine (Kaaba) and its restoration to worship of the one true God (Allah), Wahhabi puritanism spared neither the sacred tombs of Muhammad and his Companions in Mecca and Medina nor the Shiite pilgrimage site at Karbala (in modern Iraq). This pilgrimage site housed the tomb of Hussein, son of Ali, the first Shii Imam and third caliph, who with his followers was slaughtered in the Battle of Karbala and is remembered as "the martyr of martyrs." The destruction of this venerated site has never been forgotten by Shii Muslims and contributed to the historic antipathy between the Wahhabi of Saudi Arabia and Shii Islam both in Saudi Arabia and Iran. Centuries later, many would point to Wahhabi-inspired iconoclasm as the source behind the Taliban's wanton destruction of Buddhist monuments in Afghanistan, an action condemned by Muslim leaders worldwide.

In the early nineteenth century, Muhammad Ali of Egypt defeated the Saudis, but the Wahhabi movement and the House of Saud proved resilient. By the early twentieth century, Abdulaziz Ibn Saud recaptured Riyadh, united the tribes of Arabia, restored the Saudi kingdom, and spread the Wahhabi movement. The Kingdom of Saudi Arabia melded the political and religious in a self-declared Islamic state, using the Wahhabi interpretation of Islam as the official basis for state and society.

Internationally, the Saudis, both government-sponsored organizations and wealthy individuals, have exported their ultraconservative version of Wahhabi Islam to other countries and communities in the Muslim world and the West. They have offered development aid, built mosques, libraries, and other institutions, funded and distributed religious tracts, and commissioned imams and religious scholars. Wahhabi puritanism and financial support have been exported to Afghanistan, Pakistan, the Central Asian Republics, China, Africa, Southeast Asia, the United States, and Europe. At the same time, some wealthy businessmen in Saudi Arabia and the Gulf have provided financial support to extremist groups who follow a militant "fundamentalist" brand of Islam (commonly referred to as Wahhabi or Salafi) with its jihad culture. The challenge is to distinguish between the export of an ultraconservative theology on the one hand and militant extremism on the other. This difficulty is compounded by the propensity of authoritarian governments in Central Asia and China, especially since 9/11, to use the label "Wahhabi extremism" for all opposition, legitimate and illegitimate, and thus justify widespread repression of all who are opposed to their rule and policies.

What is Salafi Islam?

"Salafi," in its strict sense, means returning to the pristine Islam of the first generation (*salaf*, or pious ancestors) of Muslims. Like Wahhabis, Salafis idealize the period of Muhammad and his Companions as an uncorrupted time for the religious community. They believe that Islam declined after the early generations because un-Islamic innovations (*bida*) were introduced. Therefore today there must be a return to the practices of the early generations and a purge of un-Islamic and foreign influences.

The Salafis' uncompromising monotheism leads them to condemn many common Muslim beliefs and practices, and in particular Sufi and Shii doctrines, as polytheism (*shirk*). They regard most Islamic movements today as innovations or deviations from "true Islam" and therefore "heretical."

Today *Salafism* is used as an umbrella term that can be misleading because it includes many groups and shades of belief. Salafism is found in many Muslim-majority countries as well as in European and American communities where individuals see it as an attractive alternative to cultural practices of Islam and secularism. For example, Salafis include disaffected second-generation Muslim youth who want to define their identity by rejecting the foreign cultural practices of the Islam embraced by their parents and grandparents as well as the secular practices of Westernization. Salafis see themselves as embracing an authentic, original, "pure" form of Islam that transcends a specific culture and emphasizes Islam's universality instead.

What about militant Salafism? Like Wahhabi Islam, Salafi religious exclusivism can lead to intolerance of other believers, both other Muslims—in particular Shii Muslims, whom Salafis despise—and non-Muslims. In itself, a religiously exclusivist theology is not necessarily violent. An exclusivist theology merely entails a division between those who will, and those who will not, go to paradise after the Day of Judgment. An exclusive worldview, like that of other radical fundamentalisms (Christian, Jewish, or Hindu), lends itself to extremism and violence when fundamentalists claim to legitimate their political agendas as a mandate from God. Global terrorists in North Africa, Europe, the Middle East, and Asia exemplify this militant Salafi ideology and threat.

Is there a difference between Muslims and Black Muslims?

African-American Islam emerged in the early twentieth century when a number of black Americans converted to Islam, the religion that they believed was part of their original African identity. Islam was preferred over Christianity, which was seen as a religion of white supremacy and oppression, the religion of those who treated black Americans as second-class citizens and denied them their full civil rights. By contrast, Islam seemed to emphasize a brotherhood of believers, the *ummah*, which transcended race and ethnicity.

In the early 1930s Wallace D. Fard Muhammad drew on the Quran and the Bible to preach a message of black liberation in the ghettos of Detroit. Wallace D., who was called the Great Mahdi, or messiah, taught withdrawal from white society, saying that blacks were not Americans and owed no loyalty to the state. He rejected Christianity and the domination of white "blue-eyed devils" and emphasized the "religion of the Black Man" and the "Nation of Islam."

Fard mysteriously disappeared in 1934. Elijah Muhammad (formerly Elijah Poole [1897–1975]) took over and built the "Nation of Islam," an effective national movement whose members became known as "Black Muslims." Elijah Muhammad denounced white society's political and economic oppression of blacks and its results: self-hatred, poverty, and dependency. His apocalyptical message promised the fall of the white racist oppressor America and the restoration of the righteous black community, a "Chosen People." His religious teachings gave marginalized poor and unemployed people a sense of identity and community, and a program for self-improvement and empowerment. Elijah Muhammad emphasized a "Do for Self" philosophy, appealing particularly to black youth, focusing on black pride and identity, strength and self-sufficiency, strong family values, hard work, discipline, thrift, and abstention from gambling, alcohol, drugs, and pork. By the 1970s the Nation of Islam had more than one hundred thousand members.

A number of basic beliefs in the Black Muslim movement differed significantly from mainstream Islam. Elijah Muhammad announced that Wallace D. Fard was Allah, and thus that God was a black man, and that he, Elijah Muhammad, not the Prophet Muhammad, was the last messenger of God. The Nation taught black supremacy and black separatism, not Islam's brotherhood of all believers in a community that transcends racial, tribal, and ethnic differences. In addition, the Nation did not follow the Five Pillars of Islam or observe major Muslim rituals.

A key individual who rose through the ranks of the Nation of Islam to gain national prominence was Malcolm X, who accepted the teaching of the Nation of Islam while in prison. Drawn by Elijah Muhammad's black nationalism, denunciation of white racism, and promotion of self-help, Malcolm Little became Malcolm X: ex-smoker, ex-drinker, ex-Christian, and ex-slave. The "X" also stood for the unknown surname of Malcolm's slave ancestors, preferred to a name originally given by a slave owner. A gifted, charismatic speaker, Malcolm was the most visible and prominent spokesperson for Elijah Muhammad, recruiting new members (including the boxer Cassius Clay, renamed Muhammad Ali), establishing temples, and preaching the message of the Nation of Islam nationally and internationally. However, Malcolm's exposure to world events and contact with Sunni Muslims resulted in a gradual change in his own religious worldview, away from that of Elijah Muhammad and toward mainstream Islam.

In 1964, Malcolm X left the Nation of Islam to start his own organization. At this time he also went on pilgrimage to Mecca. On the pilgrimage he was deeply affected by what he experienced—the equality of all believers regardless of race, tribe, or nation. Malcolm explained his realization that "we were truly all the same (brothers)—because their belief in one God removed the 'white' from their minds, the 'white' from their behavior and the 'white' from their attitude." He also recognized that he did not know how to perform Islam's daily prayers and had not observed the other prescribed practices in the Five Pillars of Islam. Malcolm returned from the pilgrimage as El Hajj Malik El-Shabazz, a Muslim, rather than a Black Muslim. He changed his position on black nationalism, moving to pan-Africanism, which aligns African Americans with their cultural and religious ties in Africa.

On February 21, 1965, the former Malcolm X was assassinated as he spoke to an audience in New York City. Two members of the Nation of Islam were convicted of the murder.

The 1960s were a time of transition for the Nation of Islam. Not only Malcolm X but also Wallace D. Muhammad, son of Elijah Muhammad, along with his brother Akbar Muhammad, a distinguished scholar of Islam who had studied in Egypt and Scotland, questioned and challenged some of their father's teachings and strategies. Elijah Muhammad excommunicated both sons. Yet toward the end of his life Elijah Muhammad also made the pilgrimage to Mecca and began to modify some of his teachings. By the time of his death in 1975, Elijah Muhammad and the Nation were publicly acknowledged for their constructive contributions to America's inner cities and communities.

When Wallace D. Muhammad succeeded his father as Supreme Minister of the Nation, he implemented major reforms in doctrine and organizational structure, to conform them to the teachings of orthodox Sunni Islam. Wallace Fard was identified as the founder of the Nation and Elijah Muhammad as the leader who brought black Americans to his interpretation of Islam. Wallace Muhammad made the pilgrimage to Mecca and encouraged his followers to study Arabic in order to better understand Islam. Temples were renamed mosques, and their leaders were now called imams rather than ministers. Members of the community observed the Five Pillars of Islam in union with the worldwide Islamic community to which they now belonged. Black separatist doctrines were dropped as the Nation community began to participate within the American political process. Finally, the equality of male and female members was reaffirmed, and women were given more responsible positions in the ministry of the community. While the Nation continued to work for social and economic change, business ventures were cut back and religious identity and mission were given priority.

At the end of the 1970s Wallace transferred organizational leadership to an elected council of six imams and focused on his role as religious and spiritual leader. In the mid-1980s, signaling his and the Nation's new religious identity and mission, Wallace changed his name to Warith Deen Muhammad and renamed the community American Muslim Mission, integrating it within the global mainstream Islamic community and within the American Muslim community.

Media coverage of the Black Muslim movement often focuses on Louis Farrakhan, the man who led a minority of Nation members in protest against Warith's reforms. Farrakhan bitterly rejected the changes instituted by both Malcolm and Warith Deen Muhammad (d. 2008), maintaining that only he and his followers had remained faithful to the original message and mission of Elijah Muhammad. Farrakhan retained the mantle of leadership of the Nation of Islam, along with its black nationalist and separatist doctrines. Farrakhan's strident, separatist messages as well as the international connections he has established with militant leaders like those of Libya and Iran have given him and his minority of followers a disproportionate visibility.

Farrakhan's militancy and anti-Semitic statements have been widely criticized. At the same time, his charisma and energy directed to fighting crime and drugs and to rehabilitating prisoners have earned praise for the Nation. His leadership of the 1995 Million Man March in Washington, D.C., received widespread media coverage and support from Christian, as well as Muslim, leaders and organizations. In recent years, Farrakhan has moved the Nation closer to more orthodox Islamic practices, maintaining a closer identity with mainstream Islam.

Who are the Sufis?

Sufis belong to the mystical tradition of Islam known as Sufism. The name "Sufi" is derived from the Arabic word *suf* (wool), in honor of the coarse woolen garments worn by the first Sufis, resembling the garb of Christian monks and mystics in other faiths. Like other mystical movements in Christianity, Judaism, Hinduism, and Buddhism, the Sufi path seeks to discipline the mind and body in order to experience directly the presence of God. Sufis view their struggle to find God as one that takes place in the world, in contrast to the Christian monastic tradition of withdrawing from the world in order to find God.

Sufis set as their highest priority the individual spiritual effort of self-sacrifice and discipline in a struggle within oneself against greed, laziness, and ego. This struggle is known as the "greater jihad" (as opposed to the "lesser jihad" of armed struggle in the defense of Islam). This "greater jihad" is carried out by devoting oneself completely to fulfilling God's will, studying and meditating on the Quran and the Sunnah (the example of Muhammad), performing religious duties, especially prayer and fasting, focusing on the centrality of God and the Last Judgment, denying material desires that could distract one from God, and carrying out good works. A famous woman mystic, Rabia al-Adawiyya (d. 801), added the devotional love of God to Sufi practices.

Like Islamic law, Sufism began as a reform movement in response to the growing materialism and wealth of Muslim society that accompanied the expansion and increasing power of the Islamic empire. While some believed that strict adherence to Islamic law and rituals was the solution to the excesses of imperial lifestyles and luxuries, Sufis found the emphasis on laws, rules, duties, and rights to be spiritually lacking. Instead, they emphasized the "interior" path, seeking the purity and simplicity of the time of Muhammad, as the route to the direct and personal experience of God. Following the example of Muhammad in working tirelessly in the world to create the ideal Islamic society, Sufis have often played an important role in the political life of Muslims. For example, in the eighteenth and nineteenth centuries, Sufi brotherhoods led jihad movements (for example, the Mahdi in Sudan, Fulani in Nigeria, and Sanusi in Libya) that spearheaded an Islamic revivalist wave that regenerated society, created Islamic states, and fought off colonial powers.

The Sufi orders also played an important role in the spread of Islam through missionary work. Their tendency to adopt and adapt to local non-Islamic customs and practices in new places, and their strong devotional and emotional practices, helped them to become a popular mass movement and a threat to the more orthodox religious establishment. In this way, Sufism became integral to popular religious practices and spirituality in Islam. However, their willingness to embrace local traditions also left them open to criticism by the conservative religious establishment for being unfaithful to the tenets of Islam. Indeed, popular Sufism at times slipped into magic and superstition, as well as withdrawal from the world. Some of the major Islamic revival and reform movements of the eighteenth, nineteenth, and twentieth centuries sought to eliminate superstitious practices from Sufism and bring it back into line with more orthodox interpretations of Islam.

Sufism today exists throughout the Muslim world and in a variety of devotional paths. It remains a strong spiritual presence and force in Muslim societies, in both private and public life, and enjoys a wide following in Europe and America, attracting many converts to Islam.

Who are these Islamic fundamentalists?

The term *Islamic fundamentalism* evokes many images: the Iranian revolution, the Ayatollah Khomeini, the World Trade Center and Pentagon attacks of 9/11, Osama bin Laden and al-Qaeda, and suicide bombers. For many, this term is simply equated with radicalism, religious extremism, and terrorism. But images of hostage crises, embassies under siege, hijackings, and bombings lead to simplistic understandings. The term *fundamentalist* is applied to such a broad spectrum of Islamic movements and actors that in the end it includes both those who simply want to reintroduce or restore their pure and puritanical vision of a romanticized past and others who advocate modern reforms that are rooted in Islamic principles and values.

The ranks of Islamic fundamentalists include those who provide much-needed services to the poor such as schools, health clinics, and social welfare agencies, as well as extremists. For every country where Islamic militants seek to reach their goals through violence and terrorism, there are Islamic political parties and social welfare organizations that participate in national and local elections and function effectively within mainstream society.

Though convenient, the use of the term *fundamentalism*, which originated in Christianity, can be misleading in the Islamic context, where it has been applied to a broad and diverse group of governments, individuals, and organizations. The conservative monarchy of Saudi Arabia, the radical socialist state of Libya, clerically governed Iran, the Taliban's Afghanistan, and the Islamic Republic of Pakistan have all been called "fundamentalist." The term obscures their differences. Libya and Iran, for example, have in the past espoused many anti-Western views, while Saudi Arabia and Pakistan have often been close allies of the United States. *Political Islam* and *Islamism* are more useful terms when referring to the role of Islam in politics.

Islamism, or political Islam, is rooted in a contemporary religious resurgence, which began in the late 1960s and has affected both the personal and public life of Muslims. On the one hand, many Muslims have become more religiously observant, demonstrating increased attention to prayer, fasting, dress, and family values as well as renewed interest in Islamic mysticism, or Sufism. On the other, Islam reemerged in public life as an alternative political and social ideology to secular nationalism, western capitalism, and Marxist socialism, which many believe failed to help the majority of Muslims escape poverty, unemployment, and political oppression. Governments, Islamic movements, and organizations from moderate to extremist have appealed to Islam for legitimacy and to mobilize popular support.

Islamic activists—"fundamentalists"—both extremists and mainstream come from very diverse educational and social backgrounds. They are recruited not only from the poor and unemployed living in slums and refugee camps but also from the middle class in prosperous neighborhoods. While some are from economically or politically marginalized or "oppressed" backgrounds, others are well-educated university students and professionals. Many hold degrees in the sciences, education, medicine, law, or engineering—professionals who function in and contribute to their societies.

Many Islamic activists are part of a nonviolent political and social force in mainstream society. Activists have served as prime minister of Turkey, president and speaker of the national assembly in Indonesia, and deputy prime minister of Malaysia. Cabinet officers, parliamentarians, and mayors in countries as diverse as Egypt, Sudan, Turkey, Iran, Lebanon, Kuwait, Yemen, Jordan, Pakistan, Bangladesh, Malaysia, Indonesia, and Israel-Palestine are also activists.

At the same time, a militant minority are religious extremists and terrorists: Sheikh Omar Abdel Rahman, a religious leader who was imprisoned for his involvement in plans to bomb major sites in the United States, has a doctorate

in Islamic studies; Osama bin Laden, a university graduate
and member of one of the wealthiest families in Saudi Arabia,
became a global terrorist and leader of al-Qaeda; Ayman
al-Zawahiri, right-hand man to Osama bin Laden, is a trained
surgeon from a prominent Egyptian family.

Is Islam medieval and against change?

Islam and much of the Muslim world are often seen as medieval for many reasons: cultural (for example, the existence of
strong patriarchal societies and the veiling and seclusion of
women), political (authoritarianism on the one hand and fundamentalism on the other), and economic (lack of development
and failed economies).

Yet in truth, today as in the past Muslims interpret Islam in
many different ways. Like their Abrahamic brothers and
sisters, Muslims exhibit a wide range of approaches and orientations, ranging from ultraconservative to more progressive or reformist.

The contrast between Islam and Christianity or Judaism
appears as more vivid because we usually equate Christianity
and Judaism with believers in modern Europe and America
rather than those in more traditional, premodern, and less
developed societies such as Ethiopia, Eritrea, or Sudan.
However, Ethiopian Jews and Christians, whose religion is
linked to local tribal and cultural traditions, also contrast
sharply with their Western co-believers. Such contrasts are of
course more evident among Christianity's 1.5 billion adherents
spread across the globe than among Judaism's 14 to 18 million
followers, who have a far more restricted geographic
representation.

The forces of tradition and the authority of the past have
been reinforced in Islam by a variety of historic forces and
experiences. For four centuries (the seventeenth through the
twentieth), much of the Islamic world was dominated by
European colonialism. Religions, like countries, when under

siege tend to focus on survival, preserving and protecting what they have, rather than seeking and accepting change. Thus opponents often label Islamic calls for reform as attempts to Westernize Islam.

When conservatives try to preserve Islam, they often do not distinguish between revealed sources of faith and socially conditioned human interpretations historically preserved in manuals of Islamic law and theology. In contrast, reformers stress the difference between divinely mandated beliefs, practices, and laws and human interpretations from the past as they engage in a bold process of reinterpretation and reform that reapplies Islamic guidelines to problems in the modern world.

Amidst these differing religious interpretations and orientations, change has occurred and continues to occur in a process that sometimes seems to take two steps forward and one step back. Secular and religious reformers have promoted changes affecting religious understanding and education, family laws (marriage, divorce, and inheritance), broader opportunities for women's education and employment, democratization, pluralism, and human rights. On the other hand, more conservative voices among religious leaders as well as some ultraconservative Islamic activists and organizations have often attempted to impose rigid, militant, puritanical, and intolerant beliefs, values, and attitudes.

Finally, many authoritarian governments (secular and religious) use religion to restrict freedom of thought and expression. They limit or prohibit an independent press, media, political parties, and trade unions in the name of religion.

Muslims today are at a critical crossroads. They are faced with making radical social, political, and economic changes that the Western world has had many decades to implement gradually. Amidst increasing globalization, Muslims strive to survive and compete, often with limited resources, and to preserve their identity in a world dominated (culturally as well as politically and economically) by the West. For many, the role of religion is critical in the preservation of their personal and national identities. It provides a sense of continuity between their Islamic heritage and modern life. For some, the temptation is to cling to the authority and security of the past. Others seek to follow new paths, convinced that their faith and a tradition of Islamic reform that has existed throughout the ages can play a critical role in restoring the vitality of Muslim societies.

Is Islam compatible with modernization?

The Muslim world is popularly pictured as lacking development. While some attribute this to Islam, lack of development in the Muslim world, as elsewhere, is in fact primarily due to issues of economy, limited resources, and education rather than religion. In Muslim societies around the world today, it is evident that modernization is seen as a goal worthy of pursuit and implementation. Travelers are often surprised to see television antennae or satellite dishes even in the remotest villages. The skylines of major cities are dotted with their World Trade Centers, modern factories, and corporate headquarters. People—secular and conservative, fundamentalists and reformers—equally take advantage of modern technology: cell phones, computers, the Internet, fax machines, automobiles, and planes. The absence of certain technologies such as the Internet in some Muslim countries is due not to resistance from the people but to cost or security concerns (the fears of authoritarian rulers that the Internet will take away their control).

Belief in an inherent conflict between Islam and modernization has arisen when modernization is equated with the Westernization and secularization of society. One Western expert said that Muslims must choose between Mecca and mechanization, implying that modernization necessarily threatened and eroded faith. This attitude reflects a belief that faith and reason, religion and science, are ultimately incompatible. Thus to become modern intellectually, politically, and religiously would mean a loss or watering down of faith, identity, and values.

Secular Muslims and Islamic activists exist side by side in societies and in professions. Their opposing views regarding the relationship of religious belief to society and politics do give rise to conflict. If some believe that a viable modern nation-state requires a separation of religion and politics, or mosque and state, others advocate governments and societies that are more informed by Islamic principles and values. Yet as examples from around the Muslim world (Egypt, Turkey, Malaysia, Qatar, and Indonesia) and other countries such as Japan or China have demonstrated, modernization does not have to mean the wholesale Westernization or secularization of society. Nowhere is this more clear than among so-called fundamentalists, or Islamic activists, who are also graduates of modern universities, majoring in science, medicine, law, engineering, journalism, business, and the social sciences. Many hold prominent positions in their respective professions, functioning effectively and contributing to the ongoing modernization of their societies.

Are there any modern Muslim thinkers or reformers?

Because acts of violence and terrorism grab the headlines, most of us know much more about advocates of a "clash," militant jihadists, than about those who are working toward a peaceful revolution and civilizational dialogue. Nevertheless, today intellectuals, religious leaders, and activists all over the world are addressing Islam's encounter with the West.

Like Islamic modernist movements in the early twentieth century and, later, the Islamic ("fundamentalist") movements of the Muslim Brotherhood in Egypt and the Jamaat-i-Islami in Pakistan, today's Islamically oriented intellectuals and activists are continuing the process of Islamic modernization and reform. They represent a creative new stage, a minority who are not only reformulating Islam but also implementing their ideas through their work in government and other public arenas.

Reformist and modernist Muslim Abdurrahman Wahid (d. 2009), former leader of Indonesia's Nahdatul Ulama (Renaissance of Religious Scholars) movement with thirty million members, became the first democratically elected president of Indonesia; Dr. Amien Rais, the University of Chicago–trained political scientist and former leader of Indonesia's Muhamaddiyya movement, became speaker of Indonesia's national assembly; Anwar Ibrahim, founder of ABIM, Malaysia's Islamic Youth Movement, went on to become the deputy prime minister of Malaysia; Dr. Necmettin Erbakan, a trained engineer, became Turkey's prime minister; and Mohammad Khatami, a religious scholar, was president of Iran. Many Islamically motivated professionals have served as presidents or prime ministers, in parliaments, or as mayors of major cities and are leaders in their professions (lawyers, physicians, engineers, and scientists).

Reformist thought is especially prevalent in America and Europe, where there is a free and open environment absent in many Muslim countries. In Europe we find Muslim scholars and activists like Dr. Tariq Ramadan, grandson of Hasan al-Banna, founder of Egypt's Muslim Brotherhood, a Swiss academic and activist; and Dr. Mohammed Arkoun (d. 2010) of the Sorbonne university in Paris. In America, they include Prof. Sayyid Hossein Nasr of George Washington University, an expert on Sufism and on Islam and science; Prof. Abdulaziz Sachedina of the University of Virginia, who has written extensively on Islam and democratization and human rights; Prof. Sulayman Nyang of Howard University, who is a prolific author who writes about Islam in America and Africa; Dr. Fathi Osman (d. 2010), who has written extensively on the Quran, pluralism, and Islamic reform; Prof. Amina Wadud, retired from Virginia Commonwealth University, who is author of *Quran and Woman*; and Prof. Khaled Abou El Fadl of UCLA Law School, who addresses issues of Islam, law, pluralism, gender, and violent extremism. These scholars formulate and debate new ideas, develop rationales and strategies for reform, and train the next generation in a more dynamic, progressive vision. Increasingly, their influence and impact are felt not only in the West but also in Muslim countries, as their ideas are exported through translations of their works.

Today, a two-way information superhighway spans the world. Ideas come not only from the traditional centers of Islamic scholarship in Muslim countries but also from religious scholars, leaders, and institutions in the West and from their students, who return to become professionals and leaders in their home countries. The Internet plays host to debates between progressive Muslims and more conservative voices globally, providing a venue for heated discussion of Islam's relationship to the state, Islamic banking, democracy, religious and political pluralism, family values, and gay rights, among many other topics.

Just as they were in the process of modern reform in Judaism and Christianity, questions of leadership and the authority of the past (tradition) are critical in Islamic reform. "Whose Islam?" is a major question. Who reinterprets, decides, leads, and implements change? Is it rulers and regimes, the vast majority of whom are unelected kings, military, and former military, or should it be elected parliaments? Is it the *ulama* (religious scholars) or clergy, who continue to see themselves as the primary interpreters of Islam, although many are ill prepared to respond creatively to modern realities? Or are Islamically oriented intellectuals and activists with a modern education most qualified? Too often in authoritarian societies that restrict freedom of thought and expression, and thus effective leadership, extremists like Osama bin Laden with their theology of confrontation and hate fill the vacuum.

The second major question is "What Islam?" Is Islamic reform simply a restoration of past doctrines and laws, or is it a reformation through a reinterpretation and reformulation of Islam to meet the demands of modern life? While some call for an Islamic state based upon the reimplementation of classical formulations of Islamic laws, others argue the need to reinterpret and reformulate that law in light of the new realities of contemporary society.

The process of Islamic reform is difficult. As in all religions, tradition—centuries-old beliefs and practices—is a powerful force, rooted in the claim of being based upon the teachings of the Quran or the practice (Sunnah) of the Prophet. The vast majority of religious scholars and local mosque leaders (*imams*) and preachers, who wield significant influence over the religious education and worldview of the majority of Muslims, are products of a more traditional religious education. The ideas of a vanguard of reformers will never have broad appeal and acceptance unless they are incorporated within the curricula of seminaries and schools and universities where religion is taught. A twofold process of reform, intellectual and institutional, will be required in the face of powerful conservative forces, limited human and financial resources, and a culture of authoritarianism that limits or controls freedom of thought in many countries.

ISLAM AND OTHER RELIGIONS

Do Muslims believe Islam is the only true religion?

Islam, like Christianity, is a global religion with a universal mission, calling all of humankind to worship the one true God. Historically, Muslims have believed that God sent this revelation one final time to Muhammad and the Muslim community. The community has an obligation to spread the faith: "We have sent you only to proclaim good news and to warn all mankind" (Quran 34:28).

Islam teaches that, although God first made a covenant with Moses and the Jews, and then with Jesus and the Christians, God made a final covenant with Muhammad and the Muslim community. While the Quran and Muslim belief acknowledge that God sent many prophets and messengers, Muslims, like Jews and Christians before them, believe that they possess the fullness of God's message and truth. They also believe that other faiths have an imperfect, corrupted, and distorted version of God's word due to unintentional and purposive alterations of God's revelation by the Jewish and Christian communities. Thus, many Muslims believe that just as God sent the Gospel revelation to correct the distorted version of God's revelation in the Torah, so too did God reveal the Quran to correct the corrupted text of the Bible and the Torah. The Quran is God's final revelation to humanity, uncorrupted and pure. Therefore the *ummah* is responsible for sharing this message with the world, calling all people to worship the one true God and join in this community of believers.

From earliest times, Muslims of all walks of life have engaged in propagating their faith (*dawa*, the call) wherever they went. Merchants as well as religious leaders and soldiers spread the faith as the Islamic community expanded politically. As in the past, today many Muslims stand ready to be a witness to their faith through preaching, writing, example, and providing financial support to build mosques and schools, publish materials on Islam, and assist those agencies that seek to convert non-Muslims.

What about Muslim religious intolerance?

Anyone who reads the newspapers or follows human rights reports is aware of problems with religious pluralism and tolerance in the Muslim world. Regrettably, a significant minority of Muslims, like very conservative and puritanical Christians and Jews who strongly affirm their faith, are not pluralistic in their attitudes toward other faiths. Religious minorities in the Muslim world today, who are constitutionally entitled to equality of citizenship and religious freedom, increasingly fear the erosion of those rights—and with good reason. Blasphemies against the Prophet and the desecration of the Quran have often been used to justify attacks against Christians. In addition, intra-Muslim communal intolerance and violence between Sunni and Shii extremist organizations and militias in Pakistan and Iraq have been all too common. Religious and communal tensions and conflicts, varying from discrimination to violent exchanges to destruction of villages, churches, and mosques to rape and slaughter, have flared up in Pakistan, Egypt, Sudan, Nigeria, Iran, Iraq, Afghanistan, Bangladesh, Malaysia, and Indonesia.

A key debate today about pluralism and tolerance involves the use of past Islamic doctrine to solve current problems.

Some want to protect minorities by reinstating their status as *dhimmi* (meaning protected people). The dhimmi were non-Muslims living under Muslim rule who paid a special tax (*jizya*) and in return were permitted to practice their own religion, be led by their religious leaders, and be guided by their own religious laws and customs. This treatment was very advanced at the time. No such tolerance existed in Christendom, where Jews, Muslims, and Christians who did not accept the authority of the pope were persecuted, forced to convert, or expelled.

However progressive this policy was in the past, it would amount to second-class citizenship for non-Muslims today. Therefore others insist that non-Muslims must be given full citizenship rights because of the Quran's emphasis on the equality of all humanity. They cite the Quranic passage describing God's decision to create not just a single nation or tribe but a world of different nations, ethnicities, tribes, and languages: "O humankind, We have created you male and female and made you nations and tribes, so that you might come to know one another" (49:13). The Quran's recognition of the human community's religious diversity and support of religious pluralism are found in Quranic texts such as "To everyone we have appointed a way and a course to follow" (5:48) and "For each there is a direction toward which he turns; vie therefore with one another in the performance of good works. Wherever you may be, God shall bring you all together [on the Day of Judgment]. Surely God has power over all things" (2:148).

Prominent Muslim scholars maintain that the Islamic law on apostasy, which prescribes the death penalty, was not based on the Quran but was a man-made effort in early Islam to prevent and punish the equivalent of desertion or treason at a time when the community faced enemies who threatened its unity, safety, and security. Thus apostasy was linked to rejecting not only one's faith but also one's political allegiance to the community. For example, the attempt of some Arab tribes to break their political alliance with Muhammad's followers after his death led the first caliph, Abu Bakr, to fight a series of wars characterized by later historians as "wars of apostasy." These tribes were not denouncing their faith; rather, they were breaking political ties to Muhammad's community, and what are known as wars of apostasy were really political acts of desertion or treason. Similarly, the Kharijites condemned and revolted against the Caliph Ali not because he renounced Islam but because he agreed to negotiate with Muawiyyah, the Muslim rebel governor of Syria, which they saw as an act against God's will and the consensus of the community. Reformers argue that the early Islamic community-state, surrounded by enemies, came to regard dissent, desertion, or breaking a political alliance as apostasy because it was such a political threat.

Reformers like Indonesian scholar Nurcholish Madjid argue that times have changed, and so must the law. Citing Quran 3:85, "If anyone seeks a religion other than Islam: complete devotion to God, it will not be accepted from him; he will be one of the losers in the Hereafter," Nurcholish argues that punishment for leaving the faith is not a matter for the state but God's decision on the Day of Judgment. Similarly, Sheikh Ali Gomaa, the Grand Mufti of Egypt, when asked, "Can a person who is Muslim choose a religion other than Islam?" responded, "The answer is yes, they can because the Quran says, 'Unto you your religion, and unto me my religion' [109:6], and, 'Whosoever will, let him believe, and whosoever will, let him disbelieve' [18:29], and, 'There is no compulsion in religion' [2:256]."

It is important to remember that, historically, religious exclusivism has been common in all world religions, especially in Judaism, Christianity, and Islam; each of these religions has had a tendency to act as if it alone has the one true faith. But as we face the future in which Muslims and Christians make up half the world's population, Islam and Muslims, like Christianity and Christians, are challenged to balance their sense of uniqueness with true respect for other faiths. In fact, Muslim popular opinion in America reflects movement in this direction. Responding to a question on Islam and religious pluralism in a 2008 Pew survey, while a minority (33 percent) of Muslims polled said, "My religion is the one, true faith leading to eternal life," a majority (56 percent) believed "Many religions can lead to eternal life."

How is Islam similar to Christianity and Judaism?

Judaism, Christianity, and Islam, in contrast to Hinduism and Buddhism, are all monotheistic faiths that worship the God of Adam, Abraham, and Moses—creator, sustainer, and lord of the universe. They share a common belief in the oneness of God (monotheism), sacred history (history as the theater of God's activity and the encounter of God and humankind), prophets and divine revelation, angels, and Satan. All stress moral responsibility and accountability, Judgment Day, and eternal reward and punishment.

All three faiths emphasize their special covenant with God, for Judaism through Moses, Christianity through Jesus, and Islam through Muhammad. Christianity accepts God's covenant with and revelation to the Jews but traditionally has seen itself as superseding Judaism with the coming of Jesus. Thus Christianity speaks of its new covenant and New Testament. So, too, Islam and Muslims recognize Judaism and Christianity: their biblical prophets (among them Adam, Abraham, Moses, and Jesus) and their revelations (the Torah and the Gospels). Muslim respect for all the biblical prophets is reflected in the custom of saying "Peace and blessings be upon him" after naming any of the prophets and in the common usage of the names Ibrahim (Abraham), Musa (Moses), Daoud (David), Sulayman (Solomon), and Issa (Jesus) for Muslims. In addition, Islam makes frequent reference to Jesus and to the Virgin Mary, who is mentioned more times in the Quran than in the New Testament.

However, Muslims believe that Islam supersedes Judaism and Christianity—that the Quran is the final and complete word of God and that Muhammad is the last of the prophets. In contrast to Christianity, which accepts much of the Hebrew Bible, Muslims believe that what is written in the Old and New Testaments is a corrupted version of the original revelation to Moses and Jesus. Moreover, Christianity's development of "new" dogmas such as the belief that Jesus is the Son of God and the doctrines of redemption and atonement is seen as admixing God's revelation with human fabrication.

Peace is central to all three faiths. This is reflected historically in their use of similar greetings meaning "peace be upon you": *shalom aleichem* in Judaism, *pax vobiscum* in Christianity, and *salam alaykum* in Islam. Often, however, the greeting of peace has been meant primarily for members of one's own faith community. Leaders of each religion, from Joshua and King David to Constantine and Richard the Lion-Hearted to Muhammad and Saladin, have engaged in holy wars to enlarge or defend their communities or empires. The joining of faith and politics continues to exist in modern times, though manifested in differing ways, as seen in Northern Ireland, South Africa, America, Israel, and the Middle East.

Islam is similar to Judaism in its emphasis on practice rather than belief, on law rather than dogma. The primary religious discipline in Judaism and Islam has been religious law; for Christianity it has been theology. Historically, in Judaism and Islam the major debates and disagreements have been among scholars of religious law over matters of religious practice, whereas in Christianity the early disputes and cleavages in the community were over theological beliefs: the nature of the Trinity or the relationship of Jesus' human and divine natures.

How do Muslims view Judaism? Christianity?

Both Jews and Christians hold a special status within Islam because of the Muslim belief that God revealed His will through His prophets, including Abraham, Moses, and Jesus.

> Say, We believe in God, and in what has been revealed
> to us, and in what has been sent down to Abraham and
> Ismail and Isaac and Jacob and their offspring, and what
> has been revealed to Moses and Jesus and to all the
> prophets of our Lord. We make no distinction between
> them and we submit to Him and obey. (Quran 3:84)

The Quran and Islam regard Jews and Christians as
children of Abraham and refer to them as "People of the
Book," since all three monotheistic faiths descend from the
same patrilineage of Abraham. Jews and Christians trace
themselves back to Abraham and his wife Sarah; Muslims, to
Abraham and his servant Hagar. Muslims believe that God
sent his revelation (Torah) first to the Jews through the prophet
Moses and then to Christians through the prophet Jesus. They
recognize many of the biblical prophets, in particular Moses
and Jesus, and those are common Muslim names. Another
common Muslim name is Mary. Mary's place in Islam is
reflected in the fact that chapter nine of the Quran is named
Maryam; Mary's name occurs more times in the Quran than
in the New Testament; Muslims also believe in the virgin birth
of Jesus.

However, they believe that over time the original revelations to Moses and Jesus became corrupted. The Old
Testament, more specifically the Torah, is seen as a mixture
of God's revelation and human fabrication. The same is true
for the Gospels and what Muslims see as Christianity's
development of "new" and erroneous doctrines such as that
Jesus is the Son of God and that Jesus' death redeemed and
atoned for humankind's original sin.

Why do Muslims persecute Christians in Muslim countries?

Religious conflict and persecution historically and today exist
across the religious spectrum: Hindu fundamentalists have
clashed with Muslims, Christians, and Sikhs in India,

Christian Serbs with Muslim Bosnians and Kosovars, Jews with Palestinian Muslims and Christians, Tamil (Hindu) with Sinhalese (Buddhist) in Sri Lanka, Christians with Muslims in Lebanon, Catholics with Protestants in Northern Ireland.

History teaches us that religion is a powerful force that has been used for good and for ill. From Egypt, Sudan, and Nigeria to Pakistan, Indonesia, and the southern Philippines, Muslims have clashed with Christians. Moreover, despite an impressive record of religious pluralism in the past, the situation in Southeast Asia has gotten worse rather than better. It is often difficult to identify specific conflicts as primarily motivated by religion as opposed to politics or economics.

It is useful to recall that historically Islam's attitude toward other religions, especially Judaism and Christianity, was more tolerant than that of Christianity. However, Muslim-Christian relations have deteriorated over time under the influence of conflicts and grievances, from the Crusades and European colonialism to contemporary politics. Part of the legacy of colonialism is a deep-seated Muslim belief, nurtured by militant religious leaders, that indigenous Christians were favored by and benefited from colonial rule or that they are the product of the European missionaries and their schools that converted local Muslims, and somehow retain a connection to a Christian West. The situation is compounded in areas where Christians proved more affluent or successful. The creation of the state of Israel and subsequent Arab-Israeli wars and conflicts have contributed to a deterioration of relations between Palestinian Muslims and Christians and Israeli Jews.

In recent decades, conservative and fundamentalist interpretations of Islam (as well as the Christianity preached by leaders like Pat Robertson, Franklin Graham, Jerry Falwell, John Hagee, and others) have been sources of intolerance, persecution, violence, and terrorism. Local religious leaders who espouse and preach an exclusivist and militant view of religion raise generations of narrow-minded believers who, given the right circumstances, will take to the streets and engage in intercommunal or intersectarian battles. This has led to the torching of churches and mosques in Nigeria and Indonesia, the bombing of Christian churches in Pakistan, and the slaughter of Christians in Egypt and the southern Philippines. The rise of fundamentalism has brought with it intolerant theologies of hate that have led groups like Islamic Jihad and the Gamaa Islamiyya in Egypt or Laskar Jihad in Indonesia to attack Christians. Christians have suffered under self-styled Islamic governments in Sudan and Pakistan. "Islamic laws" such as Pakistan's and Afghanistan's blasphemy laws have been used to imprison Christians and threaten them with the death penalty.

As previously noted, however, often the main sources of conflict are political and economic rather than religious. The civil war in Lebanon, which shattered the celebrated Lebanese multireligious mosaic, is one example. Lebanon's government was established on the basis of proportional representation tied to a 1932 census in which Christians, specifically Maronite Christians, predominated, followed by Sunni, Shii, and Druze. The president was a Maronite Christian, the prime minister a Sunni Muslim, and so forth. Positions in government, the bureaucracy, and the military were distributed on the basis of religious sect or community. Changing demographics led many Muslim leaders and groups to call for a redistribution of power and wealth.

At the heart of the conflict in Israel-Palestine is the creation of the state of Israel and the Palestinian demand for a Palestinian state and the right to return to their lands. At the same time, for a significant minority of Muslims and Jews, the struggle is at its heart based upon conflicting religious claims to the land. Similarly, for some among the Muslim minority in the southern Philippines, autonomy or statehood has become a rallying cry against the Christian-dominated government in Manila, whose historic practice of moving Christians from the north to the south is regarded as an unacceptable occupation of Muslim lands. In Malaysia and Indonesia, the significant economic prosperity and power of the Chinese minority, many of whom are Christian, and who constitute an extremely small percentage of the population, have been and continue to be sources of resentment and conflict.

The long struggle of Christian East Timor for independence from Muslim Indonesia is another example. This conflict, though it had a religious dimension, was primarily about political independence for the former Portuguese colony. The government of Indonesia was hardly motivated by religion in its policies toward East Timor. Finally, the long civil war between North and South in Sudan has often been cast as a conflict between the Arab Muslim North and the Christian South. Actually, the majority of people in southern Sudan are animists (people who believe in souls, especially that non-human entities, such as animals, have souls) though many of the military leaders are Christian. More important, although there is a religious dimension and Christians have suffered persecution under Sudan's "Islamic" government, the struggle has been political and economic (over control of the South's oil reserves) as much as religious.

Haven't Jews and Christians always been enemies of Islam?

The relationship of Jews and Christians to Islam, like the relationship of Christianity to Judaism, is long and complex, conditioned by historical and political realities as well as religious doctrine. Jewish and Christian tribes lived in Arabia at the time of the Prophet Muhammad. Jews and Christians were members or citizens of the early Muslim community at Medina.

In his early years, Muhammad anticipated that Jews and Christians, as "People of the Book," would accept his prophetic message and be his natural allies. The Quran itself confirms the sending of prophets and revelation to Jews and

Christians and recognizes them as part of Muslim history: "Remember, we gave Moses the Book and sent him many an apostle; and to Jesus, son of Mary, We gave clear evidence of the truth, reinforcing him with divine grace" (23:49–50; see also 5:44–46, 32:23, 40:53).

Muhammad initially presented himself as a prophetic reformer reestablishing the religion of Abraham. For example, like the Jews, the Muslims initially faced Jerusalem during prayer and fasted on the tenth day of the lunar month. Muhammad made a special point of reaching out to the Jewish tribes of Medina. The Jews of Medina, however, had political ties to the Quraysh tribe of Mecca, so they resisted Muhammad's overtures. Shortly afterward, Muhammad received a revelation changing the direction of prayer from Jerusalem to Mecca, marking Islam as a distinct alternative to Judaism.

When Muhammad consolidated his political and military control over Medina, he wrote and promulgated documents commonly referred to as the Constitution of Medina (c. 622–624), which regulated social and political life. The constitution states that the believers comprise a single community, or *ummah*, which is responsible for collectively enforcing social order and security and for confronting enemies in times of war and peace. Tribes remained responsible for the conduct of their individual members, and a clear precedent was set for the inclusion of other religions as part of the broader community led by Muslims. The Jewish population was granted the right to internal religious and cultural autonomy, including the right to observe Jewish religious law, in exchange for their political loyalty and allegiance to the Muslims.

Muslims point to the Constitution of Medina as evidence of Islam's inherent message of peaceful coexistence, the permissibility of religious pluralism in areas under Muslim rule, and the right of non-Muslims to be members of and participants in the broader Muslim community. However, relations between the early Muslim community and some Jewish tribes became strained when the Jews backed Muhammad's Meccan rivals. Judged as traitors for their support of his enemies, many were attacked and killed. This confrontation became part of the baggage of history and would continue to influence the attitudes of some Muslims in later centuries. Recently, this legacy can be seen in official statements from Hamas and Osama bin Laden. Both not only condemn Jews for Israeli occupation and policies in Palestine but also see the current conflict as just the most recent iteration of an age-old conflict dating back to the Jews' "rejection and betrayal" of Islam and the Prophet's community at Medina.

Nevertheless, in many Muslim communities at various times in history, Jews found a home where, as "People of the Book," or *dhimmi*, they lived, worked, and often thrived. Vibrant Jewish communities existed in Muslim countries like Egypt, Morocco, Turkey, and Iran. When the Catholic rulers Ferdinand and Isabella drove the Jews out of Spain, many found refuge in North Africa and the Ottoman Empire. The establishment of the state of Israel was a turning point in relations between Muslims and Jews. The political fallout from the struggle between the Palestinians and Zionism severely strained Jewish-Muslim relations in Muslim countries. As a result, the majority of those Jews emigrated or fled to Israel and other parts of the world.

The relationship of Christians and Muslims is even more complex. Despite common theological roots, Islam and Christianity were in contention from the outset. Islam offered an alternative religious and political vision. Just as Christians saw their faith as superseding the covenant of the Jews with God, Islam now declared that God had made a new covenant, revealing his word one final and complete time to Muhammad, the "seal" or final prophet. Islam, like Christianity, proclaimed a universal message and mission and thus challenged the claims of Christianity. Moreover, the remarkable spread of Islam, with its conquest of the eastern (Byzantine) wing of the

Roman Empire, challenged the political power and hegemony of Christendom.

The history of Christianity and Islam has been one of both conflict and coexistence. When Muslims conquered Byzantium, they were welcomed by some Christian sects and groups, who were persecuted as heretics by "official" Christianity, that is, Catholicism. Many Christians welcomed a Muslim rule that gave them more freedom to practice their faith and imposed lighter taxes. Despite initial fears, the Muslim conquerors proved to be far more tolerant than imperial Christianity, granting religious freedom to indigenous Christian churches and Jews.

This spirit was further reflected in the tendency of early Islamic empires to incorporate the most advanced elements from surrounding civilizations, including Byzantine and Persian Sasanid imperial and administrative practices and Hellenic science, architecture, art, medicine, and philosophy. Christians like John of Damascus held positions of prominence in the royal courts. Christian and Jewish subjects assisted their Muslim rulers with the collection and translation of the great books of science, medicine, and philosophy from both East and West.

However, the rapid expansion of Islam also threatened Christian Europe, as Muslims seemed poised to sweep across Europe until finally turned back by Charles Martel in southern France in 732. The Crusades, the Inquisition, and European colonialism represented major periods of confrontation and conflict, as did the rise and expansion of the Ottoman Empire into Europe.

The most often cited example of interreligious tolerance in history is that of Muslim rule in Spain (al-Andalus) from 756 to about 1000, which is usually idealized as a period of interfaith harmony, or *convivencia* (living together). Muslim rule of Spain offered the Christian and Jewish populations seeking refuge from the class system of Europe the opportunity to become prosperous small landholders. Christians and Jews occupied prominent positions in the court of the caliph in the tenth century, serving as translators, engineers, physicians, and architects. The Archbishop of Seville commissioned an annotated translation of the Bible for the Arabic-speaking Christian community.

Islamic history also contains positive examples of interfaith debate and dialogue, beginning in the time of Muhammad. Muhammad himself had engaged in dialogue with the Christians of Najran, resulting in a mutually agreeable relationship whereby the Najranis were permitted to pray in the Prophet's mosque. The fifth Sunni caliph, Muawiyyah (ruled 661–669), regularly sent invitations to the contending Jacobite and Maronite Christians to come to the royal court to discuss their differences. During the Middle Ages, debates involving both Muslims and Jews occurred in Spanish Muslim courts, and in the sixteenth century an interreligious theological discussion between Catholic priests and Muslim clerics was presided over by the Mughal emperor Akbar. These debates were not always conducted between "equals" (indeed, many were held precisely in order to "prove" that the other religion was "wrong," which was also the case for dialogues initiated by Christians). The fact that the debate was permitted and encouraged, however, indicates some degree of open exchange between faiths, a significant stage of educational and cultural achievement in the Muslim world.

Furthermore, Muslims maintained an open-door policy to Jews escaping from persecution in Christian Europe during the Inquisition. During the Crusades, despite their conflict, Muslims tolerated the practice of Christianity—an example that was not emulated by the other side. In the thirteenth century some treaties between Christians and Muslims granted Christians free access to sacred places then reoccupied by Islam. For example, the great Christian saint Francis of Assisi met the Muslim leader Salah al-Din's nephew Sultan al-Malik al-Kamil in 1219. The sultan granted freedom of worship to his more than thirty thousand Christian prisoners when hostilities were suspended, as well as offering them the choice of returning to their own countries or fighting in his armies.

The Ottoman Empire is a prime example of the positive treatment of religious minorities in a Muslim-majority context. The Ottomans officially recognized four religiously based communities, known as *millets*: Greek Orthodox, Armenian Gregorian, Muslim, and Jewish. Under the millet system, Islam assumed the prime position, but each other millet was placed under the authority of its own religious leaders and permitted to follow its own religious laws. The millet system enabled the empire to accommodate religious diversity, placing non-Muslims in a subordinate position to Muslims and offering them protected status. Members of minority religions further had the right to hold government positions in some cases. Thus, a limited form of religious pluralism and tolerance were important components of Ottoman statecraft.

In the contemporary era, religious and political pluralism has been a major issue in the Muslim world. Many of those seeking to establish Islamic states look to historical precedents to determine the status of non-Muslims. Although many call for a strict reinstatement of the gradations of citizenship that accompanied dhimmi status in the past, others recognize that this approach is not compatible with the pluralistic realities of the contemporary world and international human rights standards.

Those who advocate gradation of citizenship according to religious affiliation believe that an Islamic state, defined as one in which Islamic law is the law of the land, must necessarily be run by Muslims because only Muslims are capable of interpreting Islamic law. This has been the position of Islamization programs in Pakistan, Sudan, Afghanistan, and Iran, which have legislated that only Muslims have the right to hold senior government positions. Obviously, this is not satisfactory to non-Muslims who wish to enjoy full and equal rights of citizenship. In fact, religious minorities have been persecuted and subject to discrimination under some Muslim governments in countries like the Taliban's Afghanistan,

Pakistan, and Sudan. Thus many reformers who do not agree with the application of this classical tradition in modern times insist that non-Muslims be afforded full citizenship rights.

Advocates of reform maintain that pluralism is the essence of Islam as revealed in the Quran and practiced by Muhammad and the early caliphs, rather than a purely Western invention or ideology. They point to the Islamic empires that permitted freedom of religion and worship and protected the dhimmis as evidence of the permissibility and legality of pluralism. While many militants and mainstream conservative or traditionalist Muslims advocate classical Islam's dhimmi or the millet system, reformers call for a reinterpretation or reunderstanding of pluralism. Recognizing the need to open the one-party and authoritarian political systems that prevail in the Muslim world, many mainstream Islamists (as distinguished from extremists) also began applying the word *pluralism* to the political process. Since the 1990s, the term has been used to legitimate multiparty systems as well as modern forms of religious pluralism and tolerance.

Who won the Crusades?

Two myths pervade Western perceptions of the Crusades: first, the Crusades were simply motivated by a religious desire to liberate Jerusalem, and second, Christendom ultimately triumphed. The Crusades (from *crux*, cross) were a series of military campaigns continuing over two centuries. This religious warfare or "holy war" was initiated by Pope Urban II to restore (Latin) Christian control over Jerusalem and the Holy Land. Jerusalem was and is a sacred city and symbol for all three Abrahamic faiths, Jews, Christians, and Muslims.

Events leading up to the Crusades began in 1071 when the Seljuq (Turkish) army decisively defeated the Byzantine army. The Byzantine emperor, Alexius I, feared that all Asia Minor would be overrun, and so he called on fellow Christian rulers

and the pope to come to the aid of Constantinople by under-
taking a "pilgrimage" or crusade that would free Jerusalem
and its environs from Muslim rule.

Muslims had ruled the area since 638. During that time the
Christian population had been unharmed and Christian pilgrims were allowed continued access to their holy sites. Jews,
long banned by Christian rulers from living in Jerusalem,
returned to live and worship in the city of Solomon and
David. Muslims had built a shrine, the Dome of the Rock, and
a mosque, the al-Aqsa, near the area formerly occupied by
Herod's Temple and close to the Western (Wailing) Wall, a
remnant of the Second Temple.

For Pope Urban II, the "defense" of Jerusalem provided an
opportunity to gain recognition for his papal authority and its
role in legitimating the actions of temporal rulers. Under the
ostensible goal of uniting in a "holy war" to free the holy city,
a divided Christendom rallied as warriors from France and
other parts of Western Europe (called "Franks" by Muslims)
joined forces against the "infidel." This was ironic because, as
scholar Francis E. Peters has observed, "God may indeed
have wished it, but there is certainly no evidence that the
Christians of Jerusalem did, or that anything extraordinary
was occurring to pilgrims there to prompt such a response at
that moment in history."

In fact, Christian rulers, knights, and merchants involved
in the Crusades, driven primarily by their political and military ambitions, were focused on the promise of economic
and commercial (trade and banking) rewards and the promise
of salvation for those who died in battle that would result
from establishing a Latin kingdom in the Middle East. Among
the populace, the appeal to religion captured minds and
gained widespread support.

The contrast between the behavior of the Christian and
Muslim armies in the First Crusade has been etched deeply in
the collective memory of Muslims. In 1099, the Crusaders
stormed Jerusalem and established Christian sovereignty over

the Holy Land. They left no Muslim survivors; women and children were massacred. The Noble Sanctuary, the Haram al-Sharif, was desecrated as the Dome of the Rock was converted into a church and the al-Aqsa mosque, renamed the Temple of Solomon, became a residence for the king. Latin principalities were established in Antioch, Edessa, Tripoli, and Tyre.

What is rarely remembered is that this victory and the establishment of the Latin Kingdom of Jerusalem lasted less than a century. In 1187, Salah al-Din (Saladin), having reestablished Abbasid rule over Fatimid Egypt, led his army in a fierce battle and recaptured Jerusalem. The Muslim army was as magnanimous in victory as it had been tenacious in battle. Civilians were spared; churches and shrines were generally left untouched. The striking differences in military conduct were epitomized by the two dominant figures of the Crusades: Saladin and Richard the Lion-Hearted. The chivalrous Saladin was faithful to his word and compassionate toward noncombatants. Richard accepted the surrender of Acre, in Palestine, currently northern Israel, and then proceeded to massacre all its inhabitants, including women and children, despite promises to the contrary.

By the thirteenth century the Crusades degenerated into intra-Christian wars, papal wars against Christian enemies who were denounced as heretics and schismatics. The result was a weakening, rather than a strengthening, of Christendom. As historian Roger Savory notes, an ironic but undeniable result of the Crusades was the deterioration of the status of minority Christian sects in the Holy Land:

> Formerly these minorities had been accorded rights and privileges under Muslim rule, but, after the establishment of the Latin Kingdom, they found themselves treated as "loathsome schismatics." In an effort to obtain relief from persecution by their fellow Christians, many abandoned their Nestorian or Monophysite beliefs, and adopted either Roman Catholicism, or—the supreme irony—Islam.

By the fifteenth century the Crusades had spent their force. Although they were initially launched to unite Christendom and turn back the Muslim armies, the opposite had occurred. Amid a bitterly divided Christendom, Constantinople fell in 1453 before Turkish Muslim conquerors. This Byzantine capital was renamed Istanbul and became the seat of the Ottoman Empire.

Are Muslims involved in interfaith dialogue?

Today, Muslims and major Muslim organizations are a major presence in interreligious and intercivilizational dialogue nationally and internationally.

In the past, Muslims have been suspicious of interfaith dialogue. They wondered, "Is the real intent of those seeking dialogue with us actually our conversion?" "Is dialogue really necessary if we believe we have the final and complete revelation?" or "Will dialogue with other religions lead to relativism?" Both vivid memories of colonialism, when Christian missionaries accompanied European colonizers in order to teach what they saw as their "superior" faith, as well as contemporary globalization with its political and economic dominance of the Western world, have led Muslims to be hesitant about dialogue. They wonder, "Is talk of religious pluralism and interfaith dialogue actually 'cultural imperialism' in disguise that would undermine Islam?" Nevertheless, in a matter of decades, Muslims have become partners in interreligious dialogue. These dialogues are occurring locally, in many cities and towns around the world, as well as globally, with the Vatican, the World Council of Churches, the National Council of Churches, and the United States Conference of Catholic Bishops.

Interfaith dialogue, religious and political pluralism, and human rights have become an important part of contemporary Islamic discourse. An important Muslim initiative that mobilized Christian and Muslim religious leaders to build bridges is the widely accepted "A Common Word Between Us and You" (2007). The limited coverage it has received exemplifies the media's continued lack of interest in "good news."

"A Common Word" is a major Muslim response to an address delivered in 2006 by Pope Benedict XVI in Regensburg, Germany, which dismayed and angered many Muslims globally. In his speech, Benedict cited a fourteenth-century Byzantine emperor's remarks about the Prophet Muhammad: "Show me just what Muhammad brought that was new, and there you will find things only evil and inhuman, such as his command to spread by the sword the faith he preached." Equally offensive to Muslims was the pope's assertion that the Quranic passage "There is no compulsion in religion" (2:256) (which is often used by scholars to illustrate Islam's acceptance of freedom of religion, that other believers should not be forced to convert to Islam) was revealed during Muhammad's early years in Mecca, a period "when Mohammed was still powerless and under [threat]" and that this passage was superseded by "instructions, developed later and recorded in the Koran [Quran], concerning holy war." Unfortunately, both the pope's statements were historically incorrect. Muslims and many non-Muslim scholars strenuously rejected the pope's assertion that Muhammad commanded the spread of Islam by the sword. To prove that this statement was inaccurate, Muslims and scholars argued two things. First, the Quran does not equate jihad with holy war. This interpretation of jihad developed years later after Muhammad's death when it came to be used by rulers (caliphs) to justify their wars of imperial expansion and rule in the name of Islam. Second, many scholars have verified that Quran 2:256 is not an early Meccan verse but is in fact from the later Medinan period.

A month after the Regensburg speech, thirty-eight Muslim scholars sent Pope Benedict XVI an open letter, expressing their concerns about the speech. On the first anniversary of that letter, some 138 prominent Muslim leaders (muftis, academics, intellectuals, government ministers, authors) from across the world, recognizing the need for better mutual understanding, sent another open letter, "A Common Word Between Us and You," to the heads of the world's major Christian churches. This initiative was launched simultaneously at news conferences in Dubai, London, and Washington. The purpose and heart of their message was this:

> Muslims and Christians together make up well over half of the world's population. Without peace and justice between these two religious communities, there can be no meaningful peace in the world...The basis for this peace and understanding already exists...: love of the One God, and love of the neighbour...found over and over again in the sacred texts of Islam and Christianity. The Unity of God, the necessity of love for Him, and the necessity of love of the neighbour is thus the common ground between Islam and Christianity.

The signers noted the expression of the Two Great Commandments in the Torah, New Testament, and Quran, and they emphasized: "With the terrible weaponry of the modern world; with Muslims and Christians intertwined everywhere as never before, no side can unilaterally win a conflict between more than half of the world's inhabitants. Thus our common future is at stake. The very survival of the world itself is perhaps at stake."

The response to "A Common Word" from Christian leaders and scholars was immediate and global. The Archbishop of Canterbury, Pope Benedict XVI, Orthodox Patriarch Alexei II of Russia, the presiding bishop of the Lutheran World Federation, and many others acknowledged its importance, as did many individuals and groups who posted their comments and criticisms on the official Web site of "A Common Word." Over three hundred leading American mainline and evangelical leaders as well as scholars responded in an open letter endorsing a statement, "Loving God and Neighbor Together," published in the *New York Times* and elsewhere. The number of Muslim leaders and scholars who signed the initiative increased from the original 138 to over 300, with more than 460 Islamic organizations and associations also endorsing it. As a follow-up to the letter, international conferences of religious leaders, scholars, and NGOs occurred at Yale University, Cambridge University, and Georgetown University as well as at the Vatican to explore the theological, biblical, and social implications of this initiative.

In response to Muslim reaction to the pope's speech, the Vatican invited Muslim leaders to a three-day summit to seek deeper understanding between the largest religions in the world. Roman Catholics account for just over half the world's 2 billion Christians, while Islam has 1.5 billion followers. Under the theme "Love of God, Love of Neighbor," some fifty papal officials, Islamic leaders, and scholars met in 2008 at a historic summit. At the end of the meeting the pope met with delegates in a frank discussion.

The Grand Mufti of Bosnia-Herzegovina, Mustafa Ceric, led the Muslim delegation, and Cardinal Jean-Louis Tauran, leader of the Vatican's delegation, called the meeting a "new chapter in a long history." The Vatican stressed specific issues of concern: that emphasis on shared beliefs and values not gloss over real differences and issues, in particular what it terms "reciprocity"—the freedom of Christians in countries like Saudi Arabia to build churches and practice their religion freely. The three-day meeting issued a manifesto that called for a new dialogue between Muslim and Christian leaders, underscoring the values shared by Islam and Christianity.

Following "A Common Word," an important dialogue between Muslims and evangelicals ensued. It focuses on exploring common values (peace, justice, compassion, and mercy). A group of mainstream evangelical leaders have initiated multifaith dialogues and projects dealing with common concerns, from social issues like poverty and the environment to security. A sampling of the insights that bring Christians and Muslims together in mutual understanding can be found in "10 Terms Not to Use with Muslims" by Chris Seiple, president of the Institute for Global Engagement:

- "Clash of civilizations" creates an "us as good guy and them as bad guy" scenario when the only clash is between those for civilization and those against it.
- "Secular" to Western ears represents separation of church and state needed for democracy and to Muslims often connotes a "godless society."
- Instead, "pluralism" "encourages those with (and those without) a God-based worldview to have a welcomed and equal place in the public square."
- "Integration" suggests that "all views, majority and minority, deserve equal respect as long as each is willing to be civil with one another...in the public square of a shared society."
- "Integration" is more effective than "assimilation," which suggests a majority European or North American Christian culture that minority Muslims "need to look like."
- "Tolerance," meaning "allowing someone's existence or behavior," will not build the trust and relationships needed to face global challenges in the twenty-first century.
- Only true respect for each other will help us to "name our differences and commonalities" and to recognize our "inherent dignity...as creations of God" whose different faiths call us "to walk together in peace and justice, mercy and compassion."

CUSTOMS AND CULTURE

Why does Islam separate men and women?

Many, though not all, Muslim societies practice some gender segregation—the separation of men and women—to various degrees, in public spaces such as mosques, universities, and the marketplace. Thus in many mosques men and women have separate areas for prayer or are separated by a screen or curtain. Unmarried men do not mix with unmarried women outside of very specific contexts, such as family gatherings or a meeting between two potential spouses that occurs in the presence of a chaperone. Seclusion, which differs from the public segregation of the sexes, is the practice of keeping women within the home so that they have no contact with public space.

Although gender segregation and seclusion are practiced in some Muslim societies, in many Muslim countries, from Egypt and Tunisia to Malaysia and Indonesia, men and women, especially in cities and towns, increasingly study and work together. In our modern, globalizing world, where two incomes are often necessary to maintain a household, women are increasingly joining the workforce and breaking down traditional notions of gendered space.

The practice of separation has both religious and cultural origins. The Prophet's Medina did not practice sexual segregation. Although an integral part of the community, because of their special status, Muhammad's wives were told by the Quran, "O wives of the Prophet! You are not like any of the other women. If you fear God, do not be complaisant in speech so that one in whose heart is a sickness may covet you, but speak honorably. Stay with dignity in your homes and do not display your finery as the pagans of old did" (33:32–33). The Quran later tells Muhammad's wives to place a barrier between themselves and unrelated males. Muslim men are told, "And when you ask [his wives] for anything you want, ask them from before a screen. That makes for greater purity for your hearts and for theirs" (33:53).

There have been many debates about how these verses concerned with modesty and segregation should be interpreted with respect to Muslim women in general. Modern scholars have pointed out that they specifically address only the wives of the Prophet rather than all of womankind. They maintain that until the modern age jurists relied primarily on Prophetic traditions (*hadith*), as well as the belief that women are a source of temptation (*fitnah*) for men, to support women's segregation. In recent decades, more ultraconservative/fundamentalist Muslim leaders, sometimes influenced and supported by Wahhabis (see page 53, "What is Wahhabi Islam?"), have maintained that the verses addressing the wives of the Prophet apply to all Muslim women, who are supposed to emulate the behavior of Muhammad's wives.

However, opinions today vary about the necessity of separation of the sexes, from those who believe in the absolute separation of the sexes to those who think that modesty requirements can be met by dressing appropriately and acting modestly in mixed company. This holds true even in the religious realm, since women have come to play a more visible and important role in mosque and society. They not only attend services and pray with men but are also religious scholars who interpret Islam, teach Quran classes, and lead women in prayer. Most recently, women are serving as muftis in some countries, and run for and hold elected political office. Women also have governed as prime ministers or presidents, served in cabinets and parliaments, and represented various countries as diverse as Egypt, Senegal, Turkey, Bahrain, Kuwait, Iraq, Iran, Pakistan, Afghanistan, Bangladesh, Malaysia, and Indonesia as ambassadors.

Are women second-class citizens in Islam?

The status of women in Muslim countries has long been looked to as evidence of "Islam's" oppression of women in matters ranging from the freedom to dress as they please to legal rights in divorce. The true picture of women in Islam is far more complex.

The revelation of Islam raised the status of women by prohibiting female infanticide, abolishing women's status as property, and establishing women's legal capacity. This includes granting women the right to receive their own dowries, which changed marriage from a proprietary to a contractual relationship, and allowing women to retain control over their property and use their maiden names after marriage. The Quran also granted women financial maintenance from their husbands and controlled the husband's free ability to divorce.

The Quran declares that men and women are equal in the eyes of God; man and woman were created to be equal parts of a pair (51:49). The Quran describes the relationship between men and women as one of "love and mercy" (30:21). Men and women are to be like "members of one another" (3:195), or like each other's garment (2:187).

Men and women are equally responsible for adhering to the Five Pillars of Islam. Quran 9:71–72 states, "The Believers, men and women, are protectors of one another; they enjoin what is just, and forbid what is evil; they observe regular prayers, pay zakat and obey God and His Messenger. On them will God pour His mercy: for God is exalted in Power, Wise. God has promised to Believers, men and women, gardens under which rivers flow, to dwell therein." This verse draws added significance from the fact that it was the last Quran verse to be revealed that addressed relations between men and women. Some scholars argue on the basis of both content and chronology that this verse outlines the ideal vision of the relationship between men and women in Islam—one of equality and balance.

Most Islamic societies have been patriarchal, and women have long been considered to be the culture-bearers within these societies. Prior to the twentieth century, men interpreted the Quran, *hadith* (traditional stories of the Prophet), and Islamic law. These interpretations therefore reflect this patriarchal environment. Women were not actively engaged in interpreting the Quran, hadith, or Islamic law until the twentieth century. Since then, however, reformers have argued that Quranic verses favoring men need reinterpretation in light of the new social, cultural, and economic realities of the twentieth and twenty-first centuries.

Often Muslim scholars have interpreted Quran 4:34 as indicating that women have been assigned second-class status in Islam, "Men have responsibility for and priority over women, since God has given some of them advantages over others and because they should spend their wealth [for the support of women]." However, contemporary scholars have noted that the "priority" referred to in this verse is based upon men's socioeconomic responsibilities for women. It does not say women are incapable of managing their own affairs, controlling themselves, or being leaders. Nowhere in the Quran does it say that all men are superior to, preferred over, or better than all women. God's expressed preference for certain individuals in the Quran is based upon their faith, not their gender. Thus, the noted Quran expert and translator M. Abdel Haleem has therefore rendered this verse as "Husbands should take good care of their wives, with [the bounties] God has given to some more than others and with what they spend out of their own money."

Quranic interpretation is at the center of many debates. Some note that the Quran itself specifically distinguishes between two types of verses: those that are universal principles and those that were responding to specific social and cultural contexts or questions and were subject to interpretation (3:7). They believe that those verses that assign greater rights to men (such as 2:223 and 2:228) reflect a patriarchal context in which men were dominant and solely responsible for supporting women. Today, rather than being interpreted literally, these verses should be reformulated to reflect the interests of public welfare. Reformers further argue that gender equality is the intended order established by God, because God does not make distinctions based upon gender in matters of faith.

However, Muslims who advocate a literal interpretation of the Quran believe that the gender inequalities it prescribes apply to every time and place as God's revealed social order. Biology is often used as a justification; because only women can bear children, they argue, the man must provide for and maintain the family so that the woman can do her job of bearing and raising children.

Another apparent example of second-class status for women appears in the Quranic stipulation (2:282) that two female witnesses are equal to one male witness. If one female witness errs, the other can remind her of the truth: "And call to witness two of your men; if two men are not available then one man and two women you approve of, so that if one of them is confused, the other would remind her." Over time, this was interpreted by male scholars to mean that a woman's testimony should always count for one-half of the value of a man's testimony. Contemporary scholars have revisited this question also, offering several observations about the socio-historical context in which the verse was revealed.

First, the verse specifies that witnessing is relevant in cases of a written transaction, contract, or court case. At the time the Quran was revealed, most women were not active in business or finance. A woman's expertise in these fields would most likely have been less than a man's. Another interpretation argues that the requirement for two female witnesses to equal the testimony of one man was based upon the concern that male family members might pressure a woman into testifying in their favor.

Some contemporary female scholars have argued that the requirement of two female witnesses demonstrates the need for women to have access to education, both secular and religious, in order to receive the training and experience to be equal to men in a business environment—something that is not prohibited by the Quran. In light of the right of women to own property and make their own investments, this interpretation is in keeping with broader Quranic values.

One other area in which gender discrimination has been apparent historically is the matter of divorce. Women have had little right to initiate divorce, whereas men did not have to provide any justification or reason for declaring a divorce. However, the Quran counsels compassion and tolerance as well as mediation in divorce and stresses that spouses "be generous towards one another" (2:237). Ideally, divorce is a last resort, discouraged rather than encouraged, as reflected in a tradition of the Prophet, "Of all the things permitted, divorce is the most abominable with God." Historically this ideal has been undermined and compromised by the realities of patriarchal societies. This situation has been compounded by the fact that women have been unable to exercise their rights either because they were unaware of them or because of pressures in a male-dominated society. In many Muslim countries, modern reforms have been introduced to limit a husband's rights and expand those of women. However, these reforms have been limited and challenged by more conservative and fundamentalist forces.

The Quran has also served as a reference point for restricting the practice of polygamy. Quran 4:3 commands, "Marry women of your choice, two or three or four; but if you will not be able to deal justly [with them] only one." A corollary verse (4:129) states, "You are never able to be fair and just between women even if that is your ardent desire."

Contemporary reformers have argued that these two verses together prohibit polygamy and that the true Quranic ideal is monogamy.

The twenty-first century has brought numerous significant reforms for women's rights in both the public and the private spheres. In the overwhelming majority of Muslim countries, women have the right to public education, including at the college level. In many countries, they also have the right to work outside of the home, vote, and hold public office. Particularly notable in recent years have been reforms in marriage and divorce laws.

Among the most important of these reforms are the abolition of polygamy in some countries and its severe limitation in others. Women have received expanded rights within marriage as well; they can participate in contracting their marriage and stipulate conditions favorable to them in the marriage contract. Reforms also increased the minimum age for marriage for both spouses, prohibiting child marriage. In regard to divorce, women have the right to financial compensation, to require that the husband provide housing for his divorced wife and children as long as the wife holds custody over the children, and to have custody over their older children.

What do Muslims say about women's rights?

No one should be complacent about the condition of women in many Muslim (and many Western) societies. Americans certainly are not. When asked the open-ended question "What do you admire least about the Muslim or Islamic world?" among the top responses is "gender inequality," associated with veiling, female segregation, illiteracy, and powerlessness. Patriarchy and its legacy, legitimated in the name of religion, remain alive in various Muslim countries, although also being challenged on many levels.

The realities of women in the Arab and Muslim worlds present a complex picture of individuals in different situations and varied social contexts. Many are unfairly subject to powerful forces of patriarchy and religion, but significant numbers of other women are far more empowered and respected in their own cultures than blanket stereotypes might lead us to believe. The status and roles of women in the Muslim world vary considerably, influenced as much by literacy, education, and economic development as by religion. Men and women in Muslim societies grapple with many gender issues, ranging from the extent of women's education and employment to women's role in the family and the nature of their religious leadership and authority in Islam.

Today Islamic scholars and activists, men and women representing many ideological orientations, are increasingly speaking out. They are empowering themselves not just as defenders of women's rights but also as interpreters of the Islamic tradition. Many argue that patriarchy as much as religion, or patriarchy linked to religion, accounts for customs that became long-standing traditions affecting gender relations and women's status in society.

When it comes to popular Muslim attitudes about women's rights, the facts are not always what one might expect. As the 2007 Gallup World Poll reveals, majorities of Muslims, some in the most conservative Muslim societies, support women's equal rights. Majorities in virtually every country surveyed say women should have the same legal rights as men to serve in the highest levels of government. In addition, majorities of both men and women in dozens of Muslim countries around the world (61 percent of Saudis, 85 percent of Iranians, and nearly 90 percent in Indonesia, Turkey, Bangladesh, and Lebanon) say that men and women should have the same legal rights. Majorities also support a woman's right to work outside the home in any job for which a woman qualifies (90 percent in Malaysia, 86 percent in Turkey, 85 percent in Egypt, and 69 percent in Saudi Arabia) and a woman's right to vote without interference from family members (80 percent in Indonesia, 89 percent in Iran, 67 percent in Pakistan, 90 percent in Bangladesh, 76 percent in Jordan, 93 percent in Turkey, and 56 percent in Saudi Arabia).

At the same time, the complexities surrounding women's status are illustrated by country-specific contradictions:

- Women in Egypt today have access to the best education and hold responsible professional positions in virtually every sector. Yet, like women in most Muslim societies, until recently they needed a male family member's permission to travel.
- While women cannot vote in Saudi Arabia, in almost every other Muslim country, women do vote. They also run for political office and serve in many parliaments. A woman has been a head of state or vice president in Iran, Pakistan, Turkey, Indonesia, and Bangladesh.
- Saudi women own 70 percent of the savings in Saudi banks and own 61 percent of private firms in the kingdom; they own much of the real estate in Riyadh and Jeddah and can own and manage their own businesses. Yet they are sexually segregated, restricted to "appropriate" professions, and forbidden to drive a car.
- In nearby Kuwait, women freely function in society and hold responsible positions in many areas, but until only a few years ago they could not vote.
- In Afghanistan and in some areas of Pakistan, the Taliban, in the name of Islam, has forced professional women to give up their jobs and prohibited girls from attending school.
- In Iran, where women must cover their hair and wear long-sleeved, ankle-length outfits in public, they constitute the majority of university students, hold many professional positions, and serve in parliament. A woman is one of the vice presidents in this Islamic republic.
- In modern-day Egypt, women could not until recently serve as judges, but in Morocco, more than 20 percent of judges are women.

Both the causes of women's lack of empowerment and inequality and the winds of change can be seen in women's basic literacy and education. In Yemen, women's literacy is only 28 percent vs. 70 percent for men; in Pakistan, it is 28 percent vs. 53 percent for men. Percentages of women pursuing postsecondary educations dip as low as 8 percent and 13 percent in Morocco and Pakistan respectively (comparable to 3.7 percent in Brazil, or 11 percent in the Czech Republic).

In sharp contrast, women's literacy rates in Iran and Saudi Arabia are 70 percent and as high as 85 percent in Jordan and Malaysia. In education, significant percentages of women in Iran (52 percent), Egypt (34 percent), Saudi Arabia (32 percent), and Lebanon (37 percent) have postsecondary educations. In the UAE, as in Iran, the majority of university students are women.

In many Muslim countries and communities today, women lead and participate in Quran study groups, run mosque-based educational and social services, and are religious scholars and even muftis. The growing empowerment of women is reflected in increased educational and professional opportunities (to become physicians, journalists, lawyers, engineers, social workers, university professors, and entrepreneurs), as well as in legal reforms and voting rights.

What kinds of roles did women play in early Islam?

Women played important roles in the early Muslim community and in the life of Muhammad. Historical and other evidence indicates that a woman (Muhammad's wife Khadija) was the first to learn of the Quranic revelation. Moreover, she owned her own business, hired Muhammad, and later proposed to him. This precedent led jurists to recommend that women could propose to men if they so desired. Women fought in battles and nursed the wounded during the time of the Prophet. They were consulted about who should succeed Muhammad after his death. Women also contributed to the collection and compilation of the Quran and played an important role in the transmission of numerous *hadith* (Prophetic traditions).

The fact that women prayed regularly along with men in the mosque is also evidence of their equality in public life during the early period of Islam. Women in the early Muslim community owned and sold property, engaged in commercial transactions, and were encouraged to seek and provide educational instruction. Many women were instructed in religious matters in Muhammad's own home. Muhammad's daughter Fatima, his only surviving child, played a prominent role in his community. She was the wife of Imam Ali and mother of Imams Hussein and Hassan, immaculate and sinless, the pattern for virtuous women and object of prayer and petition. Like her son Hussein she embodies a life of dedication, suffering, and compassion. Muhammad's wife Aisha also played a unique role in the community, as an acknowledged authority on history, medicine, poetry, and rhetoric, as well as one of the most important transmitters of hadith.

In political affairs, women independently pledged their oath of allegiance (*bayah*) to Muhammad, often without the knowledge or approval of male family members, and in many cases distinguished women converted to Islam before the men in their family. The second caliph, Umar Ibn al-Khattab, appointed women to serve as officials in the marketplace of Medina. The Hanbali school of law (see page 158, "What is Islamic law?") supports the right of women to serve as judges. The Quran holds up the leadership of Bilqis, the queen of Sheba, as a positive example (27:23–44). Rather than focusing on gender, the Quranic account of this queen describes her ability to fulfill the requirements of her office, her purity of faith, her independent judgment, and her political skills, portraying a woman serving as an effective political leader.

Why do Muslim women wear veils and long garments?

The word *veiling* is a generic term used to describe the wearing of loose-fitting clothing and/or a headscarf. The Quran emphasizes modesty, although there is no specific prescription for covering one's head. The custom of veiling is associated with Islam because of a passage that says, "Say to the believing women that they should lower their gaze and guard their modesty. They should draw their veils over their bosoms and not display their beauty" (24:31). Specific attire for women is not stipulated anywhere in the Quran, which also emphasizes modesty for men: "Tell the believing men to lower their gaze and be modest" (24:30).

The Islamic style of dress is known by many names (*hijab, burqa, chador, galabeya,* etc.; see glossary for descriptions) because of the multitude of styles, colors, and fabrics worn by Muslim women in countries extending from Morocco to Iran to Malaysia to Europe and the United States, and because of diverse customs and interpretations of the Quranic verses.

Veiling of women did not become widespread in the Islamic empire until three or four generations after the death of Muhammad. Veiling was originally a sign of honor and distinction. During Muhammad's time, Muhammad's wives and upper-class women wore the veil as a symbol of their status. Generations later, Muslim women adopted the practice more widely. They were influenced by upper- and middle-class Persian and Byzantine women, who wore the veil as a sign of their rank, to separate themselves not from men but from the lower classes. The mingling of all classes at prayer and in the marketplace encouraged use of the veil among urban Muslim women.

The veil is often seen as a symbol of women's inferior status in Islam. Opponents link veiling with backwardness and oppression, and Western dress with individuality and freedom. Critics of veiling, Muslim and non-Muslim, stress the importance of self-expression, which they associate with the distinctive way in which a woman dresses and wears her hair. They believe that any person or religion or culture that requires a mature woman to dress in a certain way infringes on her rights and freedom. They question those who say the veil is for women's protection, and ask why not put the burden on the men to control themselves.

Supporters of veiling explain that they choose to wear the hijab because it provides freedom from emphasis on the physical and from competing with other women's looks. Further, it keeps women from being sex objects for males to reject or approve. It enables women to focus on their spiritual, intellectual, and professional development. Some scholars have argued that in returning to Islamic dress, particularly in the 1980s, many Muslim women were attempting to reconcile their Islamic tradition with a modern lifestyle, redefining their identities as modern Muslim women.

Islamic dress is also used as a sign of protest and liberation. It has developed political overtones, becoming a source of national pride as well as resistance to Western dominance (cultural as well as political) and to authoritarian regimes. Many young Muslim women have adopted Islamic dress to symbolize a return to their cultural roots and rejection of a Western imperialist tradition that in their view shows little respect for women. These young women think that Western fashions force women into uncomfortable and undignified outfits that turn them into sexual objects lacking propriety and dignity. Women who wear Islamic dress thus find it strange or offensive for people to condemn their own modest fashions as imprisoning and misogynist. The West should not condemn the hijab or Islam, they say, but rather a social system that promotes an unrealistic ideal, makes young girls obsessive about their physical beauty and their weight, and teaches young boys to rate girls based on that ideal.

Western and Muslim critics of Islamic dress, on the other hand, question those who say it is their free choice to wear the veil. They see such women as under the sway of an oppressive patriarchal culture or as just submitting to the dictates of their religion. Critics also argue that since the hijab has been used to control and segregate women, as in Afghanistan under the Taliban, the veil is a symbol of conformity and confinement that reflects on any woman who wears it.

Some Muslims, however, would say that Western women only believe they are free. They do not see how their culture exploits them when they "choose" to spend countless hours on their appearance, wear uncomfortable skin-tight clothes and dangerous high-heeled shoes, and allow themselves to be displayed as sexual objects to sell cars, shaving cream, and beer. These Muslims say that Westerners condemn the veil because they themselves are not free to choose.

Since the 1970s, a significant number of "modern" women from Cairo to Jakarta have turned or returned to wearing Islamic dress. Often this is a voluntary movement led by young, urban, middle-class women, who are well educated and work in every sector of society. New fashions have emerged to reflect new understandings of the status and role of women. Indeed, designing contemporary Islamic dress has become a profitable enterprise. Some Muslim women have started their own companies specializing in the design and marketing of fashionable and modest outfits featuring varied flowing garments and matching veils.

Women who wear the scarf complain that, instead of asking what the hijab means to them, people simply assume that veiled women are oppressed. This assumption, they say, oppresses Muslim women more than any manner of dress ever could. Even if a woman wearing the veil is strong and intelligent, many people who are reluctant to get to know her or invite her to participate in activities automatically discount her value. They point out that women of many other cultures and religions—Russian women, Hindu women, Jewish women, Greek women, and Catholic nuns—often wear head coverings. They ask why these women are not viewed as oppressed. If opponents assume that women of other cultures who cover their heads are liberated, why can't they imagine freedom for Muslim women who wear a veil? Muslim women often talk about what the hijab symbolizes: religious devotion, discipline, reflection, respect, freedom, and modernity. But too often nobody asks them what the scarf means to them.

Why do Muslim men wear turbans or caps?

Not all Muslim men wear turbans, and not all men who wear turbans are Muslims. Sikhs, for example, wear turbans as a religious requirement. Many Muslim men do not wear any head covering at all. Head coverings tend to be associated with culture, rather than with religion.

Head coverings for Muslim males who choose to wear them include turbans, fezzes, prayer caps or skullcaps, keffiyahs, and traditional Arab head coverings. Turbans are most often associated with the Taliban of Afghanistan and Iranian clerics. The color of the turban often indicates the status of the wearer: black marks the wearer as a *sayyid*, or descendant of Muhammad, while white signifies that the wearer is not a descendant of Muhammad. The fez was the traditional head covering of Turkish men during the late Ottoman era. It was forcibly replaced with a European-style brimmed hat in the early twentieth century. Keffiyahs tend to be associated with Jordan and Palestine and are often worn today to indicate sympathy for the Palestinian national cause. Traditional Arab head coverings, such as those worn in Saudi Arabia, were originally designed to protect the head and neck from the sun. Prayer caps and skullcaps are typically found in Pakistan and among some African American Muslims.

Why do Muslim men wear beards?

Many Muslim men wear beards in honor of the Prophet Muhammad, who had a beard. Some believe that the beard should be left untrimmed in the style of Muhammad, but many do not accept this assertion; thus differing styles of beards abound, ranging from full beards covering the entire jaw and cheeks to neatly trimmed goatees covering only the chin area. Only in Afghanistan under the Taliban regime were men absolutely required to wear full, untrimmed beards.

Many other Muslim men do not wear beards and do not believe it is a religious requirement. Some who live in Muslim countries that repress any form of Islamic activism or fundamentalism do not wear them because they are more likely to be subject to suspicion and arrest if they do. Some in the West, particularly post–September 11, avoid wearing a beard because bearded Muslim men tend to be associated with extremism.

Does Islam require circumcision?

As in Judaism, circumcision for males is required in Islam according to both tradition and Muhammad's example (Sunnah). Many Muslims believe that circumcision is required for male converts to Islam. Symbolically, circumcision represents the religious process of submission to God's will and commands and the submission of base passions to the higher spiritual requirements of Islam. In other words, the physical modification of the male organ symbolizes submission of even sexual matters to God.

Socially, circumcision is an important rite of passage for boys and, when carried out at the age of ten or twelve, marks the transition to adulthood and the assumption of male responsibilities, including regular attendance at public prayer. Furthermore, a male who is circumcised at an older age is no longer permitted to mingle as freely with unrelated women.

In the Middle East, the ritual of circumcision is typically carried out somewhere between the ages of two and twelve. In many Muslim countries, the occasion of circumcision is a celebratory event paralleling wedding rituals, including the bringing of gifts and feasting. In Europe and the United States, circumcisions are typically done in the hospital immediately after birth.

Female circumcision is neither an Islamic practice nor widespread among Muslims. Rather, it appears to be an African tradition that remains in practice in countries like Sudan and Egypt, among Muslims and non-Muslims alike.

Is the practice of Muslim arranged marriages changing?

Marriage is a sacred duty in Islam, an act that traditionally was not and is not only between two individuals but between the two families of the prospective bride and groom. Traditionally arranged marriages have been the norm in most Muslim societies. Parents draw on a number of sources in the family and community to find suitable spouses for their children, from relatives and close family friends to matrimonial brokers. The prospective spouse is thoroughly investigated by contacts with teachers, professors, employers, friends, neighbors, and colleagues to learn about his or her character.

While this system continues to exist, change is occurring slowly in many Muslim countries and in Muslim communities in the West. Some parents and their children in Europe and America may look to their homeland for an appropriate spouse; others engage in alternative methods for finding a spouse, including meetings at family and community social events and exploring Muslim social networks or contacts at university. Some engage in what some have termed *halal* (Islamically permissible) dating with chaperones. Many other young Muslim professionals advertise in the matrimonial pages of Muslim publications or on Muslim Internet sites.

It is important to note that even in the case of halal dating, observant Muslims are more accurately described as "courting," meeting with the explicit intention of finding a suitable spouse and not merely for casual or uncommitted companionship. Some young Muslims, who are interested in more casual dating, are rethinking traditional Islamic guidelines in light of what they see as new relationship paradigms, seeking a suitable middle ground between modern relationship norms and traditional sensibilities. Of course, as in other religious communities, other young people simply assimilate to the wider society and ignore traditional as well as modern religious guidelines.

Can Muslim men have more than one wife?

The practice of polygamy, or more correctly polygyny (marriage to more than one wife), is a controversial subject in Islamic societies. Many modern Islamic nations have either outlawed or strictly regulated polygamy in a variety of ways (requiring a court review and approval, requiring a wife's permission, etc.). Although polygamy is practiced in some Muslim societies, the vast majority of Muslims today are monogamous.

Although it is found in many religious and cultural traditions, we tend to identify polygamy or polygyny particularly with Islam. In fact, historically polygyny was practiced in Semitic societies in general and Arab culture in particular. It was common among the nobles and leaders in Arabian society and, although less common, can also be seen in biblical Judaism; Abraham, David, and Solomon all had multiple wives.

Polygamy was common in pre-Islamic Arabia; marriage was uncontrolled. A man could have as many wives as he wanted; women were considered inferior, had no rights, and were treated like servants. Seventh-century Arabia was the scene of frequent tribal wars and combat. When men were killed in battle, it was almost impossible for their widows and orphans, or unmarried sisters or nieces, to survive without their male protector. In this context, the revelations in the Quran regarding marriage, like other Quranic revelations and reforms regarding inheritance, divorce, serving as a witness, etc., tended to improve women's position.

The Quran permits a man to marry up to four wives, provided that he is able to support and treat them equally:

"Give orphans their property, and do not exchange the corrupt for the good; and devour not their property with your property; surely that is a great crime. If you are afraid you will not be able to deal justly with the orphans, marry women of your choice, two or three or four; but if you will not be able to deal justly [with them] only one" (4:3). This Quranic command restricts a male's right to an unlimited number of wives, while also using the umbrella of marriage as a protection for women in a violent society. As Quran 24:32 says, "Marry the spouseless among you, and your slaves and handmaidens that are righteous; if they are poor God will enrich them of his bounty; God is All-Embracing, All-Knowing."

Another verse, "You are never able to be fair and just between women even if that is your ardent desire" (4:129), has been used in modern times by reformers to reject the possibility of equal justice among wives and to argue that the Quran really preaches that monogamy is the ideal, as monogamy is stressed in the later chapters of Quranic revelation. More conservative Muslims reject this interpretation as un-Islamic and say that it reflects the tendency of reformers to imitate the West.

Can Muslims marry non-Muslims?

Marriage regulations in Islam revolve around concerns regarding the faith of the children who will result from the union. Marriage between a Muslim man and someone from a community not possessing a revelation is considered unlawful. While it is preferable for Muslim men to marry Muslim women, they are allowed to marry Christian or Jewish women, because these women are "People of the Book," those who have a divine revelation. Compatibility of belief is understood to be critical to a harmonious marriage and family life. Whatever the male's official role as head of the household, women tend to spend the most time with the children, particularly when they are small, so children are more likely to be exposed to their mother's religion from an early age. Men therefore must select a wife who upholds monotheism and divine revelation.

Muslim women must marry a Muslim or someone who converts to Islam. Under Islamic law, the male is recognized as the head of the household, and in marriage his wife is expected to take the nationality and status given by her husband's law. The man is also responsible for the religious instruction of his older children and for serving as their guardian, particularly in matters of marriage. Thus the marriage of a Muslim woman to a non-Muslim man would represent the potential "loss" of the children from that union to Islam.

What does Islam have to say about domestic violence?

Domestic violence is a serious social problem in the West and globally, and the Muslim world is no exception. Many grassroots movements and women's organizations who work to eradicate it through education for both men and women emphasize Quranic teachings about the rights and responsibilities of men and women and about marital relations.

In some Muslim societies, men use the Quran to justify domestic violence. However, many verses in the Quran teach that men and women are to be kind to and supportive of each other. Love and justice in family relationships are emphasized, and cruelty is forbidden. Quran 30:21 states, "And among His signs is this, that He created for you mates from among yourselves, that you may dwell in tranquillity with them, and He has put love and mercy between your [hearts]: behold, verily in that are signs for those who reflect." Quran 4:19 further commands, "O you who believe! You are forbidden to inherit women against their will. Nor should you treat them with harshness. On the contrary live with them on a footing of kindness and equity. If you take a dislike to them it may be that you dislike a thing through which God brings about a great deal of good."

Chronologically, the last Quranic verse to be revealed that addressed relations between husband and wife was 9:71, in which women and men are described as being each other's protecting friends and guardians, emphasizing their cooperation in living together as partners, rather than adversaries or superiors and subordinates. Likewise, the *hadith* (Prophetic traditions) note Muhammad's respect for and protection of women. Muhammad said, "The best of you is he who is best to his wife." Muhammad's wife Aisha narrated that Muhammad never hit any servant or woman and never physically struck anyone with his own hand. Neither the Quran nor the hadith record Muhammad as ever mistreating or losing his temper with any of his wives, even when he was unhappy or dissatisfied.

Those who use the Quran to justify wife-beating point to 4:34, which says, "Good women are obedient, guarding in secret that which God has guarded. As for those from whom you fear disobedience, admonish them, then banish them to beds apart and strike them. But if they obey you, do not seek a way against them." In recent years scholars have argued that "obedience" refers to the woman's attitude toward God, not toward her husband. Furthermore, obedience in this verse is tied to the woman's guarding of her chastity, so that an obedient woman is one who does not commit sexual immorality. The word typically translated as "disobedience" (*nushuz*) refers to a disruption of marital harmony in which one spouse fails to fulfill the required duties of marriage. It is applied elsewhere in the Quran to both men and women. The end of the verse admonishes men not to mistreat women who obey them. Rather than granting men the right to strike their wives, reformers argue, this verse reminds men of their responsibility to treat women fairly.

Quran 4:34 lists three methods to be used in resolving marital disputes. First comes admonition or discussion between the husband and wife alone or with the assistance of arbiters. This practice, also recommended by 4:35 and 4:128, is also to be used for couples considering divorce. If this fails, the second option is physical separation, sleeping in separate beds, which gives the couple space for cooling off and thinking about the future of their marital relationship. The third and final method is to strike or hit. This striking takes the singular form grammatically, so that only a single strike is permissible. Quran 4:34 was revealed early in the Medinan period of Muhammad's ministry, a time and place in which cruelty and violence against women remained rampant. Thus some Muslim scholars today argue that the single strike permitted in this verse was intended as a restriction on an existing practice, not as a recommended method for dealing with one's wife.

In the major hadith collections—Muslim, Bukhari, Tirmidhi, Abu Daud, Nasai, and Ibn Majah—hadith about striking all emphasize that striking should be done in such a way as not to cause pain or harm. These sources stress that in cases where a single strike is used, it should be merely symbolic. The founder of the Shafii law school maintained that it is preferable to avoid striking altogether. Despite the fact that domestic violence continued to exist in male-dominated cultures and to be legitimated in the name of religion, neither the majority of Quranic verses nor the hadith support or permit it.

How does Islam treat divorce?

In contrast to Catholicism and other Christian denominations, in Islam marriage is a contract, not a sacrament. Islam has always recognized the right to divorce under certain circumstances. In pre-Islamic times, Arab custom enabled a man to divorce at any time and for any reason, while his wife had no rights at all. However, the Quran established new guidelines to control a husband's arbitrary actions. It considers divorce, among the permitted things, to be a last resort and encourages arbitration between the spouses. "If you fear a split between a man and his wife, send for an arbiter from his family and an arbiter from her family [thus putting the wife's interests on a equal footing with those of her husband]. If both want to be reconciled, God will arrange things between them" (4:35). The Quran admonishes husbands faced with the prospect of proceeding to divorce to "either retain them [their wives] honorably or release them honorably" (65:2).

The seriousness of the act of divorce is reflected in the requirement given in the Quran that in order to make his divorce irrevocable a husband must pronounce "I divorce you" not once but three times, once each successive month for a period of three months. This is to allow time for reconciliation between husband and wife or, if there is no reconciliation and the wife is found to be pregnant, to arrange child support for the unborn child. "When you divorce women, divorce them when they have reached their period. Count their periods... and fear God your Lord. Do not expel them from their houses... Those are limits set by God" (65:1).

Despite Quranic guidelines, an abbreviated form of divorce, which allows a man to declare "I divorce you" three times at once, became commonplace. Although considered a sinful abuse, it is nevertheless legally valid. This kind of divorce is a powerful example of how male-dominated customs overcame religious requirements and affected divorce rights in various Muslim countries for many generations.

Muslim countries have instituted a variety of laws, using the Quran and the courts, to control divorce proceedings and improve women's rights. In many countries today, Muslim women can obtain a divorce on a variety of grounds from the courts. Muslims who live in America or Europe must abide by civil law in obtaining a divorce. However, there are also many patriarchal societies where custom continues to allow extensive rights for men and more restricted rights of divorce for women. This illustrates the fact that problems with women's rights originate not from Islam but from patriarchy, which is still a strong force in many societies.

Why are Muslims reluctant to shake hands?

There are two reasons why some Muslims are reluctant to shake hands when greeting another person. Conservatives believe that unrelated men and women should avoid touching each other due to the sexual overtones potentially associated with touching.

Some Muslims, like orthodox Jews, are reluctant to shake hands due to concerns about ritual purity. Traditional Shii believe that non-Muslims are spiritually impure, so that physical contact with a non-Muslim, whether male or female, places the Muslim in a state of ritual impurity. Some Sunni Muslims also believe that non-Muslims are ritually impure, but Sunni do not require ritual purification after coming into physical contact with non-Muslims.

How do Muslims feel about pets, or petting animals?

There is no Quranic prohibition or condemnation of pets. Many *hadith* (Prophetic traditions) emphasize treating animals kindly and not overworking or beating them. One records the story of a woman who starved a cat to death and thus went to hell, while another describes a man who saved the life of a thirsty dog and thus went to heaven.

Dogs in the Islamic world are typically not allowed inside the house because they are considered to be unclean. Many Muslims believe that if anyone comes into contact with a dog's saliva, that person must repeat the ritual ablutions prior to prayer. A frequently cited hadith records that Muhammad forbade dogs inside the house for reasons of hygiene, but another hadith reports that the Prophet had a dog that used to play around him as he prayed outside his home. Cats, known for their cleanliness, lived in the household of Muhammad. He and some of his Companions were well known for their kindness to cats.

Some Muslims today argue that issues of disease that rendered dogs unhygienic in the past have largely been resolved through advances in veterinary medicine, so that contact with dogs is no longer a problem. Increasingly, Muslims, particularly those who were born in the United States and Europe, have dogs as pets. Others, however, believe that the prohibition of dogs inside the house recorded in the hadith remains applicable to every time and place.

What is Islam's attitude toward alcohol and pork?

Both alcohol and pork are forbidden in Islam. Islamic law strictly prohibits the consumption, sale, and purchase of alcohol by Muslims, although in rare cases its use is permitted for medicinal purposes. The prohibition of the consumption of alcohol is based upon Quran 5:90–91, which states, "O you who believe! Intoxicants and gambling, dedication of stones, and divination by arrows are an abomination, among the works of Satan. Abstain from such work so that you may prosper. Satan's plan is to stir up enmity and hatred between you, with intoxicants and gambling, and hinder you from the remembrance of God, and from prayer. Will you not then abstain?" The specific intoxicant mentioned in this passage is date wine. Although a few jurists have argued that, according to a literal interpretation, only date wine is therefore forbidden, the overwhelming majority have interpreted this passage as a broad prohibition against any substance that produces an altered state of mind, including alcohol and narcotics.

Many countries that have implemented the Shariah (Islamic law) have banned alcohol, usually for Muslims and non-Muslims alike. Examples include Iran, Pakistan, Sudan, Saudi Arabia, Libya, and portions of Malaysia. Some countries with secular regimes, such as Turkey and Egypt, have instituted strict laws prohibiting narcotics but have allowed controlled importation, sale, and consumption of alcoholic beverages. Islamist organizations typically support a complete ban on alcohol.

In the United States and Europe, Muslim communities today debate and differ about whether Muslims should work in places that sell, consume, or produce alcohol, including vineyards, restaurants, and grocery stores. A similar concern is whether it is permissible for a Muslim to accept an invitation to dinner knowing that alcohol may or will be served as part of the meal, whether at a restaurant or in the privacy of someone's home.

The dietary prohibition against pork also comes from the Quran. Quran 5:3 states, "You are forbidden to eat carrion, blood, and the flesh of swine, as well as whatever is slaughtered in the name of any one other than God." Quran 6:145 confirms this prohibition. Further, some Muslims believe that because the pig is an animal known to carry germs and diseases, particularly trichinosis, the consumption of pork products is unhealthy and unhygienic, in addition to being prohibited by the Quran. Physical contact with pork or pork products is believed to render a person or object impure, although washing or removing the offending substance can remove this impurity.

American Muslims generally respect the prohibition of pork and pork products. Just as with alcohol, some Muslims are reluctant to accept dinner invitations to non-Muslim homes for fear of unknowingly being served a pork product. The widespread use of pork products and by-products by American food manufacturers creates difficulties for American Muslims seeking to avoid pork. Pork lard is commonly used in the United States as shortening, so it may be concealed in seemingly harmless food items like cookies, and potato chips may be fried in it. Some American Muslims read every label carefully to verify that no pork products have been used; others believe that such detailed attention is unnecessary. This raises the further question of the permissibility of eating in restaurants, particularly fast-food restaurants that fry their foods, because the consumer does not know what oils and fats are used for frying and other cooking. Some mosques and Islamic centers circulate lists of specific products known to contain either pork or alcohol (even mustard, because some mustards are made with white wine), so that their faith communities can avoid them.

Why are Muslims against dancing?

Muslims have a variety of opinions about dancing, depending on their country of origin, how conservative their understanding of Islam is, the type of dancing in question, and where the dancing takes place. Dancing between unmarried couples is generally disapproved of, since dancing typically involves touching, an action considered inappropriate between unmarried people of opposite genders. In addition, many Muslims are concerned that permitting their children to attend American-style dances, such as those sponsored by junior and senior high schools, will lead to their dating non-Muslims or to sexual activity.

This does not mean that all dancing is forbidden in Islam. In many Middle Eastern countries, belly dancing and folk dancing have long been part of celebrations, particularly weddings. Especially popular are single-sex group dances that are performed in circular, cluster, or chain formations and consist of rhythmic stamping and stepping with the feet and clapping with the hands. Another style of dancing, particularly in tribal cultures, consists of a series of maneuvers with a weapon, such as a sword, dagger, spear, or stick.

In addition, some Sufi orders, such as the Mawlawi/ Mevlevi order, also known as the "Whirling Dervishes," use dance as a devotional tool in their quest for a direct spiritual experience of God and in imitation of the order of the universe. Islamic forms of dance tend to follow the broader Islamic artistic pattern of symmetry, geometry, and rhythm. Dance in Islamic culture has therefore tended to feature a series of individual units arranged to form a larger design, all of which are symmetrical and follow an arabesque pattern (an infinite series of circles or other shapes). This pattern is a symbolic representation of belief in the oneness of God (*tawhid*).

Why are some Muslims opposed to music?

Muslims sometimes oppose rock music because of the culture that generally tends to accompany it rather than the musical form in itself. Many young Muslims raised in the West listen to rock music because it is such a pervasive part of American youth culture.

Some Muslim parents, like many non-Muslims, object to much Western music, particularly rock music and hip-hop, because of the emphasis of the lyrics on sex, drugs, alcohol consumption, and violence. They are also concerned about allowing young people to attend rock concerts, because sex, drugs, and alcohol tend to be present.

Like the Christian rock movement, some Muslims have responded to these concerns by forming their own rock and even rap bands with lyrics that are religiously inspired. The songs of a Washington, D.C.–based group, Native Deen (*deen* is Arabic for "religion"), combine traditional Islamic messages—praying regularly, avoiding sex and violence, fasting during Ramadan, and generally struggling to be a good Muslim—with a hip-hop beat (see page 123, "What is Muslim hip-hop?). The folk singer Yusuf Islam (the former Cat Stevens), who after his conversion to Islam gave up his singing career for many years, now composes and sings "Muslim" pop music for both adults and children, such as his best-selling song "A Is for Allah." He has also put his musical talents to use in ways reminiscent of the Farm Aid concerts and the *Feed the World* album of the 1980s by hosting fund-raising concerts for Muslim causes throughout the world, including earthquake relief in Turkey and assistance to the Muslims of Bosnia.

Some ultraconservative Muslims, such as the Taliban of Afghanistan, believe that music should not be a part of Muslim life at all because they consider music to be intoxicating. In medieval times, as now, strict scholars objected to the kind of lifestyle represented by professional singers and the places where people gathered to listen to popular music.

However, historically music has been an important art form throughout the Muslim world. The most important musical form in Islam is Quran recitation, an art form in which annual competitions are held. Recordings of Quran recitation are sold throughout the Muslim world, and some of Islam's most famous singers have been Quran reciters or singers who have imitated Quran recitation in their music, such as the Egyptian singer Umm Kulthum. Likewise, the Muslim call to prayer (*adhan*) is sung or chanted, rather than strictly spoken. Music has also played an important role in religious festivals and life cycle events such as birth, marriage, and circumcision.

The Sufi orders typically use music as part of their devotions, both vocally, through repetition of words or phrases in chanting, and instrumentally. Music is a vehicle for spiritual transcendence and a means of attaining the experience of divine ecstasy.

Folk music has also been an important expression of culture throughout the Muslim world, often as a venue for heroic and love-related poetry, as well as moral and devotional themes. The music produced by the Muslims of Andalusia, like their poetry, had an enormous impact on the development of classical music in Europe. Some modern musicians, such as Cheb Mami, the "father" of Algerian *rai* music who sang "Desert Rose" with the British rock star Sting, have incorporated Western instruments, particularly electronics, and techniques into their folk traditions.

What is Muslim hip-hop?

Islam is an important part of hip-hop culture in America. While the Taliban banned music and many conservative Muslims look askance at modern Western music, others, especially the younger generation, are major consumers as well as musicians producing and enjoying a broad spectrum of music, including hip-hop.

Islamic influences are pervasive in hip-hop lyrics. In Puff Daddy and the Family's 1997 album *No Way Out*, the first track opens with Sean "P. Diddy" Combs praying, the *adhan* (Muslim call to prayer) echoing in the background. Lauren Hill raps "Don't forget about the *deen* [religion/Islamic way of life], the *Sirat-ul-Mustaqim* [the Straight Path]" in her 1999 Grammy Award–winning song "Doo Wop (That Thing)." Artists like Public Enemy, Ice Cube, Queen Latifah, Eve, the Fugees, Erykah Badu, Wyclef Jean, Mos Def, Everlast, and many others also wax poetic on Islamic themes and ideas in songs that have graced the Billboard charts in the last two decades.

Islam first appeared in hip-hop during the 1970s in New York. African Americans (who represent some 35 percent of Muslims in the United States) used it for social criticism and to express their experience in America. Many influential hip-hop musicians of the '70s and '80s referred to the Nation of Islam (NOI) and the Nation of Gods and Earths (an off-shoot of NOI) in their lyrics. For instance, a line in the 1996 Fugees song "Fu-gee-la" says, "I'm a true champion, like Farrakhan [leader of NOI] reads his Daily Qur'an, it's a phenomenon, lyrics fast like Ramadan."

A second wave of Muslim hip-hop artists, emerging in the last twenty years, express their commitment to both America and Islam simultaneously. They may be less well known than some of those mentioned above, but their words provide powerful indictments and calls for social change. Popular artists like the M-Team, Lupe Fiasco, Blakstone, Mecca2Medina, and Poetic Pilgrimage are creating music with *halal* (permissible) themes and content. Gone are the profanity, sexuality, and praise for material wealth often found in mainstream forms of hip-hop like the music of Run-DMC and Tupac. In their place are lyrics peppered with Quranic verses, Arabic phrases, and the *bismillah* (the blessing "In the name of God," used before meals or to give thanks to God), all of which take hip-hop in a more religious direction. In Lupe Fiasco's popular song "Muhammad Walks" (a remake of Kanye West's Grammy

Award–winning song "Jesus Walks"), Fiasco raps on the unity between the Abrahamic traditions recorded in the Quran: "Abraham talked, Muhammad talked, and Moses split the sea, Jesus Walk with me...Now how it ought to be, Muhammad talk to me, Jesus walk with me." Another group, Native Deen, raps about praying to Allah, evoking Quranic language in their song "I Am Near": "Ya Allah—*Samee' li-duana* (the One who hears our prayers)...*Allahummah* (Dear God)."

Muslim hip-hop features many songs condemning materialism and consumerism and encouraging Muslims to seek God and *deen* (religion) instead of worldly goods. For example, in her song "Best Names," American Muslim hip-hop artist Miss Undastood raps about the names of God that appear in the Quran: "You should worship Allah alone and not man/ He's our Rahim (the Compassionate) and our Rah-man (the Gracious) /Al-Malik (the King) and Al-Salaam (the Peace), the Conqueror/ No one can do what he can/ The Creator and the Designer of the Land."

Moral conduct is another important theme. In his song "Put Some Clothes On!" California native Kumasi uses images from nature to criticize the immodesty of women living in the West: "You can search in the earth to see that diamonds are covered/ The pearls in the shells of the ocean are covered/ And the gold in the mines are hidden and covered." Other artists encourage Muslims to unite together as a community, avoiding all divisions. In "Just for You," the group Born Tragedy says, "Black men talking about Black Supremacy/ None of that belong in the deen/ You know it true to be/ Every race, creed, color/ We all brothers."

Staying true to the original catalyst for hip-hop, the M-Team from New York tackles social justice: poverty, racism, human rights, freedom for political prisoners, and the devaluing of women. Capital D criticizes the war in Iraq, while Amir Sulaiman denounces the justice system in the United States. The Australian group The Brotherhood raps about the current Islamophobic view of Muslims and being regarded with suspicion in the West post-9/11. In "Why," they ask: "Why when something blows up on the TV/ People look at me as if it was my family?"

Muslim hip-hop culture is met with some resistance. The diversity of Muslims is clearly evident in their responses to music, from declaring it forbidden (*haram*) to arguing that it is permissible (*halal*) if it doesn't violate Islamic principles. Most agree that music with un-Islamic or sensual themes is prohibited, and some question if Muslim hip-hop is an appropriate form for an Islamic message or if the *bismillah* and *shahada* (profession of faith) can legitimately be put to hip-hop rhythm. In addition, just as many in the United States criticize the hip-hop lyrics of non-Muslim artists for endorsing substance abuse and gang violence, some Muslims criticize Muslim hip-hop for encouraging Muslim youth to join a jihadi organization. Because Muslim hip-hop is in English, it can provide jihadist organizations with a new recruitment base for their terrorism. For example, the popular group Soldiers of Allah used lyrics that endorsed creating an Islamic state and that divided people into *kafir* (unbelievers) and Muslims, a theme that Muslim terrorists use to justify violence. Though the group has since disbanded, it is still popular on the Internet and in chat room discussions. However, the majority of Muslim hip-hop renounces terrorism, interpreting jihad as an inner, not an outer, struggle. As Born Tragedy raps in the song "Just for You," "Gotta fight your inner, before you fight the outside. First you gotta fight to strive for Allah."

Muslim hip-hop is a global phenomenon that takes messages beyond a local community to the entire world. It serves as a voice of protest for the burgeoning younger generations of Muslims worldwide. In Gaza more than half the population is under twenty, and nearly 40 percent of Pakistan's population is under 15. Historian and musician Mark LeVine vividly describes the popularity of alternative music among Muslims, from Morocco, where hip-hop draws tens of thousands of fans, to Iran, where underground musicians use the Internet for popular social protest.

A prominent element of this music is the artists' opposition to violence, and their use of words as their weapons. Pakistan's famous Salman Ahmad from the band Junoon describes his "Sufi rock" music as his "jihad." B-Boy of the group G-Town, on the West Bank, says, "Hip-hop for me...is a way to resist. Instead of using guns and stones, maybe words are going to bring me a solution. Or maybe just make me feel better." Palestinian Ibrehiem Ghoneem says, "The violence never seems to change anything, so maybe people will listen to us this way." Israeli hip-hop artist Sagol 59 agrees: "With hip-hop you start a dialogue, Jews and Palestinians. You go to the heart of the problem." Hip-hop artists often elicit empathy rather than anger or fear, as in "Try Not to Cry," a heart-breaking song for the world's suffering children recorded as a duet with Sami Yusuf by Denmark's Outlandish, a group that describes themselves as deeply religious. Their 2005 album "Closer than Veins" uses a Quranic verse (50:16) to describe that God is closer to us than our jugular veins.

Through the rhyme, rhythm, and rap, Muslim hip-hop helps Muslims to criticize their society, to try to reform it, and to carve out their own place within it as they also describe how Islam has empowered them to live better lives.

How do Muslims greet each other, and why?

Muslims greet each other with the Arabic phrase *As-salam alaykum*, "Peace be upon you," to which the appropriate response is *Wa-alaykum as-salam*, "And upon you, peace." The Quran commands Muslims to greet each other in this way as a reflection of the peaceful relationships that are intended to exist between Muslims, based upon their common faith and submission to the will of God.

Quran 10:10 records that Muslims who enter heaven will greet each other in this way: "Their cry there will be, 'Glory to you, O God!' and 'Peace!' will be their greeting therein!" Quran 14:23 also records, "But those who believe and work righteousness will be admitted to Gardens beneath which rivers flow—to dwell there forever with their Lord's permission. Their greeting therein will be: 'Peace!' "

Why do Muslims say "Peace be upon him?" What does PBUH mean?

PBUH stands for "Peace be upon him." Muslims repeat this every time they refer to Muhammad or any of the prophets (Jesus, Moses, etc.). Some Muslims use the longer phrase "God's blessings and peace be upon him," which is the English for the Arabic phrase *Salah Allah alayi wa-salam*. This is abbreviated as SAAS. These abbreviations are used in written documents throughout the Muslim world, both privately and publicly, including in government documents in some countries.

The use of PBUH or the repetition of the phrase "Peace be upon him" in speech reflects the belief that Muslims should at all times remember the special role of the Prophet and request God's blessings upon him in order to obtain blessings for themselves. The Quran commands this remembrance. Quran 33:56 states, "God and His angels send blessings on the Prophet. O you who believe! Send blessings on him, and salute him with all respect."

This phrase also reflects the important role Muhammad plays in Islam as the living embodiment of the revelation contained in the Quran. It is through Muhammad's life, love for God and for humanity, and vision of how human beings should live in this world that Muslims believe they can know the will of God.

How does Islam handle burial and cremation?

Guidelines for burial and funeral rites are explicitly defined in Islamic law. The burial process is to begin as promptly as possible, usually within twenty-four hours after death. The body is first washed, often by family members or members of the community who are of the same sex, in a manner similar to the ablutions for prayer, and then wrapped entirely in a white cloth or shroud, tied at the head and feet. The body is then transported to another site where a special congregational prayer (*Salat al-Janazah*) is performed. It is distinct from other Muslim prayer services. It is very brief, never lasting more than a few minutes; most of it is not recited aloud, and the entire prayer is conducted while the congregation is standing (not bowing or prostrating).

After the prayer, the body is taken to the cemetery and laid in the grave without a coffin, with the head of the deceased positioned to face Mecca. No casket is used unless there is a need for it. Each mourner then shares symbolically in filling the grave by pouring in three handfuls of soil. Tombstones and other large markers are discouraged, as are excessive forms of mourning such as loud lamentations.

Cremation is forbidden in Islam because it is considered to be disrespectful to the deceased. Some religious scholars who believe cremation is contrary to the teachings of Islam and is a violation of Islamic law cite Quran 80:21, "Then He causes him to die, and places him in his grave," and a *hadith* in which the Prophet is reported to have said, "The way of honoring the deceased is to bury him." Thus, it is considered an obligation of Muslims as a community to ensure that every Muslim who dies is properly washed, shrouded, and buried according to the teachings of Islam.

What does Islam say about the environment?

In recent years many Muslims, like believers of other faiths, have become increasingly concerned about the environment and have looked to Islam's scriptural and doctrinal resources for a theology of the environment.

The Quran teaches that creation is the first revelation of God, the Creator of the heavens, earth, plants, animals, and humans, creating everything with a purpose. But creation does not belong to humans—it belongs to God (Quran 16:48). Human beings are God's representatives on earth who have a sacred duty to protect and care for God's creation, utilizing the earth's resources while not exploiting or destroying them. The Quran warns us against thinking that we are better than animals and the environment, because all creation is equal. While God invites humans to partake of the earth's fruits, we are reminded not to be wasteful and to avoid extravagance (Quran 6:141).

The Prophet Muhammad expressed great concern for the environment, especially for the sustainability of agriculture and the cultivation of unused land. He frequently instructed followers to plant trees and vegetation. "There is none among the believers who plants a tree, or sows a seed, and then a bird, or a person, or an animal eats thereof, but it is regarded as having given a charitable gift (for which there is great recompense)."

The Islamic tradition teaches respect for animals, which, like humans, are also creatures of God: "There is not an animal on earth or a bird that flies but are communities like you" (Quran 6:38). Sayings of the Prophet emphasize respect and compassionate treatment of animals. Muslims are instructed not to neglect or overwork animals, or to hunt or have animals fight for sport. Animals are to be killed humanely, without needless suffering. The Prophet is reported to have said, "Whoever kills a sparrow or anything bigger than that without a just cause, Allah will hold him accountable on the Day of Judgment."

Ibrahim Abdul-Matin, who writes about "green deen" (green faith), captures the religious worldview of a growing movement of Muslims motivated by their faith and concerned about the environment: "In Islam, humans are stewards of the Earth with a responsibility ... to leave the planet in a condition better than we found it. In Islam, the Earth is a mosque. Mosques are sacred, to be kept clean, and to be used for worship of the Creator. If the Earth is a mosque, it, too, is sacred, and must be kept clean, and to be used for worship. The way we treat the planet is a reflection of the way we treat ourselves. It is time for Muslims, and the rest of the 6.7 billion people on the earth, to learn to love themselves." As Abdul-Matin concludes: "Green Muslims are relevant, they are vibrant, they are green, and they are poised to transform the way we manage water, waste, and energy."

Recognizing that overconsumption has led to the pollution of the land, air, and water, and endangered plants and animals, a growing number of Muslims are part of a movement to address this issue. The heroes of Green Muslims are passionate scholars with eco-sermons and halal butchers who are as much concerned about how the animal was raised and what it was fed (free-range and organic) as the manner in which it was slaughtered so that it is halal.

While some Muslims can now order halal, organic, grass-fed, farm-raised meat online and have it shipped to them, others are becoming vegetarians and vegans. In August 2010, Saffron Road, the packaged food brand of American Halal Co., began to place certified all-natural halal frozen Indian entrees in Whole Foods Market stores nationwide.

The Islamic Foundation for Ecology and Environmental Sciences (IFEES), an internationally recognized charity based in Birmingham, U.K., utilizes Islamic principles to create and promote activities to preserve the environment and fight the ecological crisis. The group researches Islamic solutions to environmental problems and organizes conferences and training sessions, based on the Quran and focused on improving the environment through organic farming, waste recycling, and solar power. It also publishes materials for Muslims worldwide to raise awareness about the environmental crisis and introduce strategies to address the problem. One of its most recent publications, "A Muslim Green Guide," tells Muslims how to reduce climate change by making different household decisions. Working with a variety of NGOs, international organizations, governments, and universities, IFEES projects include ecological resource management in Indonesia, reclaiming traditional Islamic water conservation principles in

Yemen, and the Green Mosque project, which encourages Muslims worldwide to build eco-friendly mosques.

Wisdom in Nature (WIN), another U.K.-based group, organizes educational events, ecological justice activities, and nature outings to inform and mobilize Muslims (and others) to improve the environment. Educational events include workshops on Islam and ecology, climate change, and nature in mosques, Islamic centers, interfaith gatherings, and schools. Through WIN, Muslims volunteer in programs like Resource Recycle and Fast for the Planet and participate in marches and demonstrations for environmental improvement.

Governments in the Arab and Muslim world, which like many others have until recently pursued development without concern for ecology, are now developing policies to protect their environment. The Malaysian government has implemented Vision 2020, intended to make Malaysia a fully developed country by the year 2020. City planners wanting Islamic principles to be part of this process created the Total Planning and Development Doctrine (TPDD). TPDD integrates moral and spiritual values into city planning and development programs, requiring that all micro- and macro-urban decisions made by the public and city planners be guided by theocentric principles and aim to produce peace and prosperity.

Saudi Arabia has implemented Agenda 21 to reduce pollution and improve management of natural resources. In collaboration with Agenda 21, the Meteorology and Environmental Protection Administration (MEPA) recently prepared a plan for Saudi coastal regions to preserve and protect the marine ecosystem. MEPA has also formulated a plan to improve the quality of the water and air in Jeddah.

Jordan, Egypt, Lebanon, and Syria are among a number of Middle Eastern countries that have joined the International Renewable Energy Agency (IRENA) and are committed to cultivating renewable energy forms.

VIOLENCE AND TERRORISM

What is jihad?

Jihad (exertion or struggle) is sometimes referred to as the Sixth Pillar of Islam. The importance of jihad is rooted in the Quran's command to struggle (the literal meaning of the word *jihad*) in the path of God and in the example of the Prophet Muhammad and his early Companions.

The history of the Muslim community from Muhammad to the present can be read within the framework of what the Quran teaches about jihad. These Quranic teachings are significant to Muslim self-understanding, piety, mobilization, expansion, and defense. Jihad as struggle pertains to the difficulty and complexity of living a good life: struggling against the evil in oneself—to be virtuous and moral, making a serious effort to do good works and help to reform society. Depending on the circumstances in which one lives, it also can mean fighting injustice and oppression, spreading and defending Islam, and creating a just society through preaching, teaching, and, if necessary, armed struggle or holy war.

The two broad meanings of jihad, nonviolent and violent, are contrasted in a well-known Prophetic tradition. It is said that when Muhammad returned from battle he told his followers, "We return from the lesser jihad [warfare] to the greater jihad." The greater jihad is the more difficult and more important struggle against one's ego, selfishness, greed, and evil.

In its most general meaning, jihad refers to the obligation incumbent on all Muslims, individuals and the community, to follow and realize God's will: to lead a virtuous life and to extend the Islamic community through preaching, education, example, writing, etc. Jihad also includes the right, indeed the obligation, to defend Islam and the community from aggression. Throughout history, the call to jihad has rallied Muslims to the defense of Islam. An example of this is the Afghan *mujahidin* who fought a decade-long jihad (1979–89) against Soviet occupation.

Jihad is a concept with multiple meanings, used and abused throughout Islamic history. Although it is not associated with the words *holy war* anywhere in the Quran, Muslim rulers, with the support of religious scholars and officials, have historically used the concept of armed jihad to legitimate wars of imperial expansion. Early extremist groups also appealed to Islam to legitimate rebellion, assassination, and attempts to overthrow Muslim rulers.

In recent years religious extremists and terrorists have insisted that jihad is a universal religious obligation and that all true Muslims must join the jihad to promote a global Islamic revolution. A radicalized minority have combined militancy with messianic visions to mobilize an "army of God" whose jihad is to "liberate" Muslims at home and abroad. They have engaged in acts of violence and terror in their attempts to topple Muslim governments and, like Osama bin Laden and others, engaged in a global jihad.

Is there a global jihad today?

Although jihad has been throughout the centuries and still is an important belief and practice, since the last half of the twentieth century, a globalization of jihad has occurred in religious thought and in action. On the one hand, jihad's primary Quranic religious and spiritual aspects—the "struggle" or effort to follow God's path, to lead a good life—

remain central to Muslim spirituality. On the other hand, the concept of armed jihad has became more widespread, and has been used by resistance and liberation movements, as well as by extremist and terrorist organizations to legitimate, recruit, and motivate their followers.

From the late 1970s to the early 1990s, Muslim extremist groups primarily focused their attention locally, within their own countries. With the exception of bombings at the World Trade Center in 1993 and in Paris in 1995, most attacks against Westerners occurred within Muslim countries, from Morocco, Egypt, Saudi Arabia, and Turkey to Iraq, Yemen, Pakistan, and Indonesia. America and Europe remained secondary targets, "the far enemy." But because of their military and economic support for oppressive regimes, hatred and fear of Western nations continued to build.

The 1979–89 Soviet-Afghan war marked a turning point; jihad went global in an unprecedented way. The globalization of the war in Afghanistan could be seen in the countries that supported it, the mass communications that covered it, and the way in which the mass media made it an immediate reality around the world. It took place during the Cold War, at a time when Western and many Muslim nations feared both the spread of Communism and Khomeini's export of the Iranian revolution. While many in America, Europe, Pakistan, Saudi Arabia, and the Gulf States condemned Iran's "evil" jihad, both Western and Muslim governments embraced and were anxious to support Afghanistan's "good" jihad against the Soviets with money, weapons, and advisers. The globalization of communications, technology, and travel heightened a new consciousness of the transnational identity and interconnectedness of the Islamic community (*ummah*). Events in Afghanistan were followed across the Muslim world on a daily, hourly basis. This reinforced a sense of solidarity and identification with this righteous struggle. The *mujahidin* holy war drew Muslims from many parts of the world. Regardless of their national origin, these fighters came to be called the Afghan Arabs.

In the aftermath of the Afghan war, the new global jihad became the common symbol and rallying cry for holy and unholy wars. The mujahidin and Taliban in Afghanistan and Muslims in Bosnia, Chechnya, Kashmir, Kosovo, the southern Philippines, and Uzbekistan cast their armed struggles as jihads. Hizbollah, Hamas (the Islamic Resistance Movement), and Islamic Jihad Palestine have characterized violence and opposition against Israel as jihad. Al-Qaeda (the Base), through leader Osama bin Laden, claimed to be waging a global jihad against corrupt Muslim governments and the West.

Afghan Arabs moved on to fight other jihads in their home countries and in Bosnia, Kosovo, and Central Asia. Others stayed on or were trained and recruited in the new jihadi madrasas and training camps.

An outgrowth of the Afghan war was the development of a global jihad ideology among militants who saw Afghanistan as but one step in a global war against "un-Islamic" Muslim governments and the West. The policies of many authoritarian and oppressive Muslim regimes proved to be catalysts for radicalization and terrorism both within their countries and directed toward their Western supporters.

Al-Qaeda (modern in its use of technology: computers, faxes, Internet, cell phones, weapons), its affiliates, and other radical groups represent a new form of terrorism, born of transnationalism and globalization. They are transnational in identity and recruitment and global in ideology, strategy, targets, network of organizations, and economic transactions. Individuals and groups, religious and lay, have seized the right to declare and legitimate unholy wars in the name of Islam.

Terrorists like bin Laden and others go beyond classical Islam's criteria for a just jihad and recognize no limits but their own, employing any weapons and any means. They reject Islamic law's regulations regarding the goals and means of a valid jihad: that violence must be proportional and that only the necessary amount of force should be used to repel the enemy; that innocent civilians should not be targeted; and that jihad must be declared by the ruler or head of state.

Is Islam a primary cause and driver of terrorism?

Islam, like every other world religion, neither supports nor requires illegitimate violence. The Quran does not advocate or condone terrorism. To enhance their credibility and justify their atrocities, terrorists connect their acts of violence to Islam by ignoring the extensive limits that the Quran and the Islamic tradition place on the use of violence. As happens in other faiths, a radical fringe distorts and misinterprets mainstream and normative Islamic doctrines and laws. They pay no attention to Islamic law, which draws on the Quran to set out clear guidelines for the conduct of war and provides no support for hijacking and hostage taking.

Throughout the Quran, Muslims are urged to be merciful and just. However, Islam does give guidelines to Muslims for defending their families and themselves as well as their religion and community from aggression. The earliest Quranic verses dealing with the right to engage in a "defensive" struggle, were revealed shortly after Muhammad and his followers escaped persecution in Mecca by emigrating to Medina. At a time when they were forced to fight for their lives, Muhammad was told: "Leave is given to those who fight because they were wronged—surely God is able to help them—who were expelled from their homes wrongfully for saying, 'Our Lord is God' " (22:39–40).

Like the Hebrew scriptures or Old Testament, the Quran contains verses about struggles and wars. The Islamic community developed in Arabia, in the city of Mecca, where Muhammad lived and received God's revelation. The city was assailed by cycles of tribal warfare and surrounded by constant conflicts between the Byzantine (Eastern Roman) and the Sasanian (Persian) empires. Nevertheless, the Quranic verses repeatedly stress that peace must be the norm. The Quran frequently and strongly balances permission to fight an enemy by mandating the need to make peace: "If your enemy inclines toward peace, then you too should seek peace and put your trust in God" (8:61).

Those concerned about Islam and violence often point to what some refer to as the "sword verse" (although the word *sword* does not appear in the Quran). This oft-cited verse is seen as encouraging Muslims to kill unbelievers: "When the sacred months have passed, slay the idolaters wherever you find them, and take them, and confine them, and lie in wait for them at every place of ambush" (9:5). Critics use the verse to demonstrate that Islam is inherently violent, while religious extremists twist its meaning to develop a theology of hate and intolerance and to justify unconditional warfare against unbelievers. In fact, it is a distortion to apply this passage to all non-Muslims or unbelievers; the verse is specifically referring to Meccan "idolaters" who are accused of breaking a treaty and continuously warring against the Muslims. Moreover, critics do not mention that this "sword verse" is immediately qualified by the following: "But if they repent and fulfill their devotional obligations and pay the zakat [the charitable tax on non-Muslims], then let them go their way, for God is forgiving and kind" (9:5).

The religious language and symbolism used by extremists obscures Islam's true relationship to violence and terrorism, as well as the primary causes of global terrorism. It becomes easy for policymakers and experts to point to religion as the root cause of terrorism and violence. In most cases, complex political and economic grievances are the primary catalysts for conflicts, but religion becomes a means to legitimate the cause and mobilize popular support. As we can see in the global strategy of Osama bin Laden and al-Qaeda or witness in Palestine, post-Saddam Iraq, or Kashmir, the goals

of terrorists are often basically nationalist: to end the occupation of lands, to force "foreign" military forces out of what
they see as their homeland.

Of course religion does provide a powerful source of
meaning and motivation. Its invocation lends divine
authority that increases a terrorist leader's own authority as
well as moral justification, obligation, certitude, and heavenly
reward, all of which enhance recruitment and produce the
willingness to fight and die in a "sacred struggle." Secular
movements have also hijacked religion to heighten their
appeal. Yasser Arafat, leader of a secular nationalist
movement in Palestine (PLO and then PNA), drew on the
power of religious symbolism when he was under siege in
Ramallah by using the terms *jihad* and *shahid* (martyr) to
describe his situation. The Palestinian militia (not just the
Islamist Hamas) chose to call itself the al-Aqsa Martyrs
Brigade, using the symbolism of the al-Aqsa Mosque (the
holy site for Islam and Judaism in Jerusalem) and drawing
on the imagery of jihad and martyrdom. While religious and
nonreligious organizations and movements (whether
al-Qaeda or the Marxist Tamil Tigers in Sri Lanka) may share
a common strategy, those that are Muslim often strengthen
their cause by identifying their goal as Islamic: to create an
Islamic government, a caliphate, or simply a more Islamically
oriented state and society.

Religious leaders and intellectuals can play an important
role in the ideological war on terror. Wahhabi Islam and militant Christian Right groups do not advocate violence or
terror. However, both promote exclusivist, nonpluralistic theologies of hate that condemn other faiths and can be used by
militants. Hate speech is a powerful justification for blowing
up the Twin Towers of the World Trade Center, government
buildings or abortion clinics—for assassinating "the enemies
of God." Christians and Muslims share a critical common
goal, that of addressing exclusivist theologies that are antiplu-
ralistic and weak on tolerance. For these theologies contribute

to beliefs, attitudes, and values that feed religious extremism and terrorism that affects all of us.

How can Islam be used to justify terrorism, hijacking, and hostage taking?

Although atrocities and acts of terrorism have connected Islam with terrorism, the Islamic tradition places limits on the use of violence and rejects terrorism, hijacking, and hostage taking. As happens in other faiths, mainstream and normative doctrines and laws are ignored, distorted, or co-opted and misinterpreted by a radical fringe. Islamic law, drawing on the Quran, sets out clear guidelines for the conduct of war and rejects acts of terrorism. It is quite specific in calling for the protection of non-combatants as well as for proportional retaliation.

As the Muslim community grew, questions quickly emerged about who had religious and political authority, how to handle rebellion and civil war, what was proper behavior during times of war and peace, and how to rationalize and legitimate expansion and conquest, violence and resistance. The community developed answers by referring to Quranic injunctions and the practice of Muhammad and his Companions.

The Quran provides detailed guidelines and regulations regarding war: who should fight (48:17, 9:91), when fighting should end (2:192), and how to treat prisoners (47:4). It emphasizes proportionality in warfare: "Whoever transgresses against you, respond in kind" (2:194). Other verses provide a strong mandate for making peace: "If your enemy inclines toward peace, then you too should seek peace and put your trust in God" (8:61) and "Had Allah wished, He would have made them dominate you, and so if they leave you alone and do not fight you and offer you peace, then Allah allows you no way against them" (4:90).

From the beginning, the Islamic community faced rebellion and civil wars, violence and terrorism, epitomized by groups like the Kharijites and the Assassins. The Kharijites were a pious but puritanical and militant extremist group that broke with the caliph Ali and later assassinated him. The Assassins lived apart in secret communities from which they were guided by a series of Grand Masters, who ruled from the mountain fortress of Alamut in northern Persia. The Assassins' jihad against the Seljuq Dynasty terrorized princes, generals, and *ulama* (scholars), whom they murdered in the name of the Hidden Imam. They struck such terror in the hearts of their Muslim and Crusader enemies that their exploits in Persia and Syria earned them a name and memory in history long after they were overrun and the Mongols executed their last Grand Master in 1256.

The response of Sunni Islam and Islamic law was to marginalize extremists and develop a political theory that emphasized stability over chaos and anarchy. This, of course, did not dissuade all from the extremist path. In recent decades, alongside mainstream Islamic political opposition, terrorist groups have risen up to challenge regimes, terrorize their populations, and attack foreign interests. Often they portray themselves as the "true believers" struggling against repressive regimes and in the midst of a "pagan" society of unbelief. They attempt to impose their ideological brand of Islam and "hijack" Islamic doctrines such as jihad, claiming to be defending true Islam, to legitimate their illegitimate use of violence and acts of terrorism.

In Egypt, groups like Egypt's Islamic Jihad and other extremist groups assassinated President Anwar Sadat and other government officials, slaughtered tourists in Luxor, burned churches, and killed Christians. In Algeria, the Armed Islamic Group has engaged in a campaign of terror against the Algerian government. Osama bin Laden and al-Qaeda undertook a global war of terror against Muslim governments and America, distorting Islam and issuing their own *fatwas* (legal opinions) to legitimate their war and to call for attacks against civilians (noncombatants). Although these groups tend to receive the most media coverage because of the atrocities they commit, they represent only an extremist minority, not the majority of Muslims.

Does Islam permit suicide bombers?

On February 25, 1994, Dr. Baruch Goldstein, a Jewish settler who emigrated to Israel from the United States, walked into the Mosque of the Patriarch in Hebron and opened fire, killing twenty-nine Muslim worshipers during their Friday congregational prayer. In response, Hamas (Islamic Resistance Movement) introduced a new type of warfare in the Palestinian-Israeli conflict, suicide bombing. Promising swift revenge for the Hebron massacre, the Hamas militia, the Qassem Brigade, undertook operations within Israel itself, in Galilee, Jerusalem, and Tel Aviv. In Israel-Palestine, the use of suicide bombing increased exponentially during the second (al-Aqsa) *intifada* (uprising), which began in September 2000. The most horrific examples of suicide attacks were seen in the 9/11 attacks against the World Trade Center and the Pentagon.

Traditionally, Muslims are unconditionally forbidden to commit suicide, because only God has the right to take life. There is only one phrase in the Quran that appears relevant to suicide: "O you who believe! Do not consume your wealth in the wrong way—rather only through trade mutually agreed to, and do not kill yourselves. Surely God is Merciful toward you" (4:29). Many Muslim exegetes have believed that "do not kill yourselves" can mean "do not kill each other," based on the context of the verse. The subject of suicide is therefore little discussed in exegetical literature. The Prophetic traditions (*hadith*), however, frequently, clearly, and absolutely prohibit suicide. Punishment for killing oneself consists of the unending repetition of the act by which the suicide was committed. Many commentators, however, have been reluctant to say that a person who commits suicide is necessarily condemned to hell.

Historically both Sunni and Shii Muslims have generally forbidden "sacrificial religious suicide" and acts of terrorism. The Nizari Ismailis, popularly called the Assassins, who in the eleventh and twelfth centuries were notorious for suicidal attacks on their enemies, were rejected by mainstream Islam as fanatics. In the late twentieth century the issue resurfaced as many, Shii and Sunni alike, came to equate suicide bombing with martyrdom, relinquishing one's life for the faith. Although usually associated with the Israeli-Palestinian conflict, suicide bombings have also occurred in Lebanon, Indonesia, and elsewhere. In Lebanon, Hizbollah and al-Jihad used suicide bombings in attacks against the U.S. Marine barracks and French military headquarters in Beirut in 1983, in which several hundred were killed.

In Israel-Palestine, increased Israeli violence, brutality, and targeted assassinations reinforced the belief among many Palestinians and Muslims that so-called suicide bombers were committing not an act of suicide but one of self-sacrifice, engaged in resistance and retaliation against Israeli occupation and oppression. As student posters at universities in the West Bank and Gaza declared: "Israel has nuclear bombs, we have human bombs." Or as a Palestinian fighter remarked: "The Israelis blow us up. Why shouldn't I go to Israel and take some of them with me?"

The use of religious concepts like jihad and martyrdom to justify and legitimate suicide bombing provides a powerful incentive: the prospect of being a glorified hero in this life and enjoying paradise in the next. But what about the promise of seventy virgins? There is nothing in the Quran that rewards a martyr with virgins in paradise. The Quran does speak of *houris*, dark-eyed or black-eyed heavenly companions, as a reward in paradise, but not specifically for martyrdom. Many interpreters consider these descriptions metaphorical; tradition suggests that the ultimate reward of heaven is dwelling in God's presence. The reward of seventy virgins to martyrs is based on a "weak" Prophetic tradition used in medieval times to encourage Muslims to military activities and by extremist groups in recent years to recruit and motivate suicide bombers. However, there is no mention in the Quran nor any Prophetic tradition of suicide bombers.

Suicide bombings, especially those that target innocent civilians or noncombatants, have precipitated a sharp debate in the Muslim world, garnering both support and condemnation on religious grounds. Prominent religious leaders have differed sharply in their legal opinions (*fatwas*). Sheikh Ahmad Yasin, who was the religious leader and founder of Hamas, and Akram Sabri, the Mufti of Jerusalem, as well as many other Arab and Palestinian religious leaders, have argued that suicide bombing is necessary and justified. Others, however, condemn suicide bombings, in particular those that target civilians, as terrorism.

Prominent Islamic scholars and leaders have been sharply divided in opinion. Sheikh Abdulaziz al-Sheikh, Grand Mufti of Saudi Arabia, condemned all suicide bombing as un-Islamic and forbidden by Islam. Sheikh Muhammad Sayyid Tantawi (d. 2010), the former Grand Mufti of Egypt and Grand Sheikh of al-Azhar University, drew a sharp distinction between suicide bombings that are acts of self-sacrifice and self-defense and the killing of noncombatants, women, and children, which he has consistently condemned. He stated, "Attacking innocent people is not courageous; it is stupid and will be punished on the Day of Judgment...It is not courageous to attack innocent children, women and civilians. It is courageous to protect freedom; it is courageous to defend oneself and not to attack."

Today, Sheikh Yusuf al-Qaradawi is among the most influential religious authorities in the world. Although he condemned the 9/11 attacks, he has given fatwas that recognize suicide bombing in Israel-Palestine as an act of self-defense, the giving of one's life for God with the hope that God will grant him or her paradise. Like similar-minded religious leaders, Qaradawi has legitimated the killing of civilians, arguing that Israel is a militant and military society in which both men and women serve in the military and reserves and that if an elderly person or a child is killed in such acts, it is an involuntary killing.

Qaradawi and Tantawi clashed when Tantawi condemned the suicide attack that killed twenty-six Israelis in December 2001. Qaradawi dismissively retorted:

> How can the head of Al-Azhar incriminate mujahedin [Islamic fighters] who fight against aggressors? How can he consider these aggressors as innocent civilians?...Has fighting colonisers become a criminal and terrorist act for some sheikhs?...I am astonished that some sheikhs deliver fatwas [religious rulings] that betray the mujahedin, instead of supporting them and urging them to sacrifice and martyrdom.

However, Tantawi was not alone. On December 4, 2001, Sheikh Muhammad bin Abdullah al-Subail, imam of the Grand Mosque of Mecca, also declared that killing Israelis is not permissible:

> Any attack on innocent people is unlawful and contrary to Shariah [Islamic law]...Muslims must safeguard the lives, honor and property of non-Muslims who are under their protection and with whom they have concluded peace agreements. Attacking them contradicts Shariah.

A key issue that has emerged in these debates is that of proportionality, that the response or retaliation must be in proportion to the crime committed.

Why are Muslims so violent?

The acts of Muslim extremists in recent years lead many to ask why Islam and Muslims are so violent. Islam, from the

Quran to Islamic law, does not permit terrorism and places limits on the use of violence. It does permit, and in some circumstances even requires, the use of force in self-defense or the defense of Islam and the Islamic community. However, there is often a fine line between legitimate and illegitimate use of force, defensive and offensive battle and warfare, resistance and terrorism. While religion can be a powerful force for good, historically it has also been used to legitimate violence and warfare. The three great monotheistic traditions from biblical times to the present represent long histories of the positive and negative power of religion, its ability to create and to destroy.

Muslim rulers and governments past and present have used religion to legitimate and mobilize support for political expansion and imperialism. Religious extremists from early groups such as the Kharijites to contemporary movements like Egypt's Islamic Jihad and al-Qaeda have employed a radical theological vision, based upon distorted interpretations of scripture and doctrine, to justify violence and terrorism against their own societies and the international community. They have created a world in which those who do not accept and follow their beliefs, Muslim and non-Muslim alike, are the enemy to be fought and exterminated by any means.

The violent character of many states compounds the issue of violence in Muslim societies further. Authoritarian rulers and governments, secular and religious, use force, violence, repression, and terror to assure their stability and security at home and, in some instances, to expand their influence abroad. Failed economies, high unemployment, shortages of housing, a growing gap between rich and poor, and widespread corruption exacerbate the situation, contributing to the growth of radicalism and extremist opposition. The extent to which outside powers, including America and Europe, are seen as supporting oppressive regimes or "colonizing" and exploiting Muslim societies contributes to the appeal of violence and terrorism. These conditions and grievances create a seedbed from which the Saddam Husseins and Osama bin Ladens of the world find ready recruits in their unholy wars.

Who are the "moderate" Muslims?

"Who and where are the moderate Muslims?" continues to be a hotly debated question. The term *moderate* is problematic. What are the criteria for identifying a moderate Christian or Jew, a moderate Republican or Democrat? We have a human tendency to define what is "normal" or "moderate" in terms of someone who is just like us. Deciding who is a moderate Muslim often depends on the politics or religion of those making the judgment. Politically, many Western governments and experts are searching for reflections of themselves; the litmus test for a moderate Muslim may be tied to foreign policy issues—for example, how critical one is of American, British, or French policy or one's position on Palestine/Israel or on the wars in Iraq and Afghanistan, Chechnya, or Kashmir. Authoritarian Muslim governments use the term *moderate* to refer to those who do not oppose their governments.

When the "moderate" question is asked about Muslims, is it simply used to distinguish between extremist and nonextremist Muslims? Or is it really asking whether a Muslim espouses secular liberalism or is reformist as opposed to conservative or traditionalist?

Is it correct to say that the only moderate Muslim is one who accepts secularism and separation of church and state? Or can a moderate believe in a state where no religion is privileged and the rights of all (believer and nonbeliever) are protected? Must our idea of a moderate Muslim be someone who not only promotes the equality of women and men but also opposes the wearing of a hijab?

Often, "moderate" is equated with so-called progressive or liberal Muslims and excludes conservatives or traditionalists as well as fundamentalists. Some, for example, identify as moderate those Muslims who believe that a woman should be able to lead men and women together in prayer (*salat*). However, if this were a criterion for judging who is "moderate," then many Christian and Jewish groups or denominations, and their leaders (for example, the late Pope John Paul II as well as his successor, Benedict XVI), would fail the test. Should we then add other litmus tests such as a Muslim's position on birth control, abortion, and gay rights?

Minimally, I would argue that moderate Muslims are those who live and work within society, seek change from below, and reject religious extremism, illegitimate violence, and terrorism. And as in other faiths, in Islam such moderates constitute the majority of the mainstream.

Why haven't Muslims denounced terrorism?

A common charge, which has become conventional wisdom, is that Muslims did not condemn the attacks of 9/11 and still do not condemn terrorism. This belief has persisted despite the fact that Muslim scholars and organizations have promulgated extensive condemnations (including fatwas) of the 9/11 attacks and continue to condemn later acts of terrorism. Public statements have been issued in countries ranging from Saudi Arabia to Malaysia to the United States.

While extremists applauded the attacks, the vast majority of Muslims did not. As early as September 14, 2001, the BBC reported condemnations of the 9/11 attacks as acts of terrorism by a significant, influential, and diverse group of religious leaders. Heads of major Islamic movements from Egypt to Malaysia and more than forty Muslim scholars and politicians were equally strong in the following condemnation:

> The undersigned, leaders of Islamic movements, are horrified by the events of Tuesday 11 September 2001 in the United States which resulted in massive killing,

destruction and attack on innocent lives. We express our deepest sympathies and sorrow. We condemn, in the strongest terms, the incidents, which are against all human and Islamic norms. This is grounded in the Noble Laws of Islam which forbid all forms of attacks on innocents. God Almighty says in the Holy Qur'an: "No bearer of burdens can bear the burden of another" (Surah al-Isa 17:15).

Moreover, on September 27, 2001, the Fiqh Council of North America issued a joint fatwa clearly stating that every Muslim had a duty to work to apprehend and bring to justice anyone who planned, participated in, or financed such attacks. American Muslim leaders and internationally prominent Islamic scholars signed the fatwa.

On October 17, 2001, the Becket Fund for Religious Liberty published a full-page ad in the *New York Times*, proclaiming, "Osama bin Laden hijacked four airplanes and a religion," with statements by some of the world's most prominent Muslim leaders condemning the attacks. Among those who signed were Sheikh Abdulaziz al-Sheikh (Grand Mufti of Saudi Arabia and chairman of the Senior Ulama), Zaki Badawi (principal of the Muslim College in London), King Abdullah II of Jordan, and the Organization of the Islamic Conference.

Muslim leaders and organizations have continued to respond to every major terrorist attack. Thus, for example, after the terrorist attacks in London in 2005, in Glasgow in 2007, and in Mumbai in 2008, Muslim leaders and organizations around the world issued statements condemning the terrorists and their actions. More than five hundred British Muslim religious leaders and scholars issued a fatwa in response to the London bombings expressing condolences to the families of the victims and wishing the injured a speedy recovery. This statement emphasized that Islam condemns violence and destruction of innocent lives and that suicide bombings are "vehemently prohibited."

Joining the ongoing condemnations of terrorism by Muslim leaders is the 600-page fatwa issued in 2010 by internationally known telepreacher Muhammad Qadri. He condemns suicide bombers as unbelievers and declares, "Terrorism is terrorism, violence is violence and it has no place in Islamic teaching and no justification can be provided for it, or any kind of excuses or ifs or buts." Qadri's fatwa has been seen as a powerful argument for taking Islam back from terrorists and weakening terrorist recruiting.

Mainstream Muslims across the world echo the sentiments of these leaders. The Gallup World Poll, the largest and most systematic poll of more than thirty-five Muslim countries worldwide, representing the voices of a billion Muslims, found that the vast majority of respondents (93 percent) concur with Muslim leaders who say the 9/11 attacks could not be justified. This is despite the fact that many in this group of respondents hold critical views of U.S. policy. (Forty percent are considered pro-U.S.; 60 percent view the United States' policies unfavorably.)

Why are most people unaware of all this information? Statements and positions of the mainstream Muslim majority are not headline news, and are often not even regarded as newsworthy at all. Preachers of peace or conflict resolution might, if lucky, get a little coverage buried somewhere in the back pages. Nowhere is the result of this lack of coverage more evident than in the persistent belief that Muslims have not spoken out against violence and terrorism. The media's failure to cover Muslims' public pronouncements and major statements condemning religious extremism and terrorism has allowed the question "Why don't more Muslims speak out?" to persist. The actions of a dangerous minority of Muslim extremists and terrorists have continued to be the dominant, distorted prism through which all mainstream Muslims and their religion are seen and understood.

Do Muslims have a martyrdom complex?

In Islam as in Christianity, martyrdom—a willingness to die for one's faith or in order to protect the religious community—has a long and special history. Martyrs who sacrifice their lives to establish Islamic ideals or to defend those ideals hold an important place in Islam.

To die for one's faith is the highest form of witness to God. The Arabic/Quranic word for martyr, *shahid*, means "witness," from the same root as the word for the Muslim profession of faith (*shahada*), which bears witness that "there is no God but God, and Muhammad is the messenger of God."

The Quran has many passages that support the notion of martyrdom and that comfort those left behind. For example:

> If you are killed in the cause of God or you die, the for-giveness and mercy of God are better than all that you amass. And if you die or are killed, even so it is to God that you will return. (3:157–58)

> Never think that those who are killed in the way of God are dead. They are alive with their Lord, well provided for. (3:169)

Hadith literature, stories about what Muhammad said and did, also provides many affirmations of the rewards for those who die for Islam. Muslim tradition teaches that in the life after death martyrs are distinguished from others in several ways. Their self-sacrifice renders them free of sin and therefore they are not subject to the postmortem interrogation of the angels Nakir and Munkar. They bypass "purgatory" and proceed to one of the highest locations in heaven near the Throne of God. As a token of their purity, they are buried in the clothes in which they died and do not need to be washed before burial.

Both Sunni and Shii traditions value and esteem martyrdom. Sunni Islam has historically valorized martyrdom through veneration of the struggles (*jihads*) of the early Medinan community against the Meccan Arabs. Throughout Islamic history the call to jihad in the path of God served as a rallying cry. In the seventeenth and eighteenth centuries, leaders of Islamic revivalist movements from Africa and Arabia to Southeast Asia cast their struggles as jihads. Thus those who died were guaranteed paradise as martyrs.

Shii Islam has a particularly powerful martyrdom tradition and legacy, starting with the martyrdom of the Prophet's grandson Hussein, who with his small "righteous" band of followers was slaughtered by the army of the Sunni caliph Yazid. This sacred tragedy became the paradigm for Shii theology and spirituality and is ritually reenacted annually in Shii communities. It has expressed itself in the practice of visiting graves of the martyrs and mourning and emulating the suffering of Hussein and his companions with prayer, weeping, and self-flagellation—a ritual analogous to the commemoration of the passion and death of Jesus Christ.

Since the dawn of European colonialism, a new, broader understanding of martyrdom has developed. Soldiers killed in wars of independence against European colonial powers were often called martyrs. Since the late twentieth century, Muslims have used the term *jihad* for all struggles in defense of Muslim territory; thus those who die in such battles are martyrs. Martyrdom was a powerful theme in the Iran-Iraq war. Both Sunni Iraqis and Shii Iranians relied on the promise of martyrdom to motivate their soldiers. In postrevolutionary Iran, the tradition was reflected in the creation of martyr cemeteries for those who died in the Iran-Iraq war and for the revolution's clergy and supporters who were murdered or assassinated by opposition forces.

Martyrdom, like jihad, has become a global phenomenon, a common term of praise for those who have died in struggles (*jihads*) in Palestine (whether members of secular or Islamic Palestinian groups), Iran, Egypt, and Lebanon as well as Azerbaijan, Bosnia, Chechnya, Kashmir, and the southern Philippines.

Why do they hate us?

Anti-Americanism (along with anti-Europeanism) is a broad-based phenomenon that cuts across Arab and Muslim societies. It is driven not only by the blind hatred or religious zealotry of extremists but also by frustration and anger with U.S. foreign policy among a mainstream majority in the Muslim world.

While many continue to believe anti-Americanism is tied to insurmountable religious and cultural differences, the facts undercut this simple and rather self-serving response.

Terrorists may hate America (and some European countries), but the rest of the Muslim world does not. We fail to distinguish between the hatred of extremists and a broad anti-Americanism among those who admire our accomplishments, principles, and values but denounce what they see as U.S. arrogance, unilateralism, and hegemonic designs. Terrorists want to kill us, but most Muslims want us to stop making the world an even more dangerous place.

Major polls (Gallup, PEW, Zogby, and others) of the beliefs and attitudes of a cross-section of Muslims around the world give us a good measure of their admiration as well as their resentment, which, left unaddressed, has the potential to increase radicalization.

Gallup World Polls from 2001 to 2009 in more than thirty-five Muslim countries from North Africa to Southeast Asia, representing the voices of a billion Muslims, have shown the importance of policy as the primary driver or catalyst.

Muslims do not see all Western countries as the same. They distinguish between America and Europe and between specific European nations depending on their policies, not their culture or religion. During the pivotal years in the deterioration of U.S.-Muslim relations, Muslims globally drew a sharp distinction between America and Britain, under the Bush and Blair administrations, on the one hand, and other European countries, on the other. The United States and the United Kingdom were viewed negatively, while views of France and Germany were neutral to positive. For example, while 74 percent of Egyptians had unfavorable views of the United States, and 69 percent said the same about Britain, only 21 percent had unfavorable views of France and 29 percent of Germany. Across all predominantly Muslim countries polled, an average of 75 percent of respondents associate the word *ruthless* with the United States (in contrast to only 13 percent for France and 13 percent for Germany).

The importance of foreign policy emerges starkly when we compare Muslim views of the United States with views of Canada (America without its foreign policy, one might say). Sixty-six percent of Kuwaitis have unfavorable views of the United States, but only 3 percent see Canada unfavorably. Similarly, 64 percent of Malaysians say the United States is "aggressive"; yet only one in ten associates this quality with France and Germany.

Reactions to the U.S./U.K.–led invasion of Iraq underscore the influence of foreign policy on Muslim attitudes toward the West. When people in ten predominantly Muslim countries were asked how they view a number of nations, the attributes they most associate with the United States are "scientifically and technologically advanced" (68 percent),"aggressive" (66 percent), "conceited" (65 percent), and "morally decadent" (64 percent). Majorities in most countries who were asked about the invasion of Iraq, Muslim men and women alike, believed the invasion has done a great deal more harm than good. Muslims clearly have not seen their conflict as with the West or Western civilization as a whole but rather with specific Western powers' foreign policies.

The West's espousal of self-determination, democratization, and human rights is often seen as a hypocritical "double standard" when compared to its policies, what it actually does—for instance, supporting authoritarian Muslim regimes or imposing sanctions against Pakistan for its development of a nuclear weapon while failing to press Israel and India on their nuclear development. The moral will so evident in America's helping Kosovo is seen by many Muslims as totally absent in the U.S. policy of permissive neglect in the Chechnyan and Kashmiri conflicts. On the other hand, America's stance on human rights has been undermined by the abuse of Muslim prisoners in Abu Ghraib prison in Iraq and at Guantanamo Bay.

Globalization of communications has created a situation in which Arabs (Muslims and Christians) and Muslims around the world often see more than we see. Unlike the past, today international Arab and Muslim media are no longer solely dependent on Western reporters and channels. While America's overseas media presence (reporters and overseas posts) and coverage have waned over the past decade, television stations like Al-Jazeera, Al-Arabiyya, and others provide daily coverage of the violence in many Muslim countries. They show, for example, the violence and acts of terror committed by both sides as well as the disproportionate firepower used against Palestinians by Israelis. America's record of overwhelming support for Israel— witnessed over the years in its levels of aid to Israel, the U.S. voting record in the United Nations, and official statements by the administration and State Department—has proved to be a powerful lightning rod for Muslim anger over injustice.

Why was Salman Rushdie condemned to death?

In 1988, Salman Rushdie published *The Satanic Verses*, a novel that caused an uproar among Muslims throughout the world because of its perceived disrespect for Islam, the Prophet Muhammad, and the Quran. The title of the novel refers to a story about Muhammad (which many Muslims believe to be apocryphal) in which Satan interferes with the revelation Muhammad is receiving. As a consequence of this interference, Muhammad is said to have recited two verses saying that al-Lat, al-Uzza, and Manat, three goddesses who had been worshipped by the Quraysh (the people of Muhammad's tribe), could be intermediaries between God and humans. Muhammad discovered that this message had come from Satan, and these "satanic verses" were eliminated. Muhammad then received a new revelation describing the three goddesses as figments of the imagination deserving no worship at all.

Although this story appears in the accounts of two early historians, it is not to be found in the Quran or in any of the official collections of traditions (*hadith*) compiled about Muhammad in the ninth century. Moreover, it is contradicted by other stories and by the Quran itself. In the past it had attracted more interest in the West than in the Islamic world. Rushdie's use of the title, with its suggestion of Muhammad's receiving a satanic revelation, coupled with what many regarded as blasphemous treatment of the Prophet and his wives, generated Muslim protests and demonstrations. These protests occurred first in England, where the book was initially published, and then across the Muslim world. Photocopies of the book's offensive passages describing Muhammad, his wives, and his Companions were circulated widely in the Muslim community.

The worldwide Muslim protest against *The Satanic Verses* was followed by the notorious *fatwa* (a legal opinion by a religious scholar)—a death sentence imposed upon Rushdie by Iran's Ayatollah Khomeini. Khomeini held that Rushdie had insulted the Prophet and was therefore an apostate whose life, according to Islamic law, should be forfeited. A reward was offered to whoever carried out the execution, and Rushdie was forced into hiding. Eventually, in order to placate the Muslim community, he converted to Islam, having previously identified himself as non-Muslim. Subsequently he changed his mind and again became a non-Muslim.

Muslim reaction to Khomeini's condemnation of Rushdie was varied. Some considered Rushdie an apostate and agreed that a price should be put on his head. Others, especially Muslim intellectuals in Western countries, strongly opposed Khomeini's fatwa and signed petitions calling for freedom of expression. A third group, among them the Nobel Laureate Naguib Mahfouz, condemned the fatwa but also criticized Rushdie's book as "intellectual terrorism," declaring that *The Satanic Verses* "is not an intellectual work...and a person who writes a book like this does not think; he is merely seeking consciously to insult and injure."

While it is not true that most Muslims wanted to kill Salman Rushdie, it would be wrong to think that they did not agree with the outpouring of outrage against what they considered a book intentionally written to insult their sacred beliefs and sully the image of Islam. The title *Satanic Verses* implied that the Prophet was not able to recognize malevolent "revelations" and that Islam, as its enemies have maintained, teaches that evil actions are the will of God.

The Muslim community's strong defense of Islam and the Prophet in England, where the protests started, was also an expression of frustration with what they perceived as ill treatment by a British government that would not enlarge the scope of the British law against blasphemy (which applied only to Christianity) or allow them to establish Muslim schools in the same way that British Christian and Jewish schools had been allowed and supported by public funds. (The blasphemy law was abolished in 2008, and under Tony Blair's administration seven Muslim schools received state funding.)

Worldwide, what is still remembered internationally as the Rushdie affair was fueled by the gulf of misunderstanding and differences between a liberal, secular culture, which was horrified by what was seen as a medieval threat to freedom of expression, and a more conservative Muslim community, feeling disrespected, offended, and misunderstood.

SOCIETY, POLITICS, AND ECONOMY

What is Islamic law?

Islam means submission to the will of God. Therefore Muslims put primary emphasis on obeying God as prescribed in Islamic law. Islam's worldview is a vision of individual and communal moral responsibility; Muslims must strive or struggle (*jihad*) in the path (*shariah*) of God in order to implement God's will on earth, expand and defend the Muslim community, and establish a just society. The purpose of Islamic law is to provide the guidelines and requirements for two types of interactions: those between human beings and God, or worship, and those between human beings, or social transactions. Both have private and public dimensions, and both give Islam a prominent public role in Muslim community life.

Throughout history Islamic law has remained central to Muslim identity and practice, for it constitutes the ideal social blueprint for the believer who asks, "What should I do?" It is important to note that elaborating the law was the work of religious scholars (*ulama*), rather than judges, courts, or governments. The law's comprehensive coverage including regulations ranging from religious rituals to marriage, divorce, and inheritance to setting standards for penal and international law, provided a common code of behavior and connection for all Muslim societies.

While in Christianity theology is the queen of sciences, in Islam, as in Judaism, law is the primary religious science. There is a strong distinction between Christianity's emphasis on orthodoxy (or correct doctrine or belief) and Islam's emphasis on orthopraxy (or correct action).

Sunni Muslims recognize four official sources to guide the development of Islamic law: the Quran, the Sunnah (example) of Muhammad, analogical reasoning (*qiyas*), and consensus (*ijma*). Shii accept the Quran and Sunnah as well as their own collections of traditions of Ali and other Imams whom they regard as supreme authorities and legal interpreters, and substitute reason for analogy (*qiyas*).

Quranic texts provide moral directives, setting out what Muslims should aspire to as individuals and achieve as a community. The Sunnah of Muhammad (recorded in hundreds of traditions describing the Prophet's private and public life and his individual and communal activities) illustrates Islamic faith in practice and supplements and explains Quranic principles. Qiyas is used to provide parallels between similar situations or principles when no clear text is found in the Quran or Sunnah. For example, a broad prohibition of alcohol is deduced from a specific prohibition of wine, based on the altered mental state that both substances cause. The fourth source of law, consensus (*ijma*), originated from Muhammad's reported saying "My community will never agree on an error." This came to mean that a consensus among religious scholars could determine permissibility of an action.

Concern for justice led to the development of other legal principles that guide decision making where there are several potential outcomes. Among them are equity (*istihsan*), which permits exceptions to strict or literal legal reasoning in favor of the public interest (*maslaha*) or human welfare to assure a flexibility enabling judges to arrive at just and equitable decisions. These mechanisms allowed for multiple interpretations of texts based on context, necessity, and consensus.

Differences exist between the major Islamic law schools that reflect the diverse geographic, social, historical, and cultural contexts in which the jurists were writing. In the modern world, Islamic law faces the challenge of distinguishing the divine prescriptions and eternal principles of the Quran from regulations arising from human interpretations in response to specific historical situations. Many ulama, representing the traditional and conservative strains in Islam, continue to equate God's divinely revealed law with the laws in the legal manuals developed by the early law schools. Reformers, however, call for change in laws that are the products of social custom and human reasoning. Reformers say that what is unchanging relates to the Muslim's duties and obligations to God (worship). Laws that relate to social transactions or obligations, which are contingent on social and historical circumstances, are subject to change. Consequently, reformists have reclaimed the right to *ijtihad* (independent reasoning) to reinterpret Islam to address contemporary issues and meet needs in modern societies.

Legal reforms remain a contested issue in many contemporary Muslim countries. Most Muslim states, such as Egypt, Sudan, Nigeria, Morocco, Iraq, Pakistan, Afghanistan, Malaysia, and Indonesia, have Western-inspired constitutions and legal codes blended with Islamic laws. However, family law, which is viewed as the "heart of the Shariah" and the basis for a strong, Islamically oriented family structure and society, has remained intact in most Muslim countries. Nevertheless, significant reforms in marriage and divorce laws have occurred in many countries to protect and expand women's rights, although some scholars argue that these modern gains have not gone far enough in securing women's Quranically ordained rights.

Do Muslims today want Shariah law?

The relationship of religion to the state and religion's role in politics and society are critical and contentious issues globally.

They are reflected in constitutional debates in America, where there is a "wall of separation" between the religion and government on the one hand, but a strong religious presence in presidential and congressional politics on the other. The Gallup World Poll in 2007 found that a majority of Americans want the Bible as a source of legislation: 44 percent say the Bible should be "a" source, and 9 percent believe it should be the "only" source of legislation. Prayer in the schools, the teaching of creationism, and abortion are among many religious-political issues.

Nowhere has the issue of the relationship of religion to state and society been more contested, and at times explosive, than in the Muslim world. Is the separation of church and state possible in Islam? Shariah (Islamic law) is often characterized as a medieval legal system. This is a common charge and there are good reasons for it. Self-styled Islamic governments in countries like Saudi Arabia, Iran, Sudan, and the Taliban's Afghanistan have restricted women's rights and in some mandated the stoning of women charged with adultery; they have amputated the limbs of thieves, and prosecuted Muslims who convert to another religion for apostasy and blasphemy. Christians have also suffered under self-styled Islamic governments in countries like Sudan, Pakistan, and Afghanistan. "Islamic laws" such as Pakistan's blasphemy law have been used to imprison and threaten Christians with the death penalty.

Why, then, do majorities of Muslims regard Shariah so positively, as central to their faith? Despite aberrations and abuses, for many centuries, Shariah has functioned as a positive source of guidance, a law whose principles and values provided a moral compass for individuals and society. Islamic law was developed to serve as the blueprint for an ideal Muslim society. It represents a reservoir of principles and values, created to answer the question "What should a good Muslim be doing?" It regulates a Muslim's religious duties to God such as prayer, fasting, and almsgiving, as well as his and her social obligations and social transactions such as marriage, divorce, and inheritance, business contracts, and political issues.

Strong support for Shariah, despite examples past and present of its abuse, is reflected in the Gallup World Polls in 2006 and 2007, which found that large majorities of Muslims, both women and men, in many and diverse Muslim countries from Egypt to Malaysia, wanted Shariah as "a" source of law. While they did not want a theocracy, they did want a more democratic government that also incorporated Islamic values. So what are Muslims who want Shariah as "a source," but not "the sole source," of legislation really asking for? The answer to this is as diverse as the Muslim community. Shariah has had and continues to have many meanings and applications. For some, it means that no law should be contrary to Islam, raising many questions such as: Who is to make this decision, and on the basis of what interpretation of Islam? For others, it means Islamic law should be one of the sources of a nation's legal system, along with laws derived from other legal systems and legal philosophies.

Some who have a more conservative and static view of Islamic law press for the restoration of past practice, while others who are more reform-minded see Islamic law as flexible and more subject to change and adaptation.

Will Muslims impose Shariah in the West?

One battle cry frequently raised by those who warn that Muslims will overwhelm the West is that Muslims want to impose Shariah in America and Europe. Just as critics of Islam in the West question whether Islam is compatible with democracy and whether Muslims can be loyal citizens, many Muslims, in light of the rise and increase of Islamophobia and threats to their civil liberties, ask if democracy can include Islam. Some Muslims in the West have also questioned whether they could be both good Muslims and loyal citizens in "foreign" non-Muslim states based on Western secular laws. More isolationist and militant Muslims tend to associate Western countries and societies with *kufr*, unbelief, and look upon their citizens as unbelievers to be avoided, converted, or attacked.

Devout Jews can follow Jewish law and Christians follow their doctrines and laws and at the same time be fully American citizens, but can Muslims? What are the implications of the need to follow Shariah for Muslims living in non-Muslim societies? Is there something peculiar about Islam that prevents a Muslim from living in a secular pluralistic America or Europe?

Although Shariah is often simply and falsely equated with Islamic law, by many Muslims and non-Muslims alike, it should not be. Shariah refers to God's will, laws, principles, and values, found in the Quran and the traditions of the Prophet. Islamic law is the product of early jurists who interpreted and developed it during the early Islamic centuries. Therefore, Islamic law is the product not only of revelation but also of human reason and interpretation, an attempt to formulate a blueprint for personal and public life in and for Islamic empires and societies, not for Muslims living permanently in non-Muslim societies.

So what about the role of Shariah today for Muslims living in the United States or European countries? This question is especially important since for the first time in history permanent Muslim communities exist as religious minority communities in nations across the globe. Like followers of other faiths, Muslims can and do fulfill the personal religious obligations of their faith. But what are Muslims to do about the other areas of Islamic law?

The starting point, in order to better meet the needs of the faithful in modern times, is to ask what parts of a religious tradition, in this case Islamic law, must remain unchanged (strictly "religious" observances such as prayer, fasting, and pilgrimage) and what can be changed (civil/criminal transactions regarding marriage, divorce, inheritance, crimes and punishments, and issues of war and peace). Many of these laws can be revised to meet the needs of Muslims in new historical and social contexts.

Muslims have addressed this issue in a number of ways. Many in the West look to religious leaders and muftis (authorities in Islamic law), both here and overseas through their writings, DVDs, and the Internet, for guidance and *fatwas* (authoritative opinions on specific legal issues). In the United States and Europe there are organizations and institutions like the European and North American Fiqh (law) Councils that address specific questions and issue fatwas on Islamic law and practice. They cover questions ranging from marriage, divorce, abortion, sterilization, and stem cell research to issues of war and peace, the environment, banking and finance, and gender (for example, whether a woman can lead the Friday congregational prayer). Many of these questions are similar to those that Christians and Jews address to their own religious leaders.

Many reformers note that Muslims in the West share an identity informed by multiple subcultures. Muslims are Muslim by religion and French, British, German, American by culture. Like twentieth-century Roman Catholic reformers, who faced similar questions regarding Catholic life and loyalty in a secular society where some laws and cultural practices differed from the teachings of their faith, Muslim reformers argue that to embrace secularism and an open society is not a betrayal of Muslim principles; it enables all citizens to live together and is the necessary condition for religious freedom—for Muslims and others.

The Grand Mufti of Bosnia, Mustafa Ceric, a European Muslim with a PhD in Islamic studies from the University of Chicago, counsels Muslims to recognize that the West does not have a monopoly over values, that universal values such as democracy, the rule of law, and human rights are not solely Western but also Islamic. Moreover, he believes that European

Muslims can become an example to Muslims in the Middle East.

A related and contentious question is whether European and American legal systems should accommodate some aspects of Islamic law. The explosiveness of this question could be seen in reactions in the United Kingdom to comments about Shariah law made by Rowan Williams, the Archbishop of Canterbury, in a lecture at London's Royal Courts of Justice. The archbishop set out "to tease out some of the broader issues around the rights of religious groups within a secular state, with a few thoughts about what might be entailed in crafting a just and constructive relationship between Islamic law and the statutory law of the United Kingdom."

Media headlines blared: "Archbishop calls for implementation of Shariah law in Britain." The archbishop was not calling for implementation of Shariah law for non-Muslims. Rather he was addressing the question of whether British Muslims should have the same rights and choices that Orthodox Jews and Catholics already enjoyed. For example, as he noted, the London Beth Din Jewish courts adjudicate civil disputes. An award given by the Beth Din has the full force of an arbitration award and may be enforced (with prior permission of the Beth Din) by the civil courts. Parties who submit to such courts agree, as a matter of contract, to accept their decisions. The public courts enforce awards just as they would enforce other agreements as long as they do not contradict or override British law.

The situation in the United States, where the line between church and state is more sharply drawn, is quite different. In Great Britain and some other secular European governments, church and state are not completely separate: the monarch is the head of the church or must be a member of the established church, and government funding is provided for some religious institutions and their activities. In America, Muslims, like members of other faiths, can draw on their religious law to govern internal matters and as a guide in family and social behavior as long as they do not violate civil law. At the same time, there are informal or nonjudicial areas where religious leaders and scholars are consulted by the president, Congress, and other government officials on public issues such as abortion, stem cell research, and health care. Many hospitals and physicians today consult with Muslim as well as non-Muslim scholars on sensitive religious and cultural issues in their treatment of Muslim patients, and some suggest that it might be useful to have religious arbitration councils at the service of the courts to mediate in family law disputes.

But what do Muslims do when in some instances American laws are contrary to their beliefs? The answer is that they will respond in the same way as members of other faith traditions—by recognizing the democratic process and pluralistic nature of society and, if they wish, working within the system to change it through lobbying the government concerning laws and appointments of Supreme Court judges just as many Americans, of all faiths and of no faith, have done on issues like prayer in the schools and abortion.

What is the role of a fatwa?

Until recently the words *fatwa* and *mufti* were absent from most people's vocabulary. Today they have become common terms in our media and public conversations. Osama bin Laden and other terrorists use fatwas to legitimate their acts and rally Muslims to support them; many major religious leaders issue fatwas to counter religious extremism and terrorism. Fatwas are currently playing a far more prominent and comprehensive role in Islam. What is a fatwa? What authority does it have over Muslims?

A fatwa is a formal, written legal opinion based on a mufti's (legal scholar's) interpretation of the law, given in response to a request by an individual or a court. It is authoritative, though nonbinding. Its authority is based on the mufti's education and status within the community and the persuasiveness of his opinion. The qualifications of a mufti and the rules for issuing a fatwa were developed in great detail. Theoretically, a mufti must be a *mujtahid* (an interpreter of law qualified to exercise legal reasoning). Many of the more important opinions have been included in collections of fatwas, which have become authoritative in their own right.

Muftis and their fatwas historically have been independent of the judicial system, although some muftis were officially attached to various courts. In modern times, some Muslim governments—for example, Pakistan, Egypt, and Saudi Arabia—have tried to influence and control fatwas by appointing Grand Muftis or through official consultative councils or organizations within government ministries of religion. At the same time, print and electronic media have substantially increased the role of muftis and the impact of their fatwas by making them instantly available to the public on a global basis.

Fatwas have been used extensively to challenge claims of the Islamic legitimacy of violence used for political ends. In 2010 Pakistan's Muhammad Qadri, a well-known religious scholar and popular preacher, issued a 600-page fatwa that is said to be an "absolute" condemnation of terrorism. To weaken terrorist recruiting, Qadri condemned terrorists and suicide bombers as unbelievers and declared that terrorism and violence has no place in Islamic teaching and no justification can be provided for it.

People are also able to seek advice or a fatwa from a mufti about their personal situation through web sites and television programs, with titles like *Ask the Mufti*. In recent years, for the first time, women have been trained and are functioning as muftis in Turkey, Syria, Malaysia, and Indonesia.

What does Islamic law say about marriage, divorce, and inheritance?

Because of the centrality of the community in Islam, the Muslim family as the basic unit of society enjoyed pride of place in the development and implementation of Islamic law. While rulers in early Islam and today might limit, circumvent, or replace penal and commercial laws, Muslim family law (the law governing marriage, divorce, and inheritance) has generally remained in force. The formulation of Muslim family law has endured for centuries but has been subject to reform and widespread debate and revision since the twentieth century.

The place of women in family law reform remains an important, extremely sensitive, and hotly contested issue in Islam. The special status of family law reflects Quranic concerns for the status and rights of women as well as the patriarchal structure of the societies in which Islamic law was developed and elaborated. The status of women and the family in Islamic law was the product of Arab culture, Quranic reforms, and foreign ideas and values assimilated from conquered peoples. The Quran introduced substantial reforms, providing new regulations and modifying local custom and practice. At the same time, much of the traditional pre-Islamic social structure with its extended family, the paramount position of males, the roles and responsibilities of its members, and family values was incorporated.

The three major areas of Muslim family law deal with marriage, divorce, and inheritance. Marriage and family life are the expected norm in Islam. In contrast to Christianity, in Islam marriage is not a sacrament but a contract between a man and a woman, or perhaps more accurately between their families. In the traditional practice of arranged marriages, the families or guardians, not the bride and groom, are the two primary actors. The preferred marriage is between two Muslims and within the extended family. In Islam, as in Judaism, marriage between first cousins has been quite common.

The Quran introduced a number of reforms that enhanced the status of women. It recognized a woman's right to contract her own marriage and receive the dower from her husband (4:4); thus she became a party to the contract, not just an object for sale. In a society where no limitations on polygamy existed, the Quran sought to control and regulate its practice, stipulating that a man could marry up to four wives provided he could support and treat them equally. It is important to note here that the Quran did not require that a man marry four wives but limited him to that number.

The relationship between a husband and wife in Islamic law is viewed as complementary, reflecting their differing characteristics, capacities, and dispositions as well as the traditional roles of men and women in the patriarchal family. The primary arena for the man is the public sphere; he is to support and protect the family. Woman's primary role is that of wife and mother, managing the household and supervising the upbringing and religious training of their children. While both are equal before God and equally required to lead virtuous lives, in family matters and society, women are subordinate because of their more sheltered and protected lives and a man's greater economic responsibilities in the extended family.

While divorce is permissible, both the Quran and Prophetic traditions underscore its seriousness. The Prophet Muhammad is reported to have said, "Of all the permitted things, divorce is the most abominable with God." Further, an authoritative legal manual describes divorce as "a dangerous and disapproved procedure as it dissolves marriage, but is admitted on the ground of urgency of relief from an unsuitable wife."

In Arab society, men could divorce at will and on whim, and women had no grounds for divorce. The Quran and Islamic law introduced guidelines, based on greater equity and responsibility, to constrain a man's unbridled right to divorce and to establish a woman's right to a judicial (court) divorce. However, these laws were often compromised by social realities and circumvented. Thus, for example, a husband was required by law to pronounce the formula for divorce, "I divorce you," three times, once each successive month for a period of three months, during which time reconciliation was to be pursued. In fact, some men bypassed the Quranically mandated three-month waiting period (65:1) by saying, "I divorce you, I divorce you, I divorce you," three times all at one time. While Islamic law considered such an act unapproved or deviant, it was nevertheless legally valid. The force of patriarchy was especially evident in the requirement that women, in contrast to men, go before a court and present grounds to obtain a divorce.

Patriarchy also governed the rules of inheritance in pre-Islamic Arabia, according to which all property passed to the nearest male relative of the deceased. The Quran gave rights to wives, daughters, sisters, and grandmothers of the deceased, guaranteeing them a "fixed share" before the inheritance passed to the senior male. Men still inherited more than women, a fact that reflected gender relations in a male-dominated society as well as a male's greater economic responsibilities. In practice, however, families with women who were ignorant of their rights or intimidated into not pursuing those rights often circumvented these Quranic and legal reforms.

With the creation of modern nation-states in the twentieth century, many Muslim governments implemented Western-inspired legal codes. However, except in Turkey, because of religious and cultural sensitivities, family law was subject to reform rather than replacement. Islamic reformers from the late nineteenth century had called for a reinterpretation (*ijtihad*) or reformation of Islam, including modern interpretation of the Quran, to respond to the new demands of modernity and change. Among the key areas of concern were women's status and thus educational and legal reforms regarding marriage (polygamy and child marriages), divorce, and inheritance. Many governments introduced selective changes to traditional Muslim family law that ultimately entrenched state interests and power rather than protecting those whom the law targeted. The process of reform often set in motion a struggle between governments and their

Western-oriented elite, who legislated or imposed change from above, and the *ulama* (scholars), who saw themselves as the defenders of Islam and its only qualified interpreters.

Reforms increased the minimum age for marriage, required that men obtain permission from a court to take a second wife or to divorce, and expanded the grounds for women to obtain a divorce. Faced with resistance to legal reforms, governments did not pursue systematic reform, and compromises were made. Often the penalties (fines or imprisonment) for failure to comply with the law were minimal. The force of religious tradition could be seen in the fact that failure to comply with reform laws rendered an act illegal but not invalid, since few governments were willing to replace Islamic law and be accused of abrogating the Shariah, or "God's law." Thus, if a man took another wife, his second marriage would be illegal and his progeny illegitimate in the eyes of the law but not invalid in the eyes of God, according to Islamic jurists.

Reformers continue to press for change even as more conservative forces seek to block it. Resistance has been evident in Muslim countries such as Iran and Pakistan, where conservative ulama and Islamic movements blocked significant reform, and in heated debates that accompanied the drafting of new constitutions for Iraq in 2005 and Afghanistan in 2004. Despite some reforms, in Afghanistan, where more than 50 percent of girls are married before they reach the legal age of sixteen and rape within marriage is not a legal offense, the parliament passed and President Hamid Karzai signed the Shii Family Law bill in 2009. Article 132 requires wives to submit to their husband's sexual demands.

Reformers argue that Islamic law reflects the social context and norms of the past; current experiences and circumstances must be taken into account to better meet the objectives of Shariah today, which include recognition that women and men should have equal rights and responsibilities. Turkey's promulgated new Civil Code (2001) defined the family as a union based on equal partnership, with spouses jointly running the matrimonial union with equal decision-making powers. In 2004, the government of the Justice and Development Party, many of whose members are Islamically oriented, reformed the Penal Code to strengthen gender equality and protection of women's rights. A task force set up by Indonesia's Ministry of Religious Affairs in 2004 produced an alternative draft to the country's Compilation of Islamic Law that embraces gender equality.

More piecemeal reforms have occurred across the Muslim world. Countries in the Middle East (including Iraq, Jordan, Syria, and Saudi Arabia), the Indo-Pakistan subcontinent, and Southeast Asia allow the parties to agree upon conditions in marriage contracts such that breach of a condition can be grounds for a divorce. In 2005, Saudi Arabia's top religious authorities banned the practice of forcing women to marry against their will, stating that it was un-Islamic, contravened the objectives of Shariah, disobeyed God and His Prophet, and was "a major injustice." Laws in Algeria, Iraq, Syria, Jordan, Morocco, the Philippines, and most Malaysian states also prohibit this practice.

Morocco has enacted the most sweeping and systematic reforms, in its Family Code. Among its important provisions are: husband and wife share joint responsibility for the family; a wife is no longer legally obliged to obey her husband; an adult woman is entitled to self-guardianship, rather than that of a male family member, and may exercise it freely and independently; the minimum age of marriage is eighteen for both men and women; divorce is a prerogative for both men and women, exercised under judicial supervision; and a woman has the right to impose a condition in the marriage contract requiring that her husband refrain from taking other wives.

The momentum today for greater gender equality and the growing empowerment of women continues to increase pressure for substantive reform in many Muslim societies.

What does Islam say about homosexuality?

Like Christians and Jews, Muslims consider sexual fulfillment within marriage for husband and wife to be the ideal. Sex in marriage is considered a means of communication and pleasure and is not restricted to procreation.

In Islam (as in the majority opinion of all the world's religions) homosexuality is prohibited. In some areas it is treated as a crime punishable under Islamic law, while in others homosexuality is tolerated but homosexuals are still set apart socially. Today a small minority of gay Muslims in some countries are pressing for recognition of their rights within the community.

While homosexuality is forbidden, Muslims are divided over how to respond to gay Muslims. As in other faiths, the more liberal-minded have insisted that Muslims should avoid condemning or rejecting homosexuals, insisting that one can disagree with a person's behavior (public or private) while respecting him or her as an individual. Therefore Muslims should not drive a Muslim who engages in homosexual practices out of the faith.

What does Islam say about abortion?

In Islam, procreation is considered to be one of the most important aspects of marriage. The Quran places a high value on life and its preservation. The Quran (17:31) says that neither poverty nor hunger should cause one to kill one's offspring. Punishment for the unlawful killing of a human being is imposed both in this life and in the next (4:93).

Muslim scholars agree that after the "ensoulment" (infusion of the soul) of the fetus (thought to occur after 120 days), abortion constitutes homicide and should be punished. In the case of therapeutic abortions for severe medical problems, a general principle of Islamic law, choosing the lesser of the two evils, has often been applied. Rather than lose two lives, preference is given to the life of the mother, who is the pillar of the family with important duties and responsibilities.

What does Islam say about birth control?

Islam has traditionally encouraged large families to ensure a strong and vibrant Muslim community. The Quran does not address family planning measures, but a few *hadith* (traditions) mention coitus interruptus. Some *ulama* (religious scholars) oppose birth control because they believe that it challenges the supremacy of the will of God, or that limiting the size of the Muslim community will weaken Islam, or that birth control will contribute to premarital sex and adultery.

However, the majority of ulama in the twenty-first century hold that contraception is permissible as long as husband and wife agree. If both agree, then the rights of both are guaranteed. Most Muslim religious leaders oppose sterilization on religious grounds because it permanently alters what God has created.

How does Islam respond to stem cell research?

Islam encourages the pursuit of knowledge and research aimed at improving human health, as long as it does not violate core Islamic teachings. Because stem cell research can be used to cure diseases and alleviate human suffering, some Muslims argue that it represents an Islamic imperative that should be pursued. The Islamic view of the beginning of human life, which is based on a *hadith* of the Prophet Muhammad, says that "ensoulment" (the infusion of a soul into the fetus) does not begin until the 120th day of the life of a fetus. Therefore, prior to 120 days an embryo is not considered a human life and can be used for research. Moreover, Muslim jurists make a distinction between an embryo that is within the womb of the mother (which should not be used) and one that is harvested in a laboratory, which would otherwise be destroyed and carries no potential to become a human life. Because stem cell research is a relatively new phenomenon and there is little classical scholarship to rely on, many Muslims deal with the issue cautiously, for example, advocating the use of spare embryos instead of creating new embryos for specific research purposes.

What does Islam say about slavery?

Slavery, common in pre-Islamic Arabia, the Mediterranean, and African and Asian societies, was an accepted institution in Islam as it was in Judaism and Christianity. Islam did not abolish slavery but, like Judaism and Christianity before it, set about defining it legally and morally and moderating and mitigating the condition of slaves. Islamic law prohibited the enslavement of Muslims, non-Muslims (*dhimmi*), and orphans and foundlings who lived within the realm of Islam (*dar al-Islam*). Only those bought or captured outside Islamic territory or the children of slaves already in captivity were recognized as legal slaves.

Slaves were recognized as persons as well as property. The emancipation of one's slaves was regarded as a meritorious act to be encouraged. Although slaves as property could be bought and sold, Islamic law prescribed that they were to be treated fairly, justly, and kindly. They could not be killed; male slaves could not be made eunuchs, and female slaves could not be used as prostitutes. A concubine who had a child by her master would become free upon his death. Children born of a free man and a slave woman were regarded as free, not slaves. A slave mother could not be separated from her child. Slaves could marry, own property, and lead prayers.

The Abbasid Empire introduced the institution of slave soldiers (*mamluks*), which became a staple of many Muslim regimes; slave soldiers came to hold important positions in the military, becoming powerful generals and governors of provinces. In a number of important medieval Islamic states like the Mamluk sultanate in Egypt, the Delhi sultanate in

India, and the Ghaznavid state in Central Asia, slave commanders became sultans or rulers. However, while some slaves became part of the social and political elite, others continued to live and labor under harsh conditions.

By the late nineteenth century, in part due to British efforts, the slave trade, especially of African slaves, declined. The Ottoman Empire officially ended slavery in 1887, although it continued to exist there and elsewhere. By the latter half of the twentieth century, slavery was abolished in Arabia and much of the Islamic world. Although slavery has been abolished officially in Islam, it can still be found in Saudi Arabia, the Gulf, Sudan, and Mauritania.

Is honor killing sanctioned by Islam?

Honor killings are murders, usually committed by male family members against female family members who are accused of "immoral" behavior (violating social norms, modesty and sexual codes) that is seen as breaking the "honor codes" of a family or community. As the products of strong patriarchal value systems, these codes reflect deeply rooted social and cultural concepts of honor and shame, and women are seen as fully responsible for maintaining family and community honor. The complicity of other females in the family, who often support the attacks, strengthens the community mentality that women are property and that violence against them is a family matter, not a judicial issue.

According to the 2009 United Nations Human Development Report, five thousand people, mostly women and girls, die annually as a result of honor killings. Honor killings have occurred across cultures and across religions in Afghanistan, the Balkans, Bangladesh, Brazil, Ecuador, Egypt, Great Britain, Greece, Haiti, India, Iraq, Iran, Israel, Italy, Jordan, Pakistan, Morocco, Spain, Sweden, Turkey, and Uganda.

Honor killing occurred in ancient civilizations like Babylonia, biblical Israel, and Rome, and later, for example, as a result of

the Napoleonic Penal Code. Many of those guilty of honor killings attempt to justify their actions religiously, but none of the
world's religions, including Islam, approves such murders.
Rather than religion, the primary causes of honor killings are
patriarchal tribal, clan, and cultural practices or codes of
behavior in male-dominated societies or communities. The
cultural roots of honor crimes can be seen across Asia, where
they occur among Muslim, Hindu, and Sikh communities, or
in Lebanon and some other Middle East countries, where they
are found among Christians as well as Muslims.

Honor killing is not in the Quran or in the Prophetic traditions (*hadith*), nor is it sanctioned by Islamic religion and law.
Many Muslim scholars, commentators, and organizations
condemn honor killings as an un-Islamic cultural practice.
Grand Ayatollah Mohammed Hussein Fadlallah, one of the
most prominent Shii spiritual leaders, issued a fatwa banning
honor killing, describing it as "a repulsive act, condemned
and prohibited by religion." Sheikh Ali Gomaa, Egypt's Grand
Mufti, has also spoken out forcefully against honor killings.
However, the threat of this barbaric act continues in many
countries and communities where local Muslim religious
leaders, peoples, and politicians support or allow such practices. As a result those who commit such crimes often escape
punishment or receive reduced, very light sentences.

While honor killings receive a great deal of attention,
human rights activists point to the similar dynamic behind the
deaths in India of thousands of brides whose dowries are considered insufficient or who marry outside their caste. As with
crimes of passion, which are treated leniently in Latin America
and some Western countries, when male family members kill
women it is considered understandable and excusable.

How does Islam view female genital mutilation?

Amnesty International has estimated that over 130 million
women worldwide have been affected by some form of female

circumcision or female genital mutilation (FGM), with over three million girls at risk every year. Most of those affected live in twenty-eight African countries or in areas of Asia and the Middle East where female circumcision is a deep-seated cultural tradition that exists across many societies and religions. FGM predates both Christianity and Islam. No religious text requires FGM, and it is unknown in many Muslim countries.

FGM is not a religious obligation in Islam or Christianity, but it is practiced by both Christians and Muslims and in some instances has been supported by political and religious authorities. For example, this is the case in Egypt, where FGM is widespread and practiced by Muslims and Christians alike. In 2005, UNICEF reported that 97 percent of Egyptian women between the ages of fifteen and forty-nine had been circumcised. The situation changed dramatically in June 2007, after an eleven-year-old Egyptian girl died following the operation. Both government and Muslim and Christian religious authorities moved quickly to ban the practice. Sheikh Ali Gomaa, the Grand Mufti, issued a fatwa with strong and decisive condemnation: "The harmful tradition of circumcision that is practiced in Egypt in our era is forbidden." Al-Azhar's Supreme Council of Islamic Research, the highest religious authority in Egypt, also condemned FGM. Pope Shenouda, the leader of Egypt's minority Christian community and patriarch of the worldwide Coptic Orthodox Church, did likewise, emphasizing that neither the Bible nor the Quran mentions or requires female circumcision. However, other scholars stop short of an outright ban.

Despite international condemnation, the ancient practice continues to be prevalent in primarily African countries, among Muslims and non-Muslims alike.

Why are Islamic punishments for crimes so harsh?

Much has been written in recent years about the hudud punishments. Media reports from Afghanistan under the Taliban,

Saudi Arabia, Iran, Sudan, and Nigeria have covered sensational stories of stoning of adulteresses and amputations of the hands and feet of thieves. Human rights activists have denounced these punishments as cruel and contrary to (Western) standards of human rights and international law. Hudud punishments have not been implemented in most modern Muslim states. However, with the rise of political Islam in the late twentieth century they were reintroduced in Pakistan, Iran, Sudan, Afghanistan, and Nigeria.

There are two broad types of punishments for crimes in Islam: *hudud* and *tazir*. Hudud refers to the "limits" or "prohibitions" of God that are explicitly defined in the Quran as punishments for specific crimes. Tazir are punishments that are at the discretion of a judge (*qadi*). These cover a wide range of penalties like fines or imprisonment.

The hudud punishments are limited to specific acts: sexual activity outside of marriage, whether fornication or adultery; false accusations of unchastity; theft; and the consumption of alcohol. The Quran indicates the crime as well as the punishment.

Crimes punishable by hudud are considered attacks against the established social order, threatening the cohesion and morality of the Muslim community. Adultery and fornication violate the order of marriage and the legal means for the procreation of children; theft violates the protection of property that is the right of every member of the community; the consumption of alcohol can lead to acts of aggression or immorality; and false accusations of unchastity—a crime already shown to carry a harsh penalty—are acts of dishonesty that damage the reputations of innocent people. It is because these acts constitute crimes against God and a threat to the moral fabric of the Muslim community that harsh punishments like flogging, stoning, and amputation have been prescribed. Strict regulations regarding evidence in cases involving hudud crimes have been established under Islamic law, and in such cases false accusations are seriously punished.

In some of the countries in which the hudud have been implemented, the excuse given is that the country had fallen into such a state of disorder and unlawfulness that very stern measures were needed to restore some semblance of social order and security. This was the case in Afghanistan under the Taliban, where after twenty years of civil war the social order had fallen into complete disarray. Other countries have used arguments similar to those used by supporters of capital punishment in the West, claiming that knowledge of harsh punishments for certain types of crimes will serve as a deterrent to the committing of those crimes. In the contemporary era, one of the most controversial aspects of stoning adulterers is that women tend to be singled out for punishment, while men are rarely punished, despite the Quranic injunction that both parties are to be punished. In countries such as Pakistan and Nigeria, a woman's pregnancy can be used as evidence against her. In cases where women report having been raped, their testimony can be, and in some cases has been, used to convict them of fornication or adultery.

Muslim reformers and critics have argued that implementation of the hudud can only occur in a society that enjoys a high degree of economic and social justice and not in societies where poverty, high unemployment, and lack of education may drive people to commit crimes of theft. Others argue that hudud punishments were appropriate within the historical and social contexts in which they originated but are inappropriate today and that the underlying religious principles and values need to find new expression in modernizing societies.

Why don't Muslims practice a separation of church and state?

The Muslim vision of religion and politics is based upon a reading or interpretation of the Quran as well as the example of Muhammad and the early Muslim community, in tandem with the Islamic tenet that spiritual belief and action are two sides of the same coin.

Christians often cite the New Testament injunction to render unto Caesar what belongs to Caesar and to God what belongs to God as prescribing a separation of church and state. In contrast, Muslims believe that their primary act of faith is to strive to implement God's will in both their private and public life. Throughout history, being a Muslim has meant not only belonging to a religious community of fellow believers but also living in an Islamic state governed by Islamic law (in theory if not always in practice).

Many Muslims describe Islam as a "total way of life." They believe that religion cannot be separated from social and political life, since religion informs every action that a person takes. The Quran provides many passages that emphasize the relationship of religion to state and society. It teaches that God has given the earth as a trust to humankind (2:30, 6:165). Muslims see themselves as God's representatives with a divine mandate to establish God's rule on earth in order to create a just society. The Muslim community is seen as a political entity as proclaimed in Quran 49:13, which teaches that God "made you into nations and tribes." Like Jews and Christians before them, Muslims have been called into a covenant relationship with God, making them a community of believers who must serve as an example to other nations (2:143) by creating a moral social order. "You are the best community evolved for mankind, enjoining what is right and forbidding what is wrong" (3:110).

In an ideal vision of the Islamic state, the purpose of the political authority is to implement the divine message. Thus the ideal Islamic state is a community governed by God's law rather than a theocracy or autocracy that gives power to the clergy or ruler. The state should provide security and order so that Muslims can carry out their religious duties, particularly doing good and preventing evil. Legal processes implement rules and judgments from the Shariah, rather than creating new legislation. A sense of balance should exist among three groups: the caliph, who serves as the guardian of both the faith and the community; the *ulama* (religious scholars), who provide religious and legal advice; and the *qadis* (judges), who resolve disputes in accordance with Islamic law. Over time, many Muslims came to believe that this ideal blueprint and perfect state had actually existed and should be returned to. Contemporary militant movements particularly look back to this utopia as an example to be emulated today.

While a minority of Muslims today believe that modernity requires the separation of religion and the state, many Muslims continue to maintain that religion should be integral to state and society. However, there is no clear agreement—indeed, there is considerable difference of opinion—on the precise nature of the relationship of Islam to the state. For some, it is enough to say that Islam is the official state religion and that the ruler (and perhaps those who fill most senior government positions) should be Muslim. Others call for the creation of an Islamic state. But even here, there is no single agreed-upon model of government, as attested to by the diverse examples of Saudi Arabia's conservative monarchy, Iran's clergy-run state, Sudan's and Pakistan's experiments with military-imposed Islamic governments, and the Taliban's Afghanistan. And still others reject all these experiments as un-Islamic authoritarian regimes and subscribe to more secular or Islamic democratic forms of governance.

Why does religion play such a big role in Muslim politics?

Islam is an Arabic word meaning "submission." A Muslim is one who submits to the will of God, one who is responsible not only for obeying God's will but also implementing it on earth in his or her private and public world. Being a Muslim means belonging to a worldwide community of believers (*ummah*). The responsibility of the believer to Islam and to the Muslim community overrides all other social ties and responsibilities to family, tribe, ethnicity, or nation. Politics is therefore central, since it represents the means used to carry out Islamic principles in the public sphere.

Quranic verses have been used to guide Muslim political and moral activism throughout the centuries. Twenty-first-century Islamic reformers who believe that Islam, as a comprehensive way of life, should play a central role in politics support their arguments with Quranic verses as well as the example of how Muhammad and his Companions led their lives and developed the first Muslim community. They see these primary sources and examples as a blueprint for an Islamically guided and socially just state and society.

Islam's involvement with politics dates back to its beginnings with the founding of a community-state by Muhammad in the seventh century. According to Muslim tradition, several Arab tribes challenged Abu Bakr, Muhammad's first successor, who argued that the death of Muhammad represented the end of their political allegiance to the broader Muslim community. However, Abu Bakr reminded the Arab tribes of the overarching message of Islam—that membership in and loyalty to the Muslim community transcended all tribal bonds, customs, and traditions. Abu Bakr did not accept the argument of the Arab tribes that religion and politics were two separate and unrelated entities. Rather, he said, religion was intended to guide political decisions and to provide legitimacy to a political system. All Muslims belong to a single community whose unity is based upon the interconnection of religion and the state, where faith and politics are inseparable.

Under the political leadership of Muhammad and his successors, Islam expanded from what is now Saudi Arabia into Islamic empires and cultures that stretch across North Africa, through the Middle East and into Asia and Europe. Historically Islam has served as the religious ideology for the foundation of a variety of Muslim states, including the great Islamic empires: Umayyad (661–750), Abbasid (750–1258), Ottoman (1281–1924), Safavid (1501–1722), and Mughal

(1526–1857). In each of these empires and other sultanate states, Islam informed the state's legal, political, educational, and social institutions.

Today, Islam's connection with politics varies by country and region, but there are several common reasons why religion is intimately connected to the state. First of all, by the nineteenth century most Muslim countries were in a state of internal decline, and they were vulnerable to European imperialism. Muslims experienced the defeats of their societies at the hands of Christian Europe as a religious as well as political and cultural crisis. This crisis was deepened by Christian missionaries who attributed their conquests not only to superior military technology and economic power but also to the superiority of Western Christian civilization and religion. Because religion took on these political overtones on the part of Western colonialists, it is not surprising that some Muslims looked to the combination of religion and politics for a solution. Muslim responses to European colonialism ranged from resistance or struggle, justified as jihad in the defense of Islam in the face of the Christian onslaught, to accommodation and/or assimilation with the West.

Second, in the twentieth century many Muslim societies experienced a widespread feeling of failure and loss of self-esteem. The achievement of independence from colonial rulers in the mid-twentieth century created high expectations that have not been realized. Muslims have suffered from failed political systems and economies and the negative effects of modernization: overcrowded cities lacking social support systems, high unemployment, government corruption, and a growing gap between rich and poor. Rather than leading to a better quality of life, modernization has been associated with a breakdown of traditional family, religious, and social values. Many Muslims blame Western models of political and economic development as sources of moral decline and spiritual malaise.

Third, when Muslims ask themselves what went wrong, for many the inevitable answer is that their societies have strayed from the straight path of Islam that had led them to great development and success historically. Therefore future success depends upon returning to a society whose politics are governed by Islam.

What is Islamism?

Since the 1970s, Islam, both mainstream and extremist, has emerged as a powerful force in politics. Governments and Islamic (Islamist) movements, reform or opposition movements as well as terrorists, have appealed to religion as a source of identity, legitimacy, and mobilization.

Islamism and *Islamist* are among many terms (such as *Islamic activism, revivalism, extremism, fundamentalism,* or *political Islam*) that are used to describe a political or social movement, organization, or person that believes Islam or God's will applies to all areas of life, private and public, individual and social. For Islamists, Islam is not only a religion but an ideology promoting the creation of an "Islamic state" or an Islamically informed social order. Islamists include both individuals who are mainstream/moderate and others who are militant. Mainstream Islamists, who represent a spectrum of beliefs ranging from very conservative to reformist, participate in the political system, and seek gradual change from within their societies. Militant Islamists are extremists who advocate armed struggle and who employ violence and terrorism to overthrow the established order and impose their own political agendas, threatening the freedom and security of their societies.

Islamist political parties and social institutions have become an integral part of Muslim politics and societies. Since the late twentieth century, Islamically oriented candidates and political parties in Algeria, Tunisia, Morocco, Egypt, Lebanon, Turkey, Jordan, Kuwait, Bahrain, Pakistan, Malaysia, and Indonesia have opted for reform through ballots, not bullets. They have successfully contested and won municipal and parliamentary seats, held cabinet positions, and served in senior positions including prime minister in Turkey and Iraq and president in Indonesia. They have been elected to the leadership of professional associations (physicians, lawyers, engineers) as well as journalists' guilds and trade unions. Many Islamist NGOs and groups provide schools, clinics, hospitals, day care, legal aid, youth centers, and other social services. Private (not government-controlled) mosques and financial institutions such as Islamic banks and insurance companies have also proliferated.

Religious extremist and terrorist movements today are both global and local. Militant Islamists have been responsible for attacks in the Middle East and elsewhere in the Muslim world and in the West: they range from Osama bin Laden and the al-Qaeda–led attacks in New York and Washington on 9/11 to those in London, Glasgow, and Madrid on 7/7 to Sunni and Shii militias and death squads in Iraq and Pakistan that have slaughtered innocent men, women, and children.

How to distinguish between mainstream and extremist groups is the subject of heated debate. More often than not, Western governments have looked the other way when autocratic rulers in Algeria, Tunisia, Egypt, and elsewhere have intimidated and suppressed mainstream Islamist groups or attempted to reverse their electoral successes. The challenge has been particularly complex in connection with resistance movements like Hamas and Hizbollah. Both are elected political parties with a popular base. At the same time, they are resistance movements whose militias have fought Israeli occupation and whom Israel, the United States, and Europe have labeled as terrorist organizations.

Established precedents already exist for dealing with such groups, such as the ANC in South Africa and Sinn Fein, the political wing of the IRA in Ireland, groups with which the United States has had to come to terms. The United States and Europe need to deal with democratically elected officials, from whatever political party, while also strongly condemning acts of terrorism by their militias and clearly distinguishing legitimate resistance from terrorist attacks upon civilians. At the same time, the United States must condemn Israeli attacks that kill hundreds of civilians like the 2008 Operation Cast Lead in Gaza and the 2006 assault upon Lebanon.

Why do Muslims reject secularism?

Muslim reactions to the term *secularism* have been influenced by Western history, politics, and religion, as well as fear that secularism leads to the marginalization of religion. The term *secularism* has often been misunderstood and seen as diametrically opposed to *religion*. Muslims interpreted European colonialism and attempts to introduce modernity as an attempt to impose Western secularism, separating religion from state and society and thus weakening the moral fabric of Muslim society. While some Muslims, especially among the Western-oriented elites, believed that secularism was necessary to build strong modern societies, many others saw it as a direct challenge to Islam and its heritage, in which religion had for centuries been closely associated with successful and powerful empires. Secularism was equated with unbelief and thus seen as a direct threat to the religious identity and values of Muslim societies.

The problem was compounded by the fact that Muslim languages lacked a precise equivalent word for modern secularism. Few have understood that American secularism separated religion and the state to avoid privileging any one religion and to guarantee freedom of belief or unbelief to all. Little notice was taken of the diverse forms that secularism has taken in modern Western secular countries like Britain, Germany, and Canada that have a state religion and provide state support for recognized religions.

The examples of France and Turkey, which have been anticlerical and have banned the wearing of Muslim headscarves in their schools, reinforce the belief that secularism means a state that is antireligious rather than simply religiously neutral. On the other hand, in recent years many Muslims in Turkey and India have called for a "true" secular state, one that does not privilege any religion but does ensure freedom of religious belief and practice. The Muslim leadership of the ruling AKP party in Turkey has balanced its support for this kind of secularism with freedom of religion.

Why is Jerusalem so important to Muslims?

Jerusalem is revered as a holy city by all three of the great monotheistic faiths. The importance of Jerusalem to the early Islamic community is seen in the fact that Jerusalem was the original *qibla* (location that all Muslims face when they pray). In addition, according to tradition, Jerusalem was the Prophet's destination in his Night Journey from Mecca, when he traveled with Gabriel to see everything in heaven and earth and to the Temple in Jerusalem, where he met with Abraham, Moses, Jesus, and other prophets. The Night Journey made Jerusalem the third-holiest city in Islam and affirmed the continuity of Islam with Judaism and Christianity.

Today Muslims view the creation of the state of Israel and the declaration of Jerusalem as its capital as reminders of the injustices of Western imperialism and powerful symbols of the continuing weakness of contemporary Muslim societies. The history of Jerusalem helps us to see the role the city has played in all three monotheistic faiths.

Jerusalem was originally a Canaanite settlement where, according to the Hebrew scripture, David, king of Israel, built his capital and his son Solomon built the Temple. Muslim armies took Jerusalem without resistance in 635 and immediately began to refurbish its chief holy place, the neglected Temple Mount of the Noble Sanctuary. First the congregational mosque al-Aqsa was built, and then the magnificent shrine the Dome of the Rock was completed by 692. The Dome is thought to be the destination of Muhammad's Night Journey as well as the biblical site of Abraham's sacrifice and Solomon's Temple.

During this period, Jerusalem was home to many Christians and to Jews who had been permitted by the Muslims to return to the city for the first time since their ban by the Romans in 135. Both Jews and Christians may have outnumbered the Muslims in Jerusalem at this time. The city's history was generally uneventful until the Crusades.

One event that provoked the Crusaders' invasion of Palestine in 1099 and the occupation of Jerusalem was the burning of the Christians' Holy Sepulchre Church by the Egyptian ruler al-Hakim bi-amr Allah. During the eighty-eight-year Latin Christian occupation of Jerusalem, the Crusaders converted the Dome of the Rock into a church and al-Aqsa into the headquarters of the Knights Templar. When Salah al-Din (Saladin) drove them out in 1187, he restored the Muslim holy places to their original use and, aided by popular preachers, raised Muslim appreciation of this third-holiest city in Islam, after Mecca and Medina.

Salah al-Din's successors, the Mamluks and then the Ottomans, generously supported the city, which thrived until the disintegration of the Ottoman Empire in the nineteenth century. In the First World War Turkey joined Germany against the Allies, and Jerusalem fell to the British in 1917. When the British withdrew in 1948, the Jordanians occupied the Old City, and it remained a part of Jordan until the 1967 war, when Israel took it over.

What is called the Arab world's "Six Day War" with Israel (it was actually more like a six-hour war) and the devastating failure of the combined forces of Egypt, Syria, and Jordan against tiny Israel came to be remembered in Arab literature as "the disaster." It transformed the Arab and Palestinian problem into an Islamic issue. The loss of Jerusalem and its sacred shrines was a major blow to Muslim pride, faith, and identity. The "liberation of Jerusalem" became a worldwide Islamic slogan and Muslim cause.

Is Islam compatible with democracy?

All the world's religions in premodern times supported monarchies and feudal societies, then moved to accommodate modern forms of democracy. Similarly, Muslims today are debating the relationship of Islam to democracy. While most Muslims wish for greater political participation, the rule of law, government accountability, freedoms, and human rights, there are many different ways to achieve these goals.

There are many reactions to democratization in the Muslim world. Some, from former King Fahd of Saudi Arabia to ultra-conservatives and extremists, argue that Islam has its own mechanisms and institutions, which do not include democracy. Others believe that democracy can only fully be realized if Muslim societies restrict religion to private life. Still others contend that Islam is fully capable of accommodating and supporting democracy. Engaging in a process of reform, they argue the compatibility between Islam and democracy by using traditional Islamic concepts like consultation (*shura*) between ruler and ruled, community consensus (*ijma*), public interest (*maslaha*), and "the use of human reason to reinterpret Islamic principles and values and meet the new needs of society" (*ijtihad*). These mechanisms can be used to support parliamentary forms of government with systems of checks and balances among the executive, legislative, and judiciary branches.

The facts on the ground in the Muslim world, as determined by major surveys such as the Gallup World Poll, reveal a desire for greater democratization. When asked what they admire about the West, majorities of Muslims' top three spontaneous responses were: (1) technology; (2) the West's value system, hard work, self-responsibility, rule of law, and cooperation; and (3) fair political systems, democracy, respect of human rights, freedom of speech, and gender equality. In general, Muslims see no contradiction between democratic values and religious principles. Muslims want neither a theocracy nor a secular democracy and would opt for a third model in which religious principles and democratic values coexist. Men and women support a role for *Shariah* as a source of legislation, but most do not want religious leaders directly in charge of drafting legislation.

Many believe that just as the modern democracies of America and Europe accommodate diverse relationships with religion, so too Muslims can develop their own forms of democratic states that are responsive to indigenous values. However, rulers of authoritarian states tend to ignore, discourage, or suppress movements for democratization.

Are Muslims in America more loyal to the Quran or the Constitution?

This question is often asked as an accusation rather than a simple inquiry. For many Muslims, God's revealed scripture, the Quran, is the ultimate source of authority, just as the Bible is for many Jews and Christians. Most Muslims, like other citizen-believers, accept the authority of the state and its constitution. At the same time, like others, if and when a country's legislation appears to be contrary to God's word, they reserve the right to oppose that legislation and seek to have it changed. Like people in other faiths, Muslims today hold diverse positions on many questions. Thus, on a controversial issue like abortion, many (though not all) Muslims join with their conservative Jewish and Christian counterparts in opposing legislation that permits abortions.

Many Muslims came to America to enjoy its freedoms, rights, and opportunities. They and their descendants have become lawyers, judges, members of the military or local police departments, and elected officials. Although they recognize distinctive religious and cultural differences, most nevertheless affirm the essential compatibility of Islam and the West.

Why aren't Muslim countries more democratic?

Unelected governments whose leaders are kings, military, and ex-military men rule the majority of countries in the Muslim world. However, in recent years competitive elections have occurred in countries like Indonesia, Bangladesh, Turkey, and Senegal. The absence of democracy in the Muslim world today has led many to ask whether there is something about Arab or Muslim culture that is antithetical to democracy. The answer to this question lies more in history and politics than in religion.

While the West has had centuries to make its transformation from monarchies and principalities to modern democratic states, a process that was marked by revolutionary and civil wars, the Muslim world has struggled with several centuries of colonial rule followed by authoritarian regimes installed by European powers. If we ask why much of the Muslim world today is underdeveloped or unstable, we must remember that most modern Muslim states are only several decades old and that they were carved out by European powers.

In South Asia, the British divided the Indian subcontinent into India and Pakistan, giving portions of the Muslim-majority state of Kashmir to each of them. The conflicts that resulted from these actions have led to the deaths of millions in communal warfare between Hindus and Muslims, the civil war between East and West Pakistan that led to the creation of Bangladesh, and conflicts in Kashmir over Indian rule that persist to the present day. In the Middle East, the French created modern Lebanon from portions of Syria, and the British set the borders for Iraq and Kuwait and created the totally new country of Jordan. Such arbitrary borders fed ethnic, regional, and religious conflicts including the Lebanese Civil War between Christians and Muslims, the occupation of Lebanon by Syria, and the Gulf War, which resulted from Saddam Hussein's claim to Kuwaiti territory.

In addition to influencing who came to power in emerging modern Muslim nation-states, Europe and later America forged close alliances with authoritarian regimes, tolerating or supporting their nondemocratic ways in exchange for their allegiance during the Cold War or to ensure access to oil.

Not surprisingly, Muslim rulers have been plagued with issues of identity and legitimacy. The artificial nature of many modern states and the weak legitimacy of rulers have resulted in nondemocratic governments, societies in which state power is heavily reliant on security forces, police, and military, and where freedoms of assembly, speech, and press are severely limited. Many Muslim states operate within a culture of authoritarianism that is opposed to democratization, civil society, independent political parties, trade unions, and a free press. When useful, some rulers use religion to legitimate themselves and their policies. At other times, as during the aftermath of crises like the Gulf War of 1991 and the World Trade Center and Pentagon attacks of September 11, 2001, they also use the threat of "Islamic extremism" to justify increased suppression or repression of any and all opposition to their undemocratic rule.

Does Islam reject Western capitalism?

Islam has no problem with many of the essentials of capitalism. It is important to remember that Muhammad, the preeminent model for all Muslims, was a prosperous businessman who engaged in financial and commercial transactions to make a living and that his earliest followers included successful merchants. The Quran as well as Muslim historical experience confirms the right to private property, trade, and commerce.

Mosques throughout the world, like the Umayyad mosque in Damascus and the grand mosques in old Cairo and Tehran, are often adjoined by magnificent bazaars. Traders and businessmen constituted one of the most successful sectors in

Muslim society and were often responsible for the spread of their faith.

Capitalism exists both in its homegrown forms in the Muslim world and in Western-inspired versions. However, many in the Muslim world, like many in other parts of the world, are concerned about the dark side of capitalism and the possible abuses of a free market economy, including the seeming lack of concern for the poor and weaker sectors of society. More specifically, they fear that forces of globalization will lead to greater Western economic penetration in Muslim countries. The result, they fear, will be continued Muslim dependence on the West and a free market economy that is geared only toward maximizing profits, which may increase the growing gap between rich and poor. Finally, they fear a contagious Western culture whose retail stores, advertising, music, media, and dress can erode traditional Muslim religious ideals and threaten the identity and values of Muslim youth.

However, given an even playing field, perhaps the best response to those who ask whether Islam and capitalism are compatible is to look at the lives of the millions of Muslims who live and work in our midst in America and Europe. Many have come here to enjoy the freedoms and the opportunities offered by our economic as well as our political systems. Like other religious and ethnic minorities before them, they too struggle with issues of identity and assimilation but not with their desire to enjoy the best that we represent.

What does Islam say about poverty and social justice?

One of the most striking and controversial elements of the Quran at the time when it was revealed was its firm commitment to social justice, a significant threat to the tribal power structures in place.

Rather than accepting the principle that the strongest are the most powerful, the Quran emphasized the responsibility of Muslims to care for and protect each other, regardless of

socioeconomic status. In fact, the Quran repeatedly emphasizes the need to care especially for those who were outcasts
under the tribal system—widows, orphans, and the poor. One
way of doing this was through *zakat* (almsgiving), which is
one of the Five Pillars of Islam. Zakat consists of giving 2.5
percent of one's total wealth annually to support the less fortunate. In addition, usury, or the collection of interest, was
forbidden because it served as a means of exploiting the poor.
False contracts were also denounced. The Quran and Sunnah
(example of the Prophet) further give Muslims permission to
engage in armed defense of downtrodden men, women, and
children (Quran 4:74–76) and those who have been wronged,
particularly those who have been driven out of their homes
unjustly (22:39–40).

Through all of these declarations, the Quran emphasized
the responsibility of the rich toward the poor and dispossessed. The new social order called for by the Quran reflected
the fact that the purpose of all actions was the fulfillment of
God's will, not following the desires of tribes or of self. By
asserting that all believers belong to a single universal
community (*ummah*), Muhammad sought to break the bonds
of tribalism and place Muslims under a single prophetic
leader and authority.

Issues of social justice came to the forefront of Muslim societies in the early twentieth century with the rise of industri-
alism. The influx of large numbers of peasants from the
countryside into urban areas created social and demographic
tensions that led to a crisis, particularly in Egypt. The Egyptian
Muslim Brotherhood, founded in 1928, proposed Islam as the
organizational and religious solution to poverty and assistance
to the dispossessed and downtrodden. Its founder, Hassan
al-Banna, taught a message of social and economic justice,
preaching particularly to the poor and uneducated. In
al-Banna's vision, Islam was not just a philosophy, religion, or
cultural trend but a social movement seeking to improve all
areas of life, not only those that were inherently religious.

That is, rather than being simply a belief system, Islam was a call to social action.

Another major ideologue of social justice was the Egyptian Muslim Brother Sayyid Qutb, who later became the ideologue of radical Islam. According to Qutb, Islam's understanding of social justice takes account of both the material and spiritual well-being of a person. It promotes the absolute equality of all people in the eyes of God. It calls for freedom of conscience and emphasizes the permanent responsibilities of all Muslims toward society. This combination of material and spiritual welfare recognizes that those who are hungry or who have no shelter cannot attend to spiritual matters because they are necessarily preoccupied by the struggle for daily survival. In order for a person to be capable of attention to more spiritual concerns, the absolute necessities of daily life must be provided. Therefore, one of the major responsibilities of the Muslim community must be the eradication of poverty. By caring for their poor, Muslims as individuals and the Muslim community collectively demonstrate their concern and care for their own. It is in this spirit that zakat should be understood. It is a required social responsibility intended to combat poverty and to prevent the wealthy from accumulating and holding on to all of their wealth while the poor remain poor.

The redistribution of wealth is intended to break the cycle of poverty and to verify that the daily necessities of all Muslims are cared for. This redistribution of wealth also underscores the Muslim belief that everything ultimately belongs to God. Human beings are simply caretakers, or vice-gerents, for God's property. The redistribution of wealth, therefore, is really about a fairer allocation of God's resources within the broader community.

In the contemporary era, the Islamist emphasis on Islam's message of social justice has been particularly powerful in gaining adherents from poorer and less advantaged groups, particularly in Israel-Palestine and Lebanon. Groups like Hamas and Hizbollah devote much of their budgets to social welfare activities and call for the empowerment of the poor and weak. Like Christian liberation theologians, they teach that social justice can only be achieved if the poor rise up against their oppressive conditions.

Are Muslim Americans engaged in community service?

The summer of 2009 saw a remarkable example of community service when Muslim Americans across the country participated in United We Serve: Muslim Americans Answer the Call: the call of the president; the call of the needy; and the call of God to serve Him by serving others.

The Muslim Serve campaign identified and worked with existing American Muslim organizations *already* engaged in regular community service activities in areas such as healthcare, educational aid, and community assistance (food and supplies). This campaign was initiated by Dalia Mogahed, a member of the White House Advisory Council on Faith-Based and Neighborhood Partnerships. The program was part of President Obama's United We Serve, which called upon Americans to participate in the nation's recovery and renewal by serving their communities. Muslim Serve emphasized mobilizing faith communities, especially for interfaith service. Its literature used the Quranic verse "Race one another in good works" (5:48), deriving inspiration from Islamic teachings that encourage acts of charity and "good works."

A young, Internet-savvy community, Muslim American leaders made use of online organizing tools, social networking, and massive mailing lists to get the word out and call members to action quickly. The Muslim Serve campaign began with an initial goal of involving Muslim volunteers in 1,000 individual day-long service projects, with at least 25 percent to be carried out in cooperation with another faith-based community. These goals were greatly exceeded. Volunteers participated in more than 3,600 individual days of service, and 93 percent were in cooperation with other faith-based communities.

Muslim doctors provided care at more than thirty free clinics nationwide; lawyers gave free legal advice; other Muslim professionals and organizations adopted refugee families and fed the homeless. Muslim charities donated books to underfunded Native American schools, and an army of young people cleaned rivers and parks, made buildings more environmentally friendly, and built homes for the poor.

The success of the Muslim Serve initiative exemplifies the human potential of the Muslim American community to contribute to American society, working to strengthen their country by serving those most in need. As participant Salma Hasan Ali noted: "This is our opportunity to demonstrate who we are and what we believe in through our actions, to reveal what is central to our faith through acts of service and compassion, and to reclaim our place in the American mosaic."

The following sampling of the projects run by American Muslim organizations highlights the large numbers of Muslims who are coming of age in community service, discovering their capabilities and ability to mobilize collective action for the common good. The projects highlighted below represent only a fraction of those run in communities across America.

Healthcare clinics, staffed by a combination of employees and volunteers, serve Muslim and non-Muslim members of the community alike. The University Muslim Medical Association Community Clinic (UMMA Clinic) located in the heart of South Central Los Angeles, one of the poorest and most medically underserved areas of the region, provides healthcare for the uninsured to a population made up of 73 percent Latinos and 25 percent African Americans. Other clinics include the Shifa Clinic, which provides healthcare and screenings to low-income residents in Houston, Texas, and Chicago's Inner-City Muslim Action Network (IMAN), offering free health services to over 1,200 residents of underserved neighborhoods.

Life for Relief and Development, a Muslim American humanitarian relief and development organization, partners with the Brother's Brother Foundation to distribute textbooks and educational materials to underprivileged schools on Native American reservations in Arizona, New Mexico, and Wisconsin.

For thirteen years Zaman International, a worldwide humanitarian organization based in Dearborn, Michigan, has provided food, clothing, shelter, and medicine as well as adult literacy and vocational training programs to empower women, in particular those widowed, orphaned, abandoned, abused, divorced, or the spouse of someone with a terminal illness. In 2009 Zaman launched a Mobile Food Pantry to provide daily hot meals for families with a target of feeding nine thousand individuals in 2010, which it exceeded halfway through the year. Zaman has partnered with IMC (International Medical Corps) in Bosnia, Lebanon, Gaza, New Orleans, Haiti, and in flood relief in Pakistan. It soon will break ground for the construction of a new 62,000-square-foot Hope for Humanity Center in Dearborn that will service its food bank, soup kitchen, vocational training center, and clothing distribution center. Its second phase will focus on a senior wellness center and an early childhood development program in a park setting.

The ILM Foundation, an initiative started in Los Angeles that has since expanded to cities across the United States and internationally, launched Humanitarian Day, a coordinated nationwide effort of community assistance. Volunteers provided the homeless with food, health screenings, hygiene kits, and clothing items, as well as life skills lessons. Similar nationally coordinated initiatives have been sponsored by Islamic Relief USA (Day of Dignity), the Muslim Student Association (Project Downtown), and others—all mobilizing volunteers to serve the broader community of the homeless, hungry, and underserved.

What is Islamic finance and banking?

Conventional banking has been widely established for years in the Islamic world. While many Muslims and Muslim governments continue to rely on modern interest-based Western systems of banking and finance, in recent years increasing numbers of Muslims regard charging or earning interest as *riba* (which can mean usury, unearned gain, and exploitation) forbidden by the Quran. Muslim scholars today differ on whether all interest is usury. Some argue that *riba* only refers to excessive interest or economic exploitation. Islamic scholars at Cairo's Al-Azhar University, an influential source of religious authority in the Muslim world, declared in 2002 that the Quran did not prohibit all interest payments and charges, only those that were exorbitant and crossed the line into usury. However, others regard the whole concept of interest as riba, and thus unlawful.

Muslims who believe interest is forbidden (*haram*) have faced a crisis of conscience when they purchase a home mortgage or invest in the stock market. Islamic banks and financial institutions were created to respond to this need. Although Islamic finance and banking has spread in much of the Muslim world, until recently it has been relatively invisible in America and Europe.

The development of "Shariah-compliant" products in the West has been slow not only because banking institutions lacked knowledge of Islamic law (Shariah) but because they did not see a substantial market in the Muslim community. In recent years, however, the windfall from the unexpectedly high increase in oil prices has led to a boom in Islamic finance, not only increasing the eagerness of Muslim countries like Malaysia to become major centers of Islamic finance but also attracting struggling Western markets. The global Islamic finance market has grown by 15 percent in each of the last three years. The estimated amount of Islamic assets under management is approximately $800 billion, and some project a potential market of $4 trillion.

Where are the ten largest Islamic finance banks: Saudi Arabia? Kuwait? Qatar? Malaysia, which has positioned itself to be the global capitol for Islamic banking? If you guessed any of these or indeed any country in the Muslim world, you would be wrong. While Islamic banks do exist in many Muslim countries, the ten largest Islamic finance institutions are European and American banks. UBS, HSBC, Barclays, Deutsche Bank, Standard Chartered, Lloyds TSB, Swiss Re, Citigroup, Goldman Sachs, and Morgan Stanley are some of the leading Western institutions that have rushed to the Shariah-compliant market. All have Shariah advisory boards charged with reviewing transactions.

One major and expanding product, the Muslim mortgage, responds to the need of Muslims in America and Europe who see conventional Western loans and mortgages as Islamically unacceptable. Such mortgages seek to comply with Islamic law's traditional ban on charging, earning, or paying interest on borrowed money. Banks and financial institutions have moved quickly to service this growing market. For example, in July 2003 HSBC, one of the largest banks in the United Kingdom, brought out a range of Shariah-compliant mortgages. By the end of 2005 there were five banks offering Islamic mortgages, including Lloyds TSB and the Islamic Bank of Britain. Today, Britain is the West's leading center for Islamic finance.

How does a Muslim mortgage differ from a standard Western mortgage? Islamic mortgages are conducted by having the bank purchase the property and sell it back to the mortgagee. This can be handled in various ways. In a *murahaba* transaction, the bank will purchase the property and then sell it to the buyer at a pre-agreed cost plus profit, which is paid in installments over a period of time. In a *musharaka* (sharing) arrangement, the bank (which provides the greatest share of the purchase price of the home) and the customer enter into a partnership. The customer makes monthly payments to the bank for use of the home and as contributions toward the equity of the home, which gradually increase the customer's ownership share until the mortgage is paid in full. This option can be more flexible, providing variable rather than fixed repayments that can result in lower initial repayments. In a similar *ijarah* (rent) arrangement, the bank purchases the house and leases it to the customer, who pays a monthly installment for the price of the house. A portion of each monthly payment goes toward ownership until the customer owns 100 percent of the home. Unlike a typical rental, the customer is responsible for all maintenance of the property and has all the rights and duties of a homeowner.

Muslim mortgages can involve some hurdles. Often the buyer must initially find more money than would be required if he or she were obtaining a traditional mortgage. Shariah-compliant mortgages usually involve paying a large deposit, often around 20 to 30 percent of the total cost. Some Muslims counter those who point to these drawbacks by saying that religion is not always about taking the easiest path. Just as halal food (like kosher food for Jews) may cost more than regular food, Muslims are willing to make the sacrifice to fulfill a religious obligation and realize its rewards. Some have observed that if Islamic banking standards had been in effect, the current investment and banking market crisis in America might have been avoided!

Are there Muslim televangelists-preachers?

The globalization of communications has produced Muslim media stars, including a new breed of charismatic and enormously successful preachers who reach millions, sometimes hundreds of millions, from Egypt to Indonesia. Like Christian televangelists, they fill huge auditoriums and sports stadiums and also disseminate their messages on DVDs, video and audio tapes, satellite television and radio, and the Internet. These Muslim telepreachers and their organizations provide an alternative to traditional clerics and mosques, muftis, and fatwas. Most preach a direct, down-to-earth message, dispensing advice on everyday problems, promoting a practical, concrete Islamic spirituality of empowerment and success.

Three prominent figures, the Egyptian Amr Khaled, the Pakistani Muhammad Qadri, and the Indonesian Abdullah Gymnastiar, represent somewhat different styles in this growing phenomenon.

Amr Khaled has been called "the Arab world's first Islamic tele-evangelist, a digital age Billy Graham who has fashioned himself into the anti-Bin Laden... to turn around a generation of lost Muslim youth." Clean-shaven and well-dressed in a fashionable Western suit, Khaled speaks in colloquial Arabic to millions of young Muslims, ages fifteen through thirty-five. He targets upper-middle-class Muslims in the Arab world and Arab immigrants living in the West, because he believes this audience is most capable of changing the Islamic world for the better.

Amr Khaled blends conservative religious belief with a charismatic personality and speaking style. Using management training jargon and an emotive crowd-pleasing performance full of stories, laughter, and tears, he relates Islam to everyday life. He does not talk politics, preferring to emphasize God's love while addressing issues of personal piety, daily prayer, family relationships, veiling, dating, and community responsibility. Muslim youth, in particular, are drawn to his down-to-earth religious and spiritual messages, which emphasize Muslim values and a positive, proactive attitude toward life. He replaces the negative "No, No Islam" of many Muslim preachers and fundamentalists with an affirmative "Yes to life Islam."

Khaled encourages young people to focus not on the things they cannot change but rather on what they can change, like their attitude, behavior, and character. His message is simple and direct, prescribing everyday acts that empower people and contribute to the betterment of society:

- The garbage in the streets. Get rid of it yourself.
- The pothole in front of your house. Fill it yourself.
- The broken glass at your house. Replace it.

- Clean the mosques; do not be ashamed to do it yourself; your proactive attitude will give you courage.
- Give private lessons to your neighbors' children. Teach them languages or show them how to use computers.
- Teach an illiterate person to help reduce the percentage of illiteracy.
- Housewives, start a project to help women and widows by teaching them a skill that they can work with instead of waiting for financial support from others.

Khaled uses his Web site interactively to mobilize as well as instruct, garnering an overwhelming response to his requests from countries in the Arab world, Asia, Africa, Europe, and the United States. A call for clothing for the poor drew thousands of people in twenty-six countries who collected 1.5 million bags of clothes that were distributed to those in need.

In contrast to Khaled, who previously worked as an accountant, Muhammad Qadri is a trained religious scholar as well as a popular preacher. Trained both in traditional madrasas and at Punjab University, where in 1972 he earned an MA and PhD in Islamic studies, Qadri appeals to a broad audience: traditionalists as well as those who appreciate his integration of traditional Islamic sciences with modern disciplines. Noted for his liberal and tolerant views, he promotes greater unity among Sunni and Shii Muslims, interfaith dialogue, and outreach to Pakistani Christians.

Qadri founded the Lahore-based Minhaj-ul-Quran International, an international Islamic movement with centers working in ninety countries around the world. To a degree that is unprecedented in the history of Pakistan, he relies heavily on electronic technology, using his publication house, which carries thousands of CDs and DVDs in Urdu, Punjabi, Arabic, and English featuring his speeches delivered in South Asia, the Middle East, Europe, and North America.

Qadri has an established track record of denouncing terrorism in the name of Islam. An early critic of the 9/11 attacks, he challenges the Islamic legitimacy of those who approve or use violence for religious or political ends. On March 2, 2010, he attracted worldwide attention when he issued a 600-page fatwa, described as an "absolute" condemnation of terrorism without "any excuses or pretexts," one that goes beyond all previous condemnations. He declared that terrorists and suicide bombers were unbelievers and that "terrorism is terrorism, violence is violence and it has no place in Islamic teaching and no justification can be provided for it, or any kind of excuses or ifs or buts." Qadri's fatwa, which received extensive media attention, has been hailed as a powerful argument that takes Islam back from the terrorists and weakens terrorist recruiting. At the same time, however, he was also a strong critic of the U.S. invasions of Afghanistan and Iraq.

Like their Christian counterparts, Muslim televangelists come in all sizes, shapes, and personalities. For theater and drama, few can compete with Abdullah Gymnastiar. *Time* magazine captured his dramatic, even charismatic, appeal: "In the spotlight as usual," complete with "wireless mike...dry-ice smoke...and his backing quartet," Gym's "velvet baritone is caressing the crowd...His free hand is waving,...and then is clasped to his chest in rapture." His hour-long sermon concludes with "scores of women and men...openly weeping" and a long "roar of applause."

Aa Gym was Indonesia's most popular televangelist for rich and poor, educated and uneducated, men and women, more famous than Indonesian film stars, and he still commands a following. Muslims and many Christians have been drawn by his emphasis on religious pluralism and belief that all religions ultimately preach the same message. His message is disseminated on TV and radio to sixty million people and through books, cassettes, videos, management training seminars, and aphorisms that appear on the red cans of Qolbu Cola, the soft drink he markets.

Complementing the work of Amr Khaled, Aa Gym combines religious teaching with a celebration of corporate capitalism and self-help advice, emphasizing people's ability to take control of their lives and fortunes and demonstrating this message with his enormously successful lifestyle as preacher, media star, and entrepreneur. He blends modern principles of business organization with Islamic teachings and Indonesian culture, calling it "Management by Conscience."

Like many Indonesian leaders he has been a critic of violence and religious extremism, more effective than others because of his positive and motivating style. At his religious boarding school (*pesantren*) he taught many of the children of elite society. Major firms in Indonesia sent their top executives to his Islamic training center for a program including ethics and Quranic studies that emphasizes three keys to success— honesty (to gain people's trust), professionalism, and innovation. He preached the Seven Tips for Success ("Be calm, plan well, be skillful, be orderly, be diligent, be strong and be humble") and Five Tips for a Good Product ("It should be cheap, high quality, easy to use, up-to-date and useful for both the world and hereafter").

However, like some Christian evangelists', Aa Gym's meteoric rise has been cut short by scandal. In late 2006, at the height of his enormously successful and lucrative career, it was revealed that he had taken a second wife, a single mother of three and former model, who worked for his business group. Aa's first wife and mother of their seven children, who was very popular and often accompanied him on his speaking engagements, quietly agreed to the second marriage. Shocked and disillusioned, many of Aa's followers, especially women, dropped out of his programs. Others confronted him, charging, "You have sold out your religion." Gymnastiar apologized publicly, countering unwisely: "Women tend to be monogamous, that's how their 'software' is…But men, you know…their software is different." He explained that polygamy is better than extramarital sex. He also added, "What I did should not justify other men to do the same—I do not recommend it." Like many a "fallen" Christian evangelist, Gym's credibility, ministry, and organization were deeply affected. His audiences, school enrollments, seminar attendance, and product sales dropped off precipitously; and religious, political, and corporate leaders withdrew their invitations and support.

What role does the Internet play in Islam today?

Millions use the Internet daily for news, information, shopping, research, and social networking. Muslims are no exception. Many Islamic Web sites cater to both Muslims and non-Muslims who want to learn more about Islam. The Quran, Quranic commentaries, and collections of the traditions of the Prophet are available online in languages ranging from Arabic and Urdu to Spanish and Swahili. Imams use Web sites that allow Muslims worldwide to download their Friday sermons (*khutba*) and lectures without charge. Prominent religious leaders, scholars, and preachers have their own Web sites or use Facebook, Twitter, and YouTube to attract and educate large international audiences.

Social networking is also very popular among Muslims. E-mail has improved communication between Muslims in the West and their families and friends who live in different states and countries. Websites like Facebook and LinkedIn are popular cyber spots for people to make contacts and form business relationships. Some singles rely on the Internet to find a marriage partner in the United States, Europe, the Middle East, and Southeast Asia by logging on to popular Web sites such as Companionships.org, MuslimFriends.com, and SingleMuslim.com that provide opportunities to be matched by an imam or to meet, socialize, and decide if they would like to get engaged. Other sites, forums, and chat rooms online enable Muslims to make new friends, as well as to discuss and debate religious, political, and social issues and share views on popular culture.

The Internet also provides an open, anonymous space for Muslim women to explore their interests, from women's rights and roles in family and society to fashion and music, with others in cyberspace. It also offers an opportunity for some to obtain or broaden their education and learn marketable job skills. Nonprofit groups like Women's Learning Partnership help Muslim women to gain job skills through online courses. Some use the Internet to develop their own businesses. Women from very conservative families are able to work and earn money without leaving the confines of their homes.

A few major Web sites provide all the services mentioned above with one click. Sites such as IslamiCity.com and IslamOnline.net function as virtual Islamic cities, uniting Muslims across the world into one, online Islamic community. IslamiCity.com, for instance, aims to promote understanding of Islam and Muslims and to seek peace for all people. This site serves as a one-stop-shop for information on multiple topics, from the Quran to Muslim businesses across the United States. Web surfers can also log on to the site to watch Islamic television programs or join a forum to discuss politics with other Muslims around the world. The site also provides links to a bazaar where Web users can purchase Islamic gifts and books.

Non-Muslims often use IslamiCity.com to access information on topics such as Islamic beliefs or Muslim views of women's rights, or to use a glossary of common Islamic terms. People can also send questions to an *imam* (religious leader) or *mufti* (legal scholar) on a broad range of issues. This interactive site allows both Muslims and non-Muslims to engage others on Islamic issues and to debate in an open environment.

IslamOnline.net offers both Muslims and non-Muslims accurate and reliable information on Islam. Articles on health and science, art and culture, and family give readers multiple Islamic perspectives on current issues. This site also provides webcasts and live opportunities for Muslims to dialogue with

each other or even to listen to *fatwa* (legal opinion) pronouncements. Surfers can also access online counseling with an
Islamic counselor on personal issues. Of course, while historically, muftis were able to issue fatwas based on their
knowledge of the people involved in the situation, now with
fatwas being issued over the Internet, the petitioner and often
the mufti are faceless, connected only by a computer screen,
and the relationship between the mufti and the fatwa seeker
is removed.

The benefits of the Internet are enormous. The downside is
its use by anonymous extremists and terrorists who exploit chat
rooms and forums to preach their messages of hate and violence. Often preying on the alienation and discrimination that
immigrant Muslims feel in their countries of residence, terrorists advocate militant ideologies to recruit new members to their
organizations. They participate in youth-oriented Web sites
discussing topics ranging from pop culture to sports in order to
target disenfranchised Muslims, especially young adults, and to
indoctrinate them into radical Islam. They use the speeches of
radical preachers and terrorists as well as fatwas to give religious justification to killing and terrorism in the name of Islam.
Some Muslim youth in the West, who often experience
discrimination and hostility, are targeted or drawn to these sites
and their militant messages. Youth living in Muslim countries
are also attracted to calls for jihad against their rulers or for
giving aid to fellow Muslims wanting to remove what they see
as Western military occupation from their countries.

The Internet is a double-edged sword. On the one hand, it
enables Muslims worldwide to engage and join with a global
ummah online, and it offers access to important religious
resources. Muslims can listen to Quranic recitations, sermons,
and prayers with a click of a mouse. Families and friends can
participate in each others' lives despite being oceans apart.
On the other, the Internet's anonymity permits anyone to say
or advocate anything. Legitimate religious leaders, scholars,
and preachers as well as radical clerics and terrorists use the

Internet to educate and propagandize in the battle for the hearts and minds of Muslims that is taking place in private, in public, and in virtual reality.

What are the major obstacles to Islamic reform?

While in the past Muslims looked to the *ulama* (religious scholars) and *muftis* (legal scholars) in Muslim countries for authoritative answers, today questions about the relationship of faith to politics and culture, the status and rights of minorities, pluralism, and tolerance are addressed by Muslim intellectuals, religious and lay scholars, men and women. These Muslim reformers are a vanguard, facing resistance from conservative and fundamentalist factions as they challenge long-held traditions to articulate a progressive, constructive Islamic framework that meets the needs of society today.

A lively debate exists on issues as diverse as the extent and limits of reform, the role of tradition and its relationship to change, women's empowerment, legitimate and illegitimate forms of resistance and violence, suicide bombing and martyrdom, the dangers of fundamentalism, the question of Islam's compatibility with democracy and religious pluralism, and the role of Muslims in the West. The reformers debunk entrenched perceptions: that Islam is medieval, static, and incapable of change; that Islam is a violent religion that also degrades women; that Islam and democracy are incompatible; that Muslims do not speak out against religious extremism and terrorism; that they reject religious pluralism and interfaith dialogue, and they certainly cannot be loyal citizens of non-Muslim countries.

Reform-minded Muslims are informed by a deep knowledge of their religious tradition coupled with modern educations in law, history, politics, medicine, economics, and the sciences. They are equipped to reinterpret Islamic sources and traditions to meet the challenges of modernization and development, leadership and ideology, democratization, pluralism, and foreign policy.

However, reformers are still a minority that faces formidable obstacles. Repressive authoritarian regimes see all reform, any real power-sharing and rule of law, as threatening to their power and privilege. Thus reformers struggle in weak civil societies that do not support creative or independent thought or action. Other obstacles come from religious extremists who believe they have a mandate from God to impose "their Islam" and to destroy anyone who disagrees with them. Finally, intransigent religious conservatives, who are well-meaning but wedded to medieval paradigms, are often co-opted by governments to use their authority to delegitimate reforms as deviant or "heresies."

Opponents of reform are often the religious establishment that controls the major vehicles through which many learn about Islam. They run the madrasas or seminaries that train religious leaders as well as local imams for their mosques. In many countries, they influence the religion curriculum and teach courses on Islam in schools and universities. Thus, they remain powerful determiners of the understanding of Islam both officially and among Muslim populations and families.

Despite powerful forces restraining reform efforts, in the twenty-first century other influences are driving the implementation of new ideas. These include neo-traditionalists and more liberal, modern, educated, and Islamically oriented Muslim reformers and organizations, an increasingly educated sector of the population who are critical of those who cling uncritically to past and now outdated practices, religious leaders, scholars, and telepreachers. Those who espouse these new ideas apply Islamic principles in ways that more directly relate to modern-day problems and a two-way information superhighway by means of which Western Muslims, who are able to think and write more freely, exchange their reformist ideas with those in many Muslim countries who are more constrained in their research, writing, and speaking.

Is there a clash of civilizations?

The September 11 attacks appeared to dramatically highlight the well-known thesis of a clash of civilizations that was argued by Samuel Huntington in a 1993 *Foreign Affairs* article and 1996 book, *The Clash of Civilizations and the Remaking of World Order.* Huntington maintained that cultural and religious differences had replaced the ideological conflicts of the Cold War and were emerging as the biggest threat to world peace. In a December 2001 *Newsweek* piece, he declared that "the Age of Muslim Wars" had officially begun, presaging an intensified battle between Islam and the West.

This theory of global conflict failed to appreciate the significant diversity that exists not only among but also between and *within* the countries and societies that Huntington grouped under the rubric of a given civilization—whether it is Islamic, Western, or Chinese. In *The Clash of Civilizations* Huntington posits "the West" as a monolithic formation when he writes: "The problem for Islam is not the CIA or the U.S. Department of Defense . . . It is the West, a different civilization whose people are convinced of the universality of their culture and believe that their superior, if declining, power imposes on them the obligation to extend that culture throughout the world." This misses the mark. One need not look deeply into the history of great-power conflicts to see that civilizations do not reflect cultural and political unity. World Wars I and II, which pitted Germany against much of Europe and America, are sobering testimonies to the fragility of Western civilization.

So too, within the Muslim world a litany of conflicts dispels any idea of an Islamic civilization organized around a strong central identity: the Iran-Iraq war of 1980–88, the divisions within Muslim countries during the first Gulf War of 1990–91, and conflicts between Sunni-Shii in Iraq and Pakistan represent just a few examples opposing the view of an Islamic civilization organized around any strong central idea. More misleading still was Huntington's portrayal of Islam itself as "a different civilization whose people are convinced of the superiority of their culture and are obsessed with the inferiority of their power." Strictly speaking, there is in fact no civilization that could be called "Islamic": that term refers more properly and specifically to the religion of Islam, one component among many that shape Muslim culture and politics.

While some used Huntington's rhetoric to legitimize a one-note caricature of Islam, most Muslims do not see the West as monolithic. In fact, anti-American sentiment among Muslim societies is primarily tied to opposition to American foreign policy, not Western religion and culture. In the Gallup World Poll of 2005–7, Muslim respondents expressed very negative views of foreign policies that Tony Blair and George Bush had pursued. Respondents had more positive views of Western powers such as France and Germany that dissented from those policies. For example, while 74 percent of Egyptians had unfavorable views of the United States and 69 percent said the same about Britain, only 21 percent felt unfavorably toward France and 29 percent toward Germany. These policy disagreements become especially sharp when we compare Muslims' perceptions of the United States with their views of its neighbor to the north, Canada—i.e., America without the foreign policy. Sixty-six percent of Kuwaitis in the 2006 survey reported unfavorable views of the United States, while just 3 percent agreed with unfavorable descriptions of Canada.

These attitudes contrast vividly with Huntington's conclusion that "Islam's borders *are* bloody, and so are its innards," which explicitly and simplistically attributes bloodshed to the religion of Islam—rather than to the actions of a minority of Muslim terrorists whose primary grievances are political.

After September 11, the image of a clash of civilizations was used to bolster depictions of contending forces in the "war on global terrorism," routinely described in presidential addresses and editorial pages as a war between the civilized world and terrorists in the Muslim world who "hate" Western democracy, capitalism, and freedom or as an existential struggle against "evil." In fact, extensive Gallup polling data, almost fifty thousand interviews conducted in more than thirty-five Muslim nations, showed that despite widespread anti-American and anti-British sentiment, Muslims around the world admire many of the Western qualities that analysts such as Huntington imagined they resented: technology, expertise and knowledge, and freedoms and values associated with democratic governments. Among the hopes for the future that respondents cited, economic security was a leading issue—but so was an eagerness "to have better relationships with the West."

The clash of civilizations theory flattens cultural and historical forces into a caricature distorting the societies and religious traditions. It dangerously oversimplifies the encounter between the West and the Muslim world and can become part of the problem rather than the solution.

What contributions have Muslims made to world civilizations?

Muslims have made very substantial contributions to world civilizations. Muslim societies not only preserved the ancient teachings of the Greeks, but they expanded upon them, developing new ideas in medicine, mathematics, astronomy, and social sciences. In Africa, Muslims preserved distinctive African cultural traditions in new Muslim urban societies, while in South Asia Muslim scholars adapted and developed Hindu number systems. These contributions of Muslims are not well known because what most people know about world history concentrates on the history of Western civilization from ancient Greece to the Renaissance, the Industrial Revolution, and the age of Western modernity. We may think that the "dark ages" in the West existed globally and therefore miss the rich heritage of Muslim societies' scientific, technological, and cultural achievements.

During the Middle Ages, knowledge from the ancient societies of Greece, Rome, China, India, and Persia was collected, preserved, and added to in the Muslim world. As Islam spread from the Arabian Peninsula across western Asia and North Africa, the Arabic language became the lingua franca of the region. Muslim rulers established research centers and universities where scientific, technological, and philosophical developments abounded. The achievements of Muslim societies during the ninth through fifteenth centuries greatly enhanced the theoretical and material development of world civilizations.

Muslims learned the art of paper production from the Chinese when Islam spread into China. Thus, while the West was still writing manuscripts on animal skin parchment, which was difficult to use and store, Muslims were experiencing a growth of knowledge and learning through accelerated production of books. Elite members of society patronized scholars and sought to acquire books. Great libraries, public and private, were established across the Muslim world. The Fatimids in Egypt housed over a million books, and at least eighteen thousand represented the ancient sciences. Individuals also had large private libraries. Saladin's physician, Ibn al-Mathran, had ten thousand manuscripts, while an important Jewish surgeon in Cairo, Dunasch ben Tamin, owned over twenty thousand.

Mosques also contained libraries, and private collectors commonly donated their books to mosques. Scholars would frequently dictate their works at mosques, and the general public attended to listen to them. Further, manuscripts in mosque libraries, covering topics ranging from science and medicine to philosophy and religion, were available to the public. Booksellers often stationed themselves close to the mosque, selling books to collectors, citizens, students, and merchants alike. In Marrakech, for example, the Kutubya Mosque is so named because of the two-hundred-plus book vendors (*kutubiya*) that built booths around the mosque. The accessibility of books in Muslim societies contrasted greatly with the situation in Europe, where manuscripts were kept in monasteries and dealt with highly specialized theological subjects. Muslim societies gifted world civilizations with their libraries, which revolutionized the preservation of knowledge and education in the West.

Muslim contributions in the field of medicine are among the most important. In the ninth century, Mohammad Ibn Zakariya al-Razi (864–930), one of the greatest Muslim physicians of the Middle Ages, and Ibn Sina (980–1037), one of the foremost philosophers of the period, both wrote medical encyclopedias that became key medical references in Europe for centuries. Al-Zahrawi (936–1013), known by the Latin name Albucasis, was renowned among European physicians for his treatise on eye, ear, and throat surgeries. He provided drawings of surgical tools and information on using sedatives, antiseptics, and sutures and performed the first cesarean operation.

By rooting medicine in science, Muslims made it a profession requiring extensive training and study, which helped to abolish harmful, superstitious, and very popular folk medicine. Doctors were required to take the Hippocratic oath after successfully completing a physician exam. Many hospitals were open twenty-four hours a day, and physicians were required to see every patient. In time, hospitals became centers of great learning in Muslim societies and were precursors to the research hospitals of today.

Muslim interest in medicine contributed to developments in botany and agriculture as Muslim botanists learned more about plants, irrigation techniques, fertilization, and crop rotation. Herbs and plants such as anise, caraway, spinach, cauliflower, asparagus, and artichokes were grown for medicinal purposes and eaten to improve overall health. In the Islamic civilization of al-Andalus, Spain, Ibn Awwam wrote an encyclopedia in the mid-twelfth century identifying and describing the use of 160 different plants, some unknown to Europe at the time, and improving on the classic European horticultural text by Palladius (c. 380) listing 76 different plants.

Muslim knowledge of agriculture had a significant impact on what is grown, purchased, and traded in the global economy today. Plants farmed in Muslim societies included coffee, bananas, cotton, hemp, tea, olives, watermelon, sugar cane, sesame, apricots, cherries, and peaches. Muslim botanists' and farmers' knowledge of beautiful, fragrant, and nutritious plants, fruits, and vegetables, and their farming techniques, were disseminated across Europe by Crusaders, travelers, and merchants and later transplanted to the Americas.

Botanical developments contributed to advances in both theoretical and applied chemistry in Muslim societies. For example, Muslims discovered how to make soap by mixing olive oil with plant ash, and Crusaders took this castile soap recipe back to Europe. In addition, vegetable and animal oils were used to light lamps, while flowers and herbs were chemically processed into cosmetics and perfumes.

The study of chemistry was cultivated in Muslim societies and imported to the West, where Europeans built on these concepts to develop the science of chemistry that is practiced worldwide today. In theoretical chemistry, essential chemical processes such as distillation, subliming, crystallizing, and the dissolving of substances were described in Arabic sources. The writings of Jabir Ibn Hayyan (c. 815), known as the father of Arab chemistry, were translated into Latin and became standard chemistry texts in Europe. His accomplishments include discovering aqua regia, a substance that dissolves gold and eases the extraction and purification processes. His classification of matter into spirits, metals, and stones forms the basis of naming chemicals today. Al-Razi, in addition to writing his medical encyclopedia, identified ethanol. The English word *alcohol* comes from the Arabic word for this substance.

Muslim scholars made major contributions to the field of mathematics. Muhammad Ibn Musa al-Khwarizmi

(c. 780–850) is known as Algoritimi in the West and is the father of algebra. Rather than use Roman numerals, al-Khwarizmi used Hindi numerals and introduced the Indian idea of zero into mathematics. Because al-Khwarizmi used the number scale 0–9, it was possible to express any number combination. Muslims were also the first to use the decimal point to express fractions in solving complex problems. Mathematical texts written in Arabic were later translated into Latin, and by the fifteenth century, across Europe, Arabic numerals had replaced Roman numerals in common usage.

Mathematical advances also contributed to astronomical discoveries. Al-Farghani (c. 861), for example, created important calculations on the circumference of the earth. Christopher Columbus relied on these calculations but misunderstood al-Farghani's unit of measurement. This mistake led to the discovery of the Americas. Al-Battani (c. 929) created astronomical charts (tables of the movement of bodies in the sky) and created trigonometry. He used trigonometry to measure both solar and lunar time. In Cordoba, Spain, another Muslim astronomer, al-Zarqali (d. 1087), enhanced the astrolabe, an astronomical instrument used to predict the position of the planets and the sun, keep time, and determine the location of points. Muslims also discovered stars and constellations in the sky such as the Scorpion (*al-'aqrab*) and the Goat (*al-jadi*). Other words in the English language such as *zenith, nadir,* and *azimuth* are derived from Arabic astronomical terms.

In the social sciences Ibn Khaldun (1332–1406), a Tunisian Muslim, is increasingly regarded as the first modern historian and the father of sociology because of his examination of human life and institutions. Recognizing that events do not happen in a vacuum, Khaldun was the first to pay attention to socioeconomic contexts in writing history. In his famous work, *Muqaddimah,* he records information on climate, social structures, occupations, and education rather than just events such as the reigns of kings and wars. This work of universal history also considers the evolution of society, examining various societal structures and civilizational forms.

Muslims made very important contributions in philosophy. Muslims, like Jews and Christians, struggled to reconcile how Aristotle, Plato, and other Greek philosophers' concepts of reason and morality related to divine revelation and faith. From the ninth to the thirteenth centuries, important philosophical works were translated and preserved in Arabic at the House of Wisdom, a library and translation institute in Baghdad and the major intellectual center of Islam's golden age. Had these works not been maintained, they might have been lost to world civilization. Ibn Rushd (known in the West as Averroes, 1126–1198), a prominent Muslim philosopher, wrote important commentaries on Aristotle. Other Muslim philosophers such as Ibn Sina (known as Avicenna in the West) and al-Ghazali (1058–1111) also wrote on the relationship of faith and reason, encouraging Christians to contribute to the debate. The great Christian thinker Thomas Aquinas was greatly influenced by Muslim thinkers, especially Ibn Sina. These philosophers made it possible to examine the natural world, draw conclusions about it, and try to understand the natural laws of the universe. Philosophical work cultivated in Muslim societies contributed greatly to the process of scientific thought.

Finally, the educational system in Europe was changed as merchants, students, scholars, Crusaders, and travelers transmitted important ideas from Muslim cultures to the West and medical, mathematical, astronomical, and philosophical achievements made their way into Western civilization. Texts were translated from Arabic into Latin, and new knowledge gleaned from Muslims contributed to the rebirth, or Renaissance, of Europe. As Europeans rediscovered classical Greek knowledge and discovered knowledge from Muslim societies for the first time, they developed ways to improve their lives and societies.

Today, it is interesting to note the many English words having Arabic origins. For foods and drinks we have *alcohol* (*al-kohl*), *coffee* (*qahwa*), *artichoke* (*al-kharshuf*), *saffron* (*za'faran*), *lemon* (*limun*), *spinach* (*isbanakh*), *orange* (*naranj*), *sugar* (*sukkar*), and *tahini* (*tahin*). In mathematics, *algebra* (*al-jabr*) means "the restoring of a missing part." The word *algorithm* originates from the Latinization of the name al-Khwarizmi, the father of algebra. Many names of common household items such as *sofa* (*suffah*), *jar* (*jarrah*), and *talc* or *talcum power* (*talq*) come from Arabic loanwords, as do animal names such as *giraffe* (*zarafa*), *gazelle* (*ghazal*), and *gerbil* (*jarbua*). These and many other words used daily reflect Muslim influences in world civilizations.

MUSLIMS IN THE WEST

Who are the Muslims of America?

Muslim Americans are Americans who came here from sixty-eight different countries as well as indigenous African Americans and converts from a variety of ethnic backgrounds. They are one of the most diverse communities in the world, racially, economically, and politically. Although estimates of the Muslim American population vary widely, it is safe to say that there are at least five to seven million, making Islam the third largest religion (after Christianity and Judaism) in America. Many believe that in the first half of the twenty-first century Islam will become the second-largest religion in America.

In a national portrait of Muslim Americans conducted by Gallup in 2009, 28 percent of Muslims categorize themselves as "white"; 18 percent say they are Asian, and a surprising 18 percent classify themselves as "other," which may reflect their identification with more than one group. One percent say they are Hispanic. The majority (56 percent) of Muslims in America are immigrants who came to pursue political and religious freedom, economic prosperity, or education. Thirty-five percent are native-born African American Muslims, the descendants of slaves who have struggled for their civil rights as well as economic and social justice.

Muslims in America are predominantly young. Thirty-six percent are eighteen to twenty-nine years old (versus 18 percent in the general population), and 37 percent are thirty to forty-four years of age (versus 26 percent for Americans overall). The sample size of Muslims sixty-five and older was too small to report. Education is a priority for many Muslims, who, after Jews, are the most educated religious community in the United States. Most significant, students account for 31 percent of the American Muslim population, as compared to 10 percent in the general population. Many Muslims have graduated from college: 40 percent have a college degree or more, compared to 29 percent of Americans overall. Muslim women are equal to men in holding college or postgraduate degrees. Muslim women also report incomes more nearly equal to men's, compared with women in other faith groups.

Muslims include men and women spanning the socioeconomic spectrum: professionals (doctors, lawyers, engineers, and educators), corporate executives, small business owners, as well as blue-collar workers. Seventy percent have a job (paid or unpaid), compared to 64 percent of Americans overall. However, a higher proportion (24 percent) are self-employed. American Muslims' employment situation is reflected in the fact that a majority, 71 percent, a higher proportion than in the general population, agree that most people who want to get ahead in America can succeed if they are willing to work hard.

The diversity of Muslim Americans is clearly reflected in their political views. They are the religious group that is the most evenly spread along the political spectrum. Thirty-eight percent claim to be moderate, and others are equally divided on either side (29 percent liberal or very liberal and 25 percent conservative or very conservative). Contrary to the conventional wisdom, 44 percent of Muslims cited domestic policy as a more important factor in influencing their votes, versus 34 percent who cited foreign policy.

Many are not aware that Muslims have a long history in America. The explorers, traders, and settlers who visited the New World from the time of Columbus included Moriscos

(Spanish Muslims who hid their Muslim faith), and between 14 percent and 20 percent of the African slaves brought to America between the sixteenth and nineteenth centuries were Muslim, although they were forced to convert to Christianity. Other immigrants during this period, particularly Muslim Indians and Arabs, who were not slaves, were able to maintain their spiritual, cultural, and social identity.

In the nineteenth century the Muslim population increased when significant numbers of immigrants from the Arab world (Syria, Lebanon, and Jordan) settled in the Midwest and Canada as blue-collar workers. After World War II, Muslim immigrants included large numbers of Palestinians who had lost their homes after the 1948 creation of Israel, and elites from the Middle East and South Asia seeking education or professional advancement. In recent decades, significant numbers of immigrants from the Muslim world have been students as well as well-educated professionals and intellectuals from South and Southeast Asia and the Middle East who were emigrating for political and economic reasons. African American Islam originated with the Nation of Islam in 1930. (See page 57, "Is there a difference between Muslims and Black Muslims?") Many Muslims have worked hard to sustain their Islamic identity and pass it down to their children and to establish institutions and community structures—including mosques, Islamic centers, Islamic schools, Islamic publication organizations, interest-free financial institutions, and charitable organizations—to support these goals. The largest Muslim communities in the United States are in Boston, New York City, Detroit, Dearborn, Toledo, Chicago, Houston, and Los Angeles/Orange County.

Muslims are part of the fabric of American society; they have become integrated, economically and educationally, and are becoming more active in the American political process both as individuals and organizationally. Two Muslims now serve in the U.S. Congress, others are in the Obama administration and government agencies, and still others are active in local politics. Muslim organizations have also become more visible in lobbying Congress. A host of national and international organizations have been created to monitor and promote Muslim causes and interests. Among the more prominent are the Council on American-Islamic Relations (CAIR), the Muslim Public Affairs Council (MPAC), the Islamic Circle of North America (ICNA) and the Islamic Society of North America (ISNA), and the Center for the Study of Islam and Democracy (CSID).

Luis Lugo, director of the Pew Forum on Religion & Public Life, concludes, "Muslim Americans are very much like the rest of the country ... They do not see a conflict between being a devout Muslim and living in a modern society." Ninety-seven percent of Muslims polled believe they should donate to non-Muslim social service programs like aid for the homeless, and 90 percent say Muslims should participate in interfaith activities.

What kinds of problems do Muslims face in America?

Like many other immigrants of diverse religious and ethnic backgrounds, Muslims are being challenged to define their place in American society. Given their youth, educational and employment profiles, and growing population, which make them a potential political force, the future for Muslims in America can look very positive. However, this optimism can be strongly tempered by the negative attitudes toward all Muslims, influenced by 9/11 and the fears of terrorism that can be seen across America. Being Muslim, regardless of one's education or profession, seems to carry the taint of terrorism and "foreignness" that brushstrokes all Muslims as "the other."

Many former American minorities who have now "made it in America" do not empathize with what Muslims are now facing. They fail to identify the discrimination they or their ancestors encountered with Muslims' current situation. There are many reasons for this. The majority of previous religious and ethnic minorities were Judeo-Christian. In America, Islam is still an unknown, considered a foreign religion. Few think of Islam as an Abrahamic religion, part of a Judeo-Christian-Islamic tradition. Since many Americans are not familiar with Islam as a faith and are not personally acquainted with many Muslims, gaps in our knowledge, in a post-9/11 world, have also been filled with one-sided, often sensationalist media accounts, leading us to fear and ostracize these "strangers."

Living in a dominant culture that is often ignorant about or hostile to Islam, Muslims can feel marginalized, alienated, and powerless. Some are also marked as "different" because of their dress or attempts to maintain their religious practices. They wonder how to demonstrate that their acts of worship—wearing headscarves, taking off from work at noon on Friday to attend congregational prayers, building Islamic centers or mosques—do not undermine their patriotism or pride in being American. Those who want to succeed in American cultural and political environments wonder if they must give up their identity and function like strangers in their Western society in order to be accepted. This encourages some to resist assimilation because it can lead to becoming so "Westernized" that they lose their distinctive cultural identity and faith. Not only non-Muslims but also Muslims themselves are led to question whether they are Muslims who happen to live in America or American Muslims.

Two broad Muslim responses to Muslim identity in the West continue to coexist: First, some Muslim leaders advocate more isolated religious/cultural communities and imams trained in homeland countries. Like ethnic Catholics and Jews in America, who initially looked to their countries of origin for many of their priests or rabbis, Western Muslims have relied on connections to the Muslim world for religious leadership. However, this kind of support can deter the Americanization of the Muslim experience in the long run. Muslim communities can become dependent on foreign-born and -trained religious leaders who are not always aware of or sensitive to the problems of daily life that American Muslims encounter. So too, Muslim leaders must be able to face the added responsibility of helping the community to confront anti-Muslim sentiment. Thus, training indigenous imams has become a keen goal, generating new interest in developing indigenous seminaries for local religious leaders and scholars.

The second response, "we are American Muslims," represents the view of the majority of Muslims in America, whose success educationally and professionally has assisted their integration into their new mosaic society. Like other religious and ethnic groups before them, they see themselves as part of the fabric of America and have a strong desire for coexistence with their fellow citizens based on common civic, religious, and social values and interests.

Muslims recognize that making it in their adopted countries requires institution-building and reform. In the last decade there has been a great increase in the number of mosques, Islamic centers, schools, professional and social associations, and advocacy groups to monitor textbooks and the teaching of Islam to assure accuracy and objectivity and educate the media, legislators, and the general public. Western freedoms have enabled Muslim religious leaders, intellectuals, and activists to become major voices for religious, social, and political reform regarding women's roles and rights, religious pluralism and tolerance, religious extremism, becoming an American or European Muslim, and preserving Muslim civil rights and liberties.

Although great headway has been made, many obstacles remain. First, the resources, numbers, and impact of Muslim projects remain relatively small. Even more daunting is that while some non-Muslims in the West welcome the integration and institutionalization of Islam and Muslims, others do not. In Western countries' changing political and legal environments Muslims face workplace discrimination, racial and religious profiling, and overzealous security measures. Islamic institutions—mosques, charities, and NGOs—face harassment, unwarranted scrutiny, and indictment without prompt adjudication. Conservative columnists, hard-line Christian Zionist religious leaders, some of them prominent neoconservative radio and television talk show hosts with large audiences, have regularly used hate speech and dangerous invective aimed not at extremists but at Islam and Muslims in general. The result has been growth of Islamophobia, discrimination toward Muslims based on their religion or race that has led to hate crimes and other acts of violence.

The higher political profile for Muslim public institutions and political action groups has led to accusations that they are fronts for radicals supporting extremist activities abroad. As Muslim professionals try to join governing boards, participate in politics, or apply for professional positions they can be labeled as militants or terrorists. Recalling the witch hunts of the McCarthy era, many Muslims in America see it as professional suicide to have any association with major Muslim leaders or organizations (in contrast to association with major Jewish organizations like the ZOA, AJC, or the pro-Israel lobby AIPAC).

A coterie of neoconservative media (the *Weekly Standard* and the *New York Sun* as well as the *Washington Times*) and interrelated Web sites (Campus Watch, Jihad Watch, and *FrontPage*) coordinate to repeat unsubstantiated charges and claims, taking quotes out of context to create "facts on the ground." By recycling the same charges, themes, and articles, they support and enhance each other's accusations to make it look as if masses of people and groups are constantly uncovering new threats. They target not only Muslims but also non-Muslim academics, journalists, and policymakers who speak out against their bigotry and disinformation. All who criticize their actions are painted as unpatriotic, anti-Semitic apologists for Islam, or supporters of suicide bombers. The goal of these anti-Muslim individuals and organizations is to discredit and keep Muslim organizations weak and disenfranchised, and to marginalize Muslim representation in politics, government, and major American organizations.

For the foreseeable future Muslims will face the challenge of retaining their faith and identity while integrating into sometimes hostile American societies. Western countries offer many freedoms not available in much of the Muslim world, but the pluralism the West values so highly is being tested as never before. Muslims are led to wonder: What are the limits of this Western pluralism? Who is included or excluded? Is it staunchly secular or permanently Judeo-Christian? Can Americans fully accept Muslims (as well as Hindus, Sikhs, Buddhists, and others) not as "foreigners" to be tolerated, but as respected fellow citizens and neighbors with equal political and religious rights? In the past, tolerance has too often meant "suffering" the existence of others while regarding them as inferior. Today, a modern form of pluralism and tolerance must be based on mutual understanding and respect.

Who and where are the Muslims of Europe?

Twenty to twenty-three million Muslims, representing most of the major ethnic groups of the Muslim world, are estimated to be living in Western Europe. Most numerous are Turks, Algerians, Moroccans, and then Pakistanis. Because of this great ethnic diversity, it is difficult to speak of a homogenous Muslim community in any individual country, let alone across Europe. Muslims may be found in significant numbers in most Western European countries, with large populations in France, Germany, and the United Kingdom, and smaller communities in such countries as Belgium, Spain, the Netherlands, Sweden, Denmark, Norway, and Austria.

Although some immigration to Britain and France began before World War II, the major waves of Muslim migration came afterward. In contrast to America, whose Muslim population is heavily indebted to family or educational migration, and the growth of Islam among African Americans,

Europe's Muslim presence is due in large part to labor immigration and a colonial connection. When their countries achieved independence, many of those who had cooperated with European colonizers chose to emigrate, and in the 1960s and 1970s, unskilled laborers flooded into a Europe whose growing economies were in need of cheap labor. More than a million Muslims were admitted to France alone. Germany and Britain had similar stories. From the 1970s onward, increasing numbers of Muslim students came to Europe, as they did to America, to study. While many returned home, others, for political or economic reasons, chose to stay.

France has the largest Muslim population in Europe, five million Muslims, primarily from North Africa, and thirty-five thousand converts. Muslims represent almost 10 percent of the population, outnumbering Protestants and Jews and second only to Roman Catholics. There are grand mosques in major cities like Paris and Lyons and more than fifteen hundred mosques and prayer rooms throughout the country. Muslim communities have continued to grow because of their high birthrate, regulations permitting immigration to reunite families, and a continual flow of legal and illegal entrants from North Africa.

Britain's two million Muslims, primarily from the Indian subcontinent, and others from Africa, Malaysia, and the Arab world, are concentrated in the northern industrial cities and in the East End of London. More than six hundred mosques serve as prayer, education, and community centers, many built with funds from the Middle East, particularly Saudi Arabia.

Muslims who come from British Commonwealth countries enjoy British citizenship and full participation in politics as voters and candidates for elective office. Nine members of the House of Lords have a Muslim heritage, and in 2010 a record number of eight Muslim MPs—including the first women— were elected to the House of Commons. Even more Muslims have been elected to the Dutch parliament's equivalent of the

House of Commons. In contrast, France and Spain have no Muslim representatives in the national legislature, and Germany has five.

Muslim integration in European society has been more difficult than in America. While many Muslims emigrated to America with education and skills, they came to Europe primarily as laborers and blue-collar workers. As a result, many in Britain, France, Germany, and Holland with limited education, skills, and social mobility have become trapped in depressed areas with high unemployment and little access to education or job skill development. In contrast to the 70 percent of American Muslims who reported having a job in 2009, the figures for Muslims in Europe showed a radically different picture: 38 percent in the United Kingdom, 45 percent in France, and 53 percent in Germany.

These conditions feed a sense of second-class citizenship, social exclusion, marginalization, and alienation and contribute to problems with drugs and crime. Gallup polling of Muslims living in Europe reveals their problems. Sixty-nine percent of Muslims living in France and 72 percent in the United Kingdom consider themselves "struggling," while 23 percent of French Muslims and only 7 percent of Muslims in the United Kingdom say they are "thriving." Thus it is not surprising that European Muslims also struggle even more intensely than American Muslims with their identity. Because of class structure and cultural attitudes, first- and second-generation European Muslims as well as recent immigrants feel that they will never be accepted as fully and equally British, French, or German. Despite being citizens, many believe that they have at best moved from being "guests" to being "foreigners."

While many insist that Muslims totally assimilate, others argue that Muslims need to develop a distinctive European Muslim identity that blends European principles and values with Muslim faith and values. They argue that Islam is now a European religion; in fact, the second-largest religion in many

European countries. No longer predominantly first-generation immigrants, many are second- and third-generation citizens. Despite the acts of and continued threat from a very small but dangerous minority of extremists, the majority of Muslims, like their non-Muslim fellow citizens, are loyal citizens who can partner with the rest of the European population to identify and fight terrorists.

A major study of interfaith relations in Britain, France, and Germany (Gallup Coexist Index 2009: A Global Study of Interfaith Relations) reflects what some would find a surprising level of integration. Gallup found that Muslims are more likely than the general population in Britain, France, and Germany to identify strongly with their faith, *and* they are also as likely as the general public (if not more likely) to identify strongly with their countries of residence. While majorities of the public in France, Germany, and the United Kingdom either did not think Muslims were loyal to their countries of residence or were unsure, strong majorities of European Muslims thought Muslims *were* loyal to their countries of residence in Europe. Moreover, when asked how justifiable acts of violence (like those in London and Madrid) were, majorities of Muslims in all three countries (82 percent in France, 91 percent in Germany, and 89 percent in Britain) said that violence was not justifiable at all. Gallup found that people claiming that religion was important were also likely to say that violence could not be justified for a noble cause. Clear common grounds were reflected in all three countries where the public and Muslims thought that skill in the national language, employment, and education would best help immigrants to integrate into their new homes.

What kinds of problems do Muslims in Europe face?

The Muslims of Europe have faced many challenges, from issues of national and religious identity to educational, economic, and social integration. (See "Who and where are the Muslims of Europe?" above.) Their situation has been exacerbated by the growth of religious extremism and terrorism, Islamophobia, and threats to their civil liberties. Radical preachers and mosques, terrorist cells, attacks in Madrid (3/11/2008), London (7/7/2005), and Glasgow (6/30/2007), and arrests in cities across Europe have underscored the dangers of domestic terrorism. At the same time, fears of growing domestic terrorism and the sharp rise of xenophobia and right-wing nationalist, anti-immigrant political parties have fed an exponential increase in Islamophobic rhetoric—calls to ban the Quran, monitor or close mosques, question the loyalty of European Muslims, deport Muslim citizens, and halt immigration from Muslim countries.

The result is the perception and charge that Islam and Muslims represent a foreign religion and peoples incapable of being integrated into democratic, pluralistic European societies, a demographic time bomb, threatening to overwhelm Europe. Modern-day prophets of doom predict that Europe will be overrun by Islam, transformed by the end of the century into "Eurabia."

News stories in Europe portray a vanishing Christian Europe endangered by a Muslim population that has grown from twelve million to twenty million in a decade. They compare the increase in mosques in Britain, Germany, France, and Italy to empty European churches and deplore the replacement of church bells with the call to prayer. Changing demographics—a shrinking "indigenous" population overtaken by high Muslim birthrates—has led many Catholic and Protestant church leaders to decry secularization and modernity, loss of faith, and moral breakdown; some warn that Christian Europe is increasingly powerless against the rise of "radical Islam."

The media, political leaders, and commentators on the right warn of a "soft terrorism" plot to take over Europe. Bernard Lewis, Middle East historian and adviser to the Bush administration on its failed Iraq policy, received widespread coverage when he chided Europeans for losing their loyalty, self-confidence, and respect for their own culture, charging that they have "surrendered" to Islam in a mood of "self-abasement," "political correctness," and "multiculturalism."

The anti-immigrant drumbeat warning of the demise of Europe's religious and cultural identity in the face of an Islamic threat has been further exacerbated by media coverage that lumps diverse identity, demographic, economic, and social conflicts together under the umbrella of religion. Because Muslims are defined simply in terms of their faith, rioting in French ghetto areas inhabited by North African Arabs is portrayed as "Muslim" rather than as protests against poverty and hopelessness. Muslim boycotts in London protesting Danish cartoons that depicted Muhammad as a terrorist with a bomb in his turban and conflicts over the hijab in France, Turkey, and Denmark are seen exclusively as "religious issues" rather than issues of civil rights and freedoms such as women's right to dress as they choose.

A common charge both with regard to Muslim-West relations and the integration of Muslims in America and Europe is that Islam is incompatible with the realities of modernity and Western culture and values. However, many of these supposed "Muslim issues," given their nature and primary causes, are problems that require social, not religious, solutions and policies.

Religious symbols like Muslim women's hijab (headscarf) or the niqab (veil that covers the face) and burqa (garment that covers the entire body) and mosque minarets have become prominent symbols for opposition to Islam and Muslims. The French government in the mid-1990s outlawed the headscarf worn by Muslim students, claiming it violated France's secular constitution and traditions. The ban was overturned by the courts but reemerged in September 2004 when France banned religious symbols and apparel in public schools. Although the ban included all overtly religious dress and signs (including Muslim headscarves, Sikh turbans, Jewish skullcaps, and large Christian crosses), the furor over the ban has focused mainly on banning Muslim hijabs.

Subsequently, in 2010, France banned the niqab and burqa, citing reasons of security, women's rights, and national culture; Belgium, Denmark, the Netherlands, and other countries debated banning them. Others argued that women should be free to decide how they wish to dress. As some have put it, does a country that gives women the right to wear very little, if they so choose, have the legal right to ban a burqa?

Following the lead of far right European parties in using religious symbols as issues to target Muslims, the Swiss far right chose the minaret. The campaign to prohibit minarets, fueled by appeals to popular emotions and fears about the demographic threat of Islam, used posters highlighting a Muslim woman in black niqab framed by minarets or depictions of minarets as weapons drawn on a "colonized" Swiss flag to underscore Islam's fundamental incompatibility with Swiss values. The Swiss far right scored a surprising election victory in November 2009.

The Swiss were not alone. Other far right European political parties also performed better than expected in 2009 elections: Geert Wilders's Freedom Party in the Netherlands, the Danish People's Party, the Austrian Freedom Party (FPÖ), Hungary's Jobbik, and the British National Party. Their "victories" in parliamentary elections emboldened their leaders to applaud the Swiss vote and encourage similar prohibitions. Wilders, who had previously warned that mass deportation of millions of Muslims from Europe might be necessary, now called for a vote to stem the "tide of Islamization" in the Netherlands.

What is Islamophobia?

We live in a world in which two great world religions with Semitic origins are often under siege: objects of discrimination, hate crimes, and acts of violence and terror. For one, the

14–18 million Jews of the world, we have a powerful term, *anti-Semitism*, and a global awareness and sensitivity that can be mobilized against anti-Semitic attitudes and acts. As history and recent experiences confirm, the term *anti-Semitism* is a potent antidote for this disease that continues to infect our societies. However, for the 1.5 billion Muslims in the world, until relatively recently we have had no comparable effective way to brand and counter the hostility, prejudice, and discrimination directed toward Islam and Muslims.

Islamophobia did not suddenly come into being after the events of 9/11. In November 1997, Britain's Runnymede Report, *Islamophobia: A Challenge for Us All*, defined Islamophobia as "the dread, hatred and hostility towards Islam and Muslims perpetrated by a series of closed views that imply and attribute negative and derogatory stereotypes and beliefs to Muslims." It results in exclusion from economic, social, and public life, and discrimination based on the perception that the religion of Islam has no values in common with and is inferior to the West, and that it really is a violent *political ideology* rather than, like the other Abrahamic religions, Judaism and Christianity, a source of faith and spirituality.

Like anti-Semitism and xenophobia, Islamophobia has long and deep historical roots. Its contemporary resurgence has been triggered by the significant influx of Muslims in the West in the late twentieth century, as well as the Iranian revolution, hijackings, hostage taking, and acts of terrorism in the 1980s and 1990s, the attacks against the World Trade Center and the Pentagon, and subsequent terrorist attacks in Europe. The victims of discrimination and hate crimes are not the extremists responsible for violence and terror but the mainstream moderate majority of Muslims in Europe and America. In recent years, far right anti-immigrant political parties and political commentators in Europe and America have demonized the religion of Islam and all Muslims. The net result has been a virulent form of cultural racism.

Kofi Annan, then secretary-general of the United Nations, convened a 2004 UN conference, "Confronting Islamophobia: Education for Tolerance and Understanding" and addressed the international scope of the problem:

> When the world is compelled to coin a new term to take account of increasingly widespread bigotry—that is a sad and troubling development. Such is the case with "Islamophobia" ... There is a need to unlearn the stereotypes that have become so entrenched in so many minds and so much of the media. Islam is often seen as a monolith ... [and] Muslims as opposed to the West ... The pressures of living together with people of different cultures and different beliefs from one's own are real ... But that cannot justify demonization or the deliberate use of fear for political purposes. That only deepens the spiral of suspicion and alienation.

Due to the lack of a collective consciousness able to identify the signs of Islamophobia in the United States, political and religious leaders and media commentators have been free to engage in a form of hate speech, asserting with impunity what would never appear in mainstream broadcast or print media about Jews, Christians, or established ethnic and racial groups in America. While the term *Islamophobia* has been used in Europe for many years, in America it has only recently gained general recognition, through the widely publicized controversy about a new Islamic cultural center (Park51) to be located two blocks from Ground Zero in New York City. This project, which was approved by all relevant government and local agencies, sparked intense opposition not only from some families of 9/11 victims but also from politicians, media, right-wing bloggers, and political pundits whose Islamophobic comments spiraled out of control. No wonder that a June 22, 2010, *New York Post* editorial attacked plans to construct new mosques in the state of New York, claiming:

There's no denying the elephant in the room. Neither is there any rejoicing over the mosques proposed for Sheepshead Bay, Staten Island and Ground Zero because where there are mosques, there are Muslims, and where there are Muslims, there are problems. Before New York becomes New Yorkistan, it is worth noting that the capital of Great Britain was London until it became known as "Londonstan," degenerated by a Muslim community predominantly from South Asia and Africa, whose first generation of "British Asians" has made the United Kingdom into a launching pad for terrorists.

Violent protests against construction of new mosques erupted across the country, as did multiple cases of hate crimes, violence, and vandalism. Protesters, taking a cue from those at the Park51 site, charged that mosques were "monuments to terrorism."

What fuels the fires of discrimination against Muslims in America and Europe? There is no lack of examples that empower Islamophobia's deep suspicion and lack of trust. Here is a sampling of comments by right-wing political pundits, preachers, and politicians, from 9/11 to Park51 and the lead-up to congressional elections in 2010: Rush Limbaugh, reacting to criticism of the abuse of Iraqi prisoners at Abu Ghraib, commented, "They're the ones who are sick... They're the ones who are perverted. They are the ones who are dangerous. They are the ones who are subhuman. They are the ones who are human debris, not the United States of America and not our soldiers and not our prison guards." Ann Coulter in the *National Review* urged, "We should invade their countries, kill their leaders and convert them to Christianity. We weren't punctilious about locating and punishing only Hitler and his top officers. We carpet-bombed German cities; we killed civilians. That's war. And this is war." Christian Right leader Pat Robertson, in an interview on Fox News' *Hannity*

& *Colmes*, charged, "This man [Muhammad] was an absolute wild-eyed fanatic. He was a robber and a brigand. And to say that these terrorists distort Islam, they're carrying out Islam...I mean, this man was a killer. And to think that this is a peaceful religion is fraudulent." Robertson also called Islam "a monumental scam" and claimed the Quran, Islam's revealed text, "is strictly a theft of Jewish theology." Jerry Falwell referred to the Prophet Muhammad as a "terrorist" on the CBS news program *60 Minutes*. Benny Hinn declared, "This is not a war between Arabs and Jews. It's between God and the devil."

Politicians in 2010 such as Newt Gingrich likened Muslims who wanted to build Park51 to Nazis planting a sign outside the Holocaust Museum in Washington, D.C., and also warned of the danger of Shariah taking over American courts. Republican state senator Rex Duncan of Oklahoma declared there is a "war for the survival of America," to keep the Shariah from creeping into the American court system. Congresswoman Sue Myrick from North Carolina and Congressman Paul Broun from Georgia charged that Muslim student interns were part of a secret infiltration of Muslim spies into key national security committees on Capitol Hill. Tennessee Republican congressional candidate Lou Ann Zelenik wrote to oppose a new mosque, "Until the American Muslim community find it in their hearts to separate themselves from their evil, radical counterparts, to condemn those who want to destroy our civilization and will fight against them, we are not obligated to open our society to any of them."

Major polls revealed the extent to which public speeches and media coverage about Islam and Muslims in the United States had deeply affected Americans' attitudes, often blurring the mainstream majority of Muslims and the acts of a small but dangerous minority of terrorists. A 2006 *USA Today/Gallup* poll found that substantial minorities of Americans admitted to having negative feelings or prejudices against people of the Muslim faith and favored using heightened security measures against Muslims as a way to help prevent terrorism. Fewer than half the respondents believed U.S. Muslims are loyal to the United States. Nearly one quarter of Americans, 22 percent, said they would not like to have a Muslim as a neighbor; 31 percent said they would feel nervous if they noticed a Muslim man on their flight, and 18 percent said they would feel nervous if they noticed a Muslim woman on the flight. About four in ten Americans favored more rigorous security measures for Muslims than those used for other U.S. citizens: requiring Muslims who are U.S. citizens to carry a special ID and undergo special, more intensive, security checks before boarding airplanes in the United States.

Four years later, no improvement can be seen. A 2010 Gallup Center for Muslim Studies report found that more than four in ten Americans (43 percent) admit to feeling at least "a little" prejudice toward Muslims—more than twice the number who say the same about Christians (18 percent), Jews (15 percent), and Buddhists (14 percent). Nine percent of Americans admitted feeling "a great deal" of prejudice toward Muslims, while 20 percent admitted feeling "some" prejudice. The result of Islamophobia, as noted by Dr. Jeremy Henzell-Thomas, chairman of the Forum Against Islamophobia and Racism (FAIR), amounts to

clichés which stigmatise the whole of Islam as fundamentalist, ideological, monolithic, static, unidimensional, implacably opposed to modernity, incapable of integration or assimilation, impervious to new ideas, retrogressive, retrograde, backward, archaic, primaeval, medieval, uncivilised, hostile, violent, terrorist, alien, fanatical, barbaric, militant, oppressive, harsh, threatening, confrontational, extremist, authoritarian, totalitarian, patriarchal, misogynist, negatively exotic, and bent on imposing on the whole world a rigid theocratic system of government which would radically overturn every principle of freedom and liberal democracy cherished by the Western world.

"I have to say," continues Henzell-Thomas, "that I don't know a single Muslim who embodies even one of these characteristics, and I have Muslim friends and colleagues in all walks of life and from many cultures all over the globe."

After 9/11 Muslims shared fears that Islamophobia among their communities, neighbors, and co-workers would grow, along with hate crimes, discrimination, and more erosion of civil liberties. Their fears have been realized as all Western Muslims have been forced to live in increasingly suspicious and hostile American and European environments. Yet this experience did compel Western Muslims to both reassess their identity and reexamine their understanding of Islam. Among the positive outcomes has been acceleration of Muslim internal discussion and debate over what it means to be a Muslim in America or Europe, greater outreach on the part of Muslims to their non-Muslim communities, and more Muslim involvement in electoral politics and public affairs.

The history of our great country has been plagued from colonial days by religious and racial prejudice and exploitation: slavery and centuries of racial discrimination, the demonization and marginalization of Native Americans, the denial of the right to build synagogues in New York and anti-Semitism in America, discrimination against ethnic Catholic immigrants, and the collective punishment of Japanese Americans during World War II. We have weathered these storms as a nation, though many lives were shattered and problems remain.

The interconnectedness of Islamophobia, multiculturalism, and pluralism is critical to the future of Muslim-West relations. Attitudes toward Muslim communities in America and Europe are part of a complex set of issues. There is no easy way to discuss pluralism, multiculturalism, and the future of Western societies without discussing the precarious place of Islam and Muslims in the debate over civic engagement and integration.

GLOSSARY

adhan   Muslim call to prayer.

Aga Khan   Leader of the Nizari Ismaili sect of Shii Muslims who oversees cultural and spiritual lives of followers.

Aisha   Muhammad's influential wife, daughter of the first Sunni caliph, acknowledged authority on history, medicine, poetry, and rhetoric, and one of the most important transmitters of *hadith*.

Ali   Muhammad's cousin and son-in-law (married to Muhammad's daughter Fatima). Shii Muslims believe that Ali was the first caliph to succeed Muhammad (Sunnis place him fourth). Shiis trace the ruling descendants of Muhammad (Imams) through him.

Allah   God.

Allahu Akbar   Literally, "God is most great." Phrase used for Muslim call to prayer.

Assassins   Eponym given to the Nizari Ismaili sect of Shii Muslims due to campaign of terror and violence, including assassinations, they carried out against the Sunni Seljuq Dynasty in the name of the Hidden Imam. Last grand master was executed in 1256 C.E.

ayatollah   Literally, "Sign of God." Highest rank of Shii Muslim clerics. Respected for knowledge and piety.

bayah   Oath of allegiance.

bida Innovation or unacceptable departure from the example of Muhammad (Sunnah).

bismillah Reference to the phrase "Bismillah al-Rahman al-Rahim," meaning "In the name of God, the Merciful, the Compassionate." Opening verse of the Quran, which is used to begin letters, books, speeches, ceremonies, and official documents throughout the Muslim world.

Black Muslim Adherent of African-American strain of Islam, member of African-American sect Nation of Islam.

burqa Garment that covers a woman's entire body.

Caliph Title for successor to Muhammad as political leader of Muslim community.

Chador Iranian term for women's veil that covers hair and body, leaving only face, hands, and feet exposed.

Constitutuon of Medina Constitution promulgated by Muhammad, which established principle of religious pluralism within single political entity.

dar al-Islam "Abode of peace." Muslim territories; territories ruled by Islamic law.

dawa Literally, "call." Missionary work.

dhimmi Person enjoying protected status due to treaty relationship with Muslims. Typically used to refer to "People of the Book," particularly Jews and Christians.

din, deen. Religion.

dua Invocation. Private prayer of petition.

Eid al-Adha Feast of the Sacrifice. Major Muslim holiday falling at the end of the pilgrimage to Mecca *(hajj)*.

Eid al-Fitr Feast of the Breaking of the Fast. Major Muslim holiday that concludes the month of Ramadan, during which Muslims fast.

Fatima Daughter of Muhammad, wife of Ali, and mother of Hassan and Hussein. Example of perfect womanhood in Islam.

fatwa   Legal opinion issued by a private religious scholar (as opposed to a judge in a court of law). May be used by a judge in rendering a legal ruling.

fez   Red cap traditionally worn by Turkish men prior to the twentieth century.

Five Pillars of Islam   The five acts required of all Muslims: profession of faith, prayer five times daily, almsgiving (*zakat*), fasting during Ramadan, and *hajj* (pilgrimage) once in a lifetime.

galabeya   Long, loose-fitting garment with long sleeves, worn by both men and women.

hadith   Traditions, reports of Muhammad's deeds and sayings, considered to be a source of scripture for Muslims.

hajj   Pilgrimage to Mecca, which Muslims are required to make at least once in a lifetime if they are physically and financially able. One of the Five Pillars of Islam.

halal   Permitted; that has been prepared in a ritually appropriate way.

Hanafi   Major Sunni Islamic law school. Predominates in the Arab world and South Asia.

Hanbali   Major Sunni Islamic law school. Predominates in Saudi Arabia.

Haram   Forbidden.

Hidden Imam   Shii belief that the twelfth Imam did not die but went into hiding or "occultation," from which he is expected to return at the end of time as a messianic figure to bring in an era of peace and justice.

hijab   Veil covering the hair and head of a Muslim woman. Can include long-sleeved, long, flowing dress as well.

hijra   Emigration. Refers to departure of Muhammad and early Muslims from Mecca for Medina, which marks first year of Muslim lunar calendar.

hudud   Literally, "limits." Refers to crimes of theft, extramarital sexual activity, false accusations of unchastity, and consumption of alcohol specified by the Quran and carrying harsh capital penalties.

Hussein   Grandson of Muhammad and son of Ali and Fatima. Massacred in Karbala, Iraq, along with followers when he tried to claim sovereignty over Muslim community in 680 C.E. Massacre set paradigm of suffering, oppression, and need to fight injustice for Shii Muslims.

ijarah   Islamic financial principle of rent/purchase, which abides by Islamic prohibition of usury.

ijma   Consensus.

Ijtihad   Independent reasoning in interpretation of Islamic law.

Imam   Prayer leader and person who delivers Friday sermon for Sunni Muslims. Shii Muslims use Imam as title for Muhammad's male descendants through Ali and Fatima. Shiis believe that Imams, although human, were divinely inspired and infallible, rendering their writings and legal interpretations additional sources of scripture.

intifada   Palestinian uprising that began in 1987. The so-called second intifada began in 2000.

Islam   Literally, "submission."

Ismaili   "Sevener" branch of Shii Islam, which recognizes seven Imams. Founders of Fatimid Empire.

istihsan   Equity; using personal judgment to mitigate literal application of law.

Ithna Ashari   "Twelver" branch of Shii Islam, which recognizes twelve Imams, the last of whom is believed to be in hiding (see "Hidden Imam"). Majority of Shiis belong to this branch.

Jafari   Major Shii school of Islamic law.

jihad   Literally, "struggle" or "exertion." "Greater" jihad is the struggle within oneself to live a righteous life and submit oneself to God's will. "Lesser" jihad is the defense of Islam and the Muslim community.

jizya   Poll or head tax paid by *dhimmis* in order to enter into protective treaty relationship with Muslims.

juma Friday congregational prayer.

Kaaba Muslim House of God. Cube containing the Black Stone, which Muslims believe was given to Abraham by the angel Gabriel and placed in the Kaaba by Abraham and Ismail. Located in Mecca. Focal point of the *hajj*.

kafir Unbeliever.

keffiyah Traditional male head covering typically associated with Palestine and Jordan.

Khadija Muhammad's first and only wife for twenty-four years, the first convert to and one of the strongest supporters of Islam.

Kharijites Extremist minority sect of Muslims who broke with the early Muslim community over Ali's willingness to compromise in conflict, which they interpreted as a failure to act within God's will. Ultimately assassinated Ali due to their belief that he had committed apostasy. Believed that the world was strictly divided into two spheres, the realm of Islam and the realm of unbelief, so that only two categories of people were possible: believers or unbelievers, who were, by definition, enemies of Muslims. Inspired contemporary movements like Islamic Jihad and al-Qaeda.

Khutba Sermon preached during Friday congregational prayer.

Mahdi Muslim messianic figure expected to return at the end of time to usher in an era of peace and justice

Maliki Major Sunni Islamic law school. Predominant in North, Central, and West Africa.

mamluk Slave soldier. Became part of social and political elite under Muslim dynasties.

masjid Mosque, place for Muslim prayer.

maslaha Public interest or public welfare. Concept that allows for consideration of public interest in interpreting Islamic law.

Mecca Holiest city in Islam. Birthplace of Muhammad and location of the Kaaba. City where Muslims go on the *hajj*. Located in Saudi Arabia.

Medina   Second holiest city in Islam. City to which Muhammad and the early Muslims emigrated (*hijra*) when they were forced to leave Mecca. City where Muhammad is buried. Located in Saudi Arabia.

mihrab   Niche in mosque wall indicating direction of Mecca, toward which all Muslims must pray.

millet   Religious or faith community officially recognized by the Ottoman Empire.

minaret   High tower in a mosque from which the call to prayer (*adhan*) is made.

minbar   Pulpit in a mosque from which the Friday sermon (*kutba*) is delivered.

mosque   Muslim house of worship, where all Muslim men are required to attend Friday prayer services.

mudaraba   Islamic financial principle of installment purchase, which abides by Islamic prohibition of usury.

muezzin   Person who issues the call to prayer (*adhan*).

mufti   Specialist in Islamic law who is capable of delivering a legal opinion (*fatwa*).

Muhammad   Prophet of Islam who received revelation of the Quran. Muslims believe that he was the perfect human being and seek to emulate his example (*Sunnah*), as recorded in the *hadith*.

mujahid (pl., mujahidin)   Soldier of God.

mujtahid   Person qualified to exercise independent reasoning (*ijtihad*) in the interpretation of Islamic law.

musharakah   Islamic financial principle of equity-sharing, which abides by Islamic prohibition of usury.

Muslim   Literally, "one who submits." Adherent of faith of Islam.

Muwahhidun   Literally, "Unitarians," or upholders of absolute monotheism. Also called Wahhabis.

Nation of Islam   African-American strain of Islam that initially preached message of black supremacy, militancy, and separatism but has become more in line with mainstream Sunni Islam since the late 1990s.

niqab   Veil that covers a woman's face.

Nizari Ismaili   Sect of "Sevener" Shiis. Historically known as Assassins. Contemporary movement is nonviolent. Leader today is known as Aga Khan.

People of the book   Religious group with a revealed scripture or divine revelation. Used by Muslims to refer to Christians and Jews.

pir   Sufi master.

qadi   Muslim judge.

qibla   Direction of Mecca as indicated by niche (*mihrab*) in wall of mosque.

qiyas   Islamic legal principle of analogical reasoning.

Quran   Literally, "recitation." Muslim scripture or holy book revealed to Muhammad.

raka   Muslim prayer unit.

Ramadan   Muslim month of fasting, which ends with celebration of Eid al-Fitr. Fasting during Ramadan is one of the Five Pillars of Islam.

riba   Usury or interest. Outlawed by Islamic law.

salam   Peace.

As-salam alaykum   Literally, "peace be upon you." Muslim greeting. Response is "And peace be upon you also" or "Wa-alaykum as-salam."

salat   Prayer. Required of all Muslims five times daily. One of the Five Pillars of Islam.

sayyid   Descendant of Muhammad.

Shaffi   Major Sunni Islamic law school. Predominant in East Africa and Southeast Asia.

Shahada   Witness or testimony. Declaration "There is no god but God, and Muhammad is His messenger." One of the Five Pillars of Islam.

Shahid Martyr.

Shariah Islamic law as established in the Quran and *hadith.*

Shii Muslims who believe that succession to the political and religious leadership of the Muslim community should be hereditary through Muhammad's daughter Fatima and her husband, Muhammad's cousin Ali. Although Shiis do not believe that these successors (Imams) are prophets, they do believe that they are divinely inspired and infallible. About 15 percent of all Muslims are Shiis.

Shirk Idolatry; polytheism.

Shura Consultation.

Sufi Muslim mystic.

Sunnah Muhammad's example as recorded in the *hadith.*

Sunni Muslims who believe that succession to the political leadership of the Muslim community should belong to the most qualified and pious person, not be hereditary. They believe that the successor is strictly a political leader and a protector of the faith, not someone who is divinely inspired. About 85 percent of all Muslims are Sunnis.

Surah Chapter of the Quran.

takfir Excommunication, exclusion for unbelief.

taqlid Unquestioned imitation or following of tradition, past legal or doctrinal precedents, the opposite of *ijtihad.*

tawhid Monothesim.

tazir Crimes punished at the discretion of a Muslim judge (*qadi*).

turban Head covering worn by some Muslim males, particularly in Afghanistan under the Taliban and in Iran.

ulama Muslim religious scholars.

ummah The worldwide Muslim community, community of believers.

umrah Lesser pilgrimage in which Muslims visit Muhammad's tomb in Medina; visitation of Muslim holy sites outside of the *hajj.*

Wahhabi Adherent of ultraconservative interpretation of Islam as practiced in Saudi Arabia.

wali Literally, "friend," "helper," or "patron." Muslim saint.

zakat Literally, "purification." Almsgiving or charitable giving consisting of 2.5 percent of a Muslim's entire wealth (not just income). One of the Five Pillars of Islam.

Zamzam Literally, "bubbling." Well in Mecca that Muslims believe was revealed to Hagar by God in order to preserve her and Ismail from dying of thirst. Drinking water from this well is one of the *hajj* rituals.

Zaydi Sect of Shii Islam also known as "Fivers" due to recognition of five Imams. Predominant in Yemen.

SUGGESTIONS FOR FURTHER READING

General Reference

Esposito, John L., editor-in-chief. *The Oxford Dictionary of Islam*. New York: Oxford University Press, 2002.

———. *The Oxford Encyclopedia of the Islamic World*. 6 vols. New York: Oxford University Press, 2009.

———. *The Oxford Encyclopedia of the Modern Islamic World*. 4 vols. New York: Oxford University Press, 1995.

Esposito, John L., ed. *The Oxford History of Islam*. New York: Oxford University Press, 1999.

Hodgson, Marshall G. S. *The Venture of Islam: Conscience and History in a World Civilization*. 3 vols. Chicago: University of Chicago Press, 1974.

Lapidus, Ira M. *A History of Islamic Societies*. 2nd ed. New York: Cambridge University Press, 2002.

Translations of the Quran

Ali, Abdullah Yusuf. *The Meaning of the Holy Qur'an*. 11th ed. Beltsville, Md.: Amana Publications, 2004.

Ali, Ahmed. *Al-Quran: A Contemporary Translation*. Princeton, N.J.: Princeton University Press, 2001.

Arberry, A. J. *The Koran Interpreted*. New York: Macmillan, 1964.

Asad, Muhammad. *The Message of the Quran*. Chicago: Kazi Publications, 1996.

Bakhtiar, Leila. *The Sublime Quran: Based on the Hanafi, Maliki, and Shafii Schools of Law*. Chicago: Kazi Publications, 2007.

Fakhry, Majid. *An Interpretation of the Qur'an*. New York: New York University Press, 2002.

———. *The Qur'an: A Modern English Version*. Berkshire, U.K.: Garnet Publishing, 1996.

Haleem, M. A. S. Abdel. *The Qur'an*. Oxford: Oxford University Press, 2008.

Pickthall, Mohammed Marmaduke. *The Meaning of the Glorious Koran.* Beltsville, Md.: Amana Publications, 1999.

Faith, Practice, Politics, and Society

Abdo, Geneive. *No God but God: Egypt and the Triumph of Islam.* New York: Oxford University Press, 2000.

Abdul-Matin, Ibrahim. *Green Deen: What Islam Teaches About Protecting the Planet.* New York: Berrett-Koehler Publishers, 2010.

Abou El Fadl, Khaled. *The Great Theft: Wrestling Islam from the Extremists.* New York: HarperOne, 2005.

———. *The Search for Beauty in Islam: A Conference of the Books.* Lanham, Md.: Rowman and Littlefield, 2005.

———. *Speaking in God's Name: Islamic Law, Authority and Women.* Oxford: Oneworld Publications, 2001.

Abou El Fadl, Khaled, Joshua Cohen, and Ian Lague. *The Place of Tolerance in Islam.* Boston: Beacon Press, 2002.

Ahmed, Leila. *Women and Gender in Islam: Historical Roots of a Modern Debate.* New Haven, Conn.: Yale University Press, 1992.

Armstrong, Karen. *The Battle for God: Fundamentalism in Judaism, Christianity, and Islam.* New York: Alfred A. Knopf, 2000.

———. *Holy War: The Crusades and Their Impact on Today's World.* New York: Doubleday, 1991.

———. *Jerusalem: One City, Three Faiths.* New York: Alfred A. Knopf, 1996.

———. *Muhammad: A Biography of the Prophet.* San Francisco: HarperCollins, 1993.

Aslan, Reza. *No God but God: The Origins, Evolution, and Future of Islam.* New York: Random House, 2005.

Bloom, Jonathan, and Sheila Blair. *Islam: A Thousand Years of Faith and Power.* New Haven, Conn.: Yale University Press, 2002.

Bunt, Gary R. *Islam in the Digital Age: E-Jihad, Online Fatwas and Cyber Islamic Environments.* London: Pluto Press, 2003.

———. *Muslims: Rewiring the House of Islam.* Chapel Hill: University of North Carolina Press, 2009.

Cesari, Jocelyne. *When Islam and Democracy Meet: Muslims in Europe and in the United States.* New York: Palgrave Macmillan, 2004.

———, ed. *Muslims in the West After 9/11: Religions, Politics and Law.* London: Routledge, 2008.

Chittick, William C. *Sufism: A Beginner's Guide.* Oxford: Oneworld, 2007.

Cragg, Kenneth. *Jesus and the Muslim: An Exploration.* Boston: Oneworld, 1999.

———. *Muhammad in the Qur'an: The Task and the Text.* London: Melisende, 2001.

———. *The Pen and the Faith: Eight Modern Muslim Writers and the Qur'an.* New York: Routledge, 2008.

———. *The Qur'an and the West.* Washington, D.C.: Georgetown University Press, 2006.

Daniel, Norman. *Islam and the West: The Making of an Image.* Rev. ed. Oxford: Oneworld, 1993.

Denny, Frederick M. *An Introduction to Islam.* Upper Saddle River, N.J.: Pearson Prentice Hall, 2006.

Esack, Farid. *The Qur'an: A Short Introduction.* Oxford: Oneworld, 2002.

———. *The Qur'an: A User's Guide.* Oxford: Oneworld, 2005.

Esposito, John L. *The Future of Islam.* New York: Oxford University Press, 2010.

———. *Islam: The Straight Path.* 4th ed. New York: Oxford University Press, 2010.

———. *The Islamic Threat: Myth or Reality?* 3rd ed. New York: Oxford University Press, 1999.

———. *Unholy War: Terror in the Name of Islam.* New York: Oxford University Press, 2002.

Esposito, John L., and Osman Bakar, eds. *Asian Islam in the 21st Century.* New York: Oxford University Press, 2007.

Esposito, John L., with Natana J. DeLong-Bas. *Women in Muslim Family Law.* 2d ed. Syracuse, N.Y.: Syracuse University Press, 2001.

Esposito, John L., Yvonne Haddad, and Jane Smith. *Immigrant Faiths: Christians, Jews, and Muslims Becoming Americans.* Walnut Creek, Calif.: AltaMira Press, 2002.

Esposito, John L., and John O. Voll. *Islam and Democracy.* New York: Oxford University Press, 1996.

———. *Makers of Contemporary Islam.* New York: Oxford University Press, 2001.

Fitzgerald, Michael L., and John Borelli. *Interfaith Dialogue: A Catholic View.* Maryknoll, N.Y.: Orbis Books, 2006.

Haddad, Yvonne Yazbeck, ed. *Muslims in the West: From Sojourners to Citizens.* New York: Oxford University Press, 2002.

Haddad, Yvonne Yazbeck, and John L. Esposito, eds. *Islam, Gender, and Social Change.* New York: Oxford University Press, 1998.

———. *Muslims on the Americanization Path?* Atlanta: Scholars Press, 1997.

Haddad, Yvonne Yazbeck, and Wadi Z. Haddad. *Christian-Muslim Encounters.* Gainesville: University Press of Florida, 1995.

Haddad, Yvonne Yazbeck, and Adair T. Lummis. *Islamic Values in the United States: A Comparative Study.* New York: Oxford University Press, 1987.

Haddad, Yvonne Yazbeck, and Jane I. Smith, eds. *Muslim Minorities in the West: Visible and Invisible.* Walnut Creek, Calif.: AltaMira Press, 2002.

Haddad, Yvonne Yazbeck, Jane I. Smith, and Kathleen M. Moore. *Muslim Women in America: The Challenge of Islamic Identity Today.* New York: Oxford University Press, 2006.

Halm, Heinz. *The Shi'ites: A Short History.* 2nd ed. Princeton, N.J.: Marcus Wiener Publishers, 2007.

Haneef, Suzanne. *What Everyone Should Know About Islam and Muslims.* 12th ed. Chicago: Kazi Publications, 1995.

Hroub, Khaled. *Hamas: Political Thought and Practice.* Washington, D.C.: Institute for Palestine Studies, 2000.

Hunter, Shireen T. *Islam, Europe's Second Religion.* Westport, Conn.: Praeger, 2002.

Klausen, Jytte. *The Islamic Challenge: Politics and Religion in Western Europe.* New York: Oxford University Press, 2005.

Kohlberg, Etan, ed. *Shi'ism.* Burlington, Vt.: Ashgate, 2003.

LeVine, Mark. *Heavy Metal Islam: Rock, Resistance, and the Struggle for the Soul of Islam.* New York: Three Rivers, 2008.

Lings, Martin. *Muhammad: His Life Based on the Earliest Sources.* London: Allen & Unwin, 1983.

———. *A Sufi Saint of the Twentieth Century.* Cambridge, U.K.: Islamic Texts Society, 1993.

———. *What Is Sufism?* 2nd ed. Berkeley: University of California Press, 1999.

Lowney, Chris. *A Vanished World: Medieval Spain's Golden Age of Enlightenment.* New York: Free Press, 2005.

MacLeod, Arlene Elowe. *Accommodating Protest: Working Women, the New Veiling, and Change in Cairo.* New York: Columbia University Press, 1991.

Mawdudi, Abdul A'la. *Towards Understanding Islam.* Chicago: Kazi Publications, 1992.

McAuliffe, Jane Dammen, ed. *The Cambridge Companion to the Qur'an.* Cambridge: Cambridge University Press, 2006.

Menocal, Maria Rosa. *The Ornament of the World: How Muslims, Jews, and Christians Created a Culture of Tolerance in Medieval Spain.* Foreword by Harold Bloom. New York: Little, Brown, 2002.

Mernissi, Fatima. *The Veil and the Male Elite: A Feminist Interpretation of Women's Rights in Islam.* Trans. Mary Jo Lakeland. Cambridge, Mass.: Perseus Books, 1992.

Mills, Paul S., and John R. Presley. *An Introduction to Islamic Finance: Theory and Practice.* New York: St. Martin's Press, 1999.

Momen, Moojan. *An Introduction to Shii Islam: The History and Doctrines of Twelver Shiism.* New Haven, Conn.: Yale University Press, 1985.

Nasr, Sayyed Hossein. *The Garden of Truth: The Vision and Promise of Sufism, Islam's Mystical Tradition.* New York: HarperOne, 2007.

———. *The Heart of Islam: Enduring Values for Humanity.* San Francisco: Harper San Francisco, 2002.

———. *Ideals and Realities of Islam.* New rev. ed. Chicago: Kazi Publications, 2000.

———. *Islam: Religion, History, and Civilization.* San Francisco: Harper San Francisco, 2003.

———. *Traditional Islam in the Modern World.* London: KPI Limited, 1987.

Nielsen, Jorgen. *Muslims in Western Europe.* 3rd ed. Edinburgh: Edinburgh University Press, 2005.

Peters, F. E. *The Children of Abraham.* New ed. Princeton, N.J.: Princeton University Press, 2004.

————. *Muhammad and the Origins of Islam*. Albany: State University of New York Press, 1994.

Peters, Rudolph. *Jihad in Classical and Modern Islam*. Princeton, N.J.: Markus Wiener Publishers, 1996.

Rahman, Fazlur. *Islam*. Chicago: University of Chicago Press, 1979.

————. *Major Themes of the Qur'an*. 2nd ed. Chicago: Bibliotheca Islamica, 1989.

Ramadan, Tariq. *In the Footsteps of the Prophet: Lessons from the Life of Muhammad*. New York: Oxford University Press, 2007.

————. *The Messenger: The Meanings of the Life of Muhammad*. London: Allen Lane, 2007.

————. *To Be a European Muslim*. Leicester, U.K.: Islamic Foundation, 2003.

————. *Western Muslims and the Future of Islam*. New York: Oxford University Press, 2004.

Renard, John. *Responses to 101 Questions on Islam*. New York: Gramercy Books, 2002.

————. *Seven Doors to Islam: Spirituality and the Religious Life of Muslims*. Berkeley: University of California Press, 1996.

————. *Understanding the Islamic Experience*. Mahwah, N.J.: Paulist Press, 2002.

————, ed. *Windows on the House of Islam*. Berkeley: University of California Press, 1998.

Rippin, Andrew, ed. *Blackwell Companion to the Qur'an*. Oxford: Wiley-Blackwell, 2006.

Rippin, Andrew, and Jan Knappert, eds. and trans. *Textual Sources for the Study of Islam*. Chicago: University of Chicago Press, 1990.

Sachedina, Abdulaziz. *The Islamic Roots of Democratic Pluralism*. New York: Oxford University Press, 2001.

————. *The Qur'an on Religious Pluralism*. Washington, D.C.: Georgetown University Press, 1999.

Said, Edward W. *Covering Islam: How the Media and the Experts Determine How We See the Rest of the World*. New York: Pantheon Books, 1981.

Sardar, Ziauddin, and Zafar Abbas Malik. *Introducing Muhammad*. New York: Totem Books, 1994.

Schimmel, Annemarie. *And Muhammad Is His Messenger*. Chapel Hill: University of North Carolina Press, 1985.

————. *Mystical Dimensions of Islam*. Chapel Hill: University of North Carolina Press, 1975.

Sedgwick, Mark J. *Sufism: The Essentials*. Cairo: American University in Cairo Press, 2000.

Sells, Michael. *Approaching the Qur'an*. Ashland, Ore.: White Cloud Press, 1999.

Smith, Jane I. *Islam in America*. New York: Columbia University Press, 1999.

Sonn, Tamara. *Islam: A Brief History of Islam*. 2nd ed. Malden, Mass.: Blackwell, 2010.

Speight, R. Marston. *God Is One: The Way of Islam.* 2nd ed. Cincinnati: Friendship Press, 2001.

Stowasser, Barbara Freyer. *Women in the Qur'an, Traditions, and Interpretations.* New York: Oxford University Press, 1996.

Thurlkill, Mary F. *Chosen Among Women: Mary and Fatima in Medieval Christianity and Shi'ite Islam.* Notre Dame, Ind.: Notre Dame University Press, 2008.

Vogel, Frank E., and Samuel L. Hayes III. *Islamic Law and Finance: Religion, Risk, and Return.* Boston: Kluwer Law International, 1998.

Wadud, Amina. *Qur'an and Woman: Rereading the Sacred Text from a Woman's Perspective.* New York: Oxford University Press, 1999.

Watt, W. Montgomery. *Islam and Christianity Today.* London: Routledge and Kegan Paul, 1983.

———. *Islamic Philosophy and Theology.* Edinburgh, United Kingdom: Edinburgh University Press, 1996.

———. *Muhammad: Prophet and Statesman.* New York: Oxford University Press, 1960.

Wolfe, Michael. *The Hadj: An American's Pilgrimage to Mecca.* New York: Grove Press, 1998.

———, ed. *One Thousand Roads to Mecca: Ten Centuries of Travelers Writing About the Muslim Pilgrimage.* New York: Grove Press, 1999.

INDEX

Abbasid Empire, 44, 51, 183
Abdullah II of Jordan (king), 149
Abdul-Matin, Ibrahim, 130
ABIM. *See* Islamic Youth Movement
ablutions (cleansing), 25
abortion, 173–74
Abraham, xv, 6–7, 12, 78
Abu Bakr, 49, 75, 183
Abu Ghraib, 237
acclamation, 32
activism, 68, 110, 183
al-Adawiyya, Rabia, 61
adhan, 19, 123, 241
Afghan-Soviet War, 42, 135
African American Islam, 57.
    See also Nation of Islam
afterlife, 29–31
Aga Khan, 51–53, 241
Aga Khan Development Network, 53
Aga Khan IV, 52
Agenda, 21, 132
agriculture, 216–17
Ahmad, Salman, 127
Aisha, 105, 115
Akbar (Mughal emperor), 85
AKP, 188
al-Andalus, 84
al-Aqsa, 88, 188
al-Aqsa Martyrs Brigade, 139
Al-Arabiyya, 155
alaykum, 127
Al-Azhar, 178
al-Battani, 218
Albucasis, 216
alcohol, 119–20, 179
al-Dajjal. *See* Great Deceiver

Alexei II (patriarch), 92
Alexius I, 87
al-Farghani, 218
al-Ghazali, 219
Algoritimi, 218
Ali, 43, 49, 241
Ali, Muhammad (boxer), 58
Ali, Muhammad (Egyptian leader), 55
Ali, Salma Hasan, 198
Al-Jazeera, 155
al-Jihad, 143
Allah, 8, 18, 241
Allah, al-Hakim bi-amr, 189
Allahu Akbar, 19–20, 26, 241
al-Lat, 156
almsgiving, 243. *See also zakat*
al-Qaeda, 46, 65, 141
    fundamentalism and, 63
    global *jihad* of, 136
    strategy of, 138
    terrorism by, 186
al-Uzza, 156
al-Zarqali, 218
American Halal Co., 131
American Muslim Mission, 60
ANC, 186
angels, 27–28, 151
aniconism, 15
animals, 118–19, 130
Annan, Kofi, 236
anti-Americanism, 153, 212–13
anti-Semitism, 235, 240
apostasy, 74–75
Aquinas, Thomas, 219
Arabic language, 9–10, 41, 215
Arafat, 23

Arafat, Yasser, 139
arbitration, 116, 165–66
Archbishop of Seville, 85
Aristotle, 219
Arkoun, Mohammed, 69
Armed Islamic Group, 141
Ask the Mufti, 167
As-salam alaykum, 247
Assassins, 141, 143, 241
assimilation, 94, 230
astronomy, 218
Austrian Freedom Party (FPÖ), 234
authoritarianism, 65–66, 71, 211
Averroes, 219
Avicenna, 219
ayatollah, 52, 241. *See also specific individuals*
azwaj, 31

Badawi, Zaki, 149
Badu, Erykah, 124
banking, 199–201
al-Banna, Hasan, 69, 195
Barclays, 201
Battle of Karbala, 54
bayah, 105, 241
beards, 109–10
Becket Fund for Religious Liberty, 149
belly dancing, 121
Benedict XVI (pope), 91, 148
ben Tamin, Dunasch, 215
Bible, 72
    Hebrew, 5
    as legislation, 161
    New Testament, 5, 8, 92, 181
    Old Testament, 5–6, 8
bida, 54, 56, 242
Bilqis, 105
bin Laden, Osama, 65, 70, 138
    Ibn Taymiyya and, 44, 46
    Islamic fundamentalism and, 63
    jihad and, 134, 136
    Judaism and, 83
    terrorism and, 141, 166, 186
    Wahhabi Islam and, 53
biology, 99
birth control, 174
bismillah, 124, 126, 242
Black Muslims, 57–58, 60, 242. *See also*
    Nation of Islam
black nationalism and separatism, 58–59
Blair, Tony, 154, 157, 213
Blakstone, 124
blasphemy, 73, 157
Book of Deeds, 29
Born Tragedy, 126
botany, 216–17

Britain, 154, 165, 229–30
British National Party, 234
The Brotherhood, 125
Brother's Brother Foundation, 198
Broun, Paul, 238
al-Bukhari, Ismail, 13
burial, 128–29
burqa, 106, 233–34, 242
Bush, George W., xv, 154, 213
Byzantine Empire, 27, 138

CAIR. *See* Council on American-Islamic
    Relations
caliphs, 43–44, 49, 182, 242
call to prayer. *See adhan*
canonization, 32
Capital D, 125
capitalism, 193–94
capital punishment, 74, 180
Catholicism, 84, 93, 116
cats, 118
Center for the Study of Islam and
    Democracy (CSID), 224
Ceric, Mustafa, 93, 164
chador, 106, 242
charity, 20, 197. *See also zakat*
chastity, 115
chemistry, 217
Chosen People, 57
Christendom, 84
Christian Right, 139
Christians and Christianity, 4, 7–9, 63, 65, 163
    African Americans and, 57
    in Europe, 232
    Islam and, 76–79, 81, 83–84
    Maronite, 80
    marriage to Muslims, 113
    as "People of the Book," 5, 78, 81
    persecution of, 78–79
    theology of, 159
    Trinity, 19, 34, 77
    vision of heaven, 30. *See also* Bible;
        Catholicism; Jesus; Judeo-Christian
        tradition; New Testament; Old
        Testament
circumambulation, 23–24
circumcision, 110
Citigroup, 201
citizenship, 86, 230
civilizations: clash of, 212–14
    contributions to, 214–15
civil war, 80–81, 192
*The Clash of Civilizations and the Remaking
    of World Order* (Huntington), 212
Clay, Cassius. *See* Ali, Muhammad
cleansing, 25

clergy, 37. *See also caliphs; imam*
Cold War, 135, 193, 212
colonialism, xiv, 65, 79, 90
    conflict and confrontation and, 84
    interpretation of, 187
    martyrdom and, 152
    response to, 184
Columbus, Christopher, 218
Combs, Sean "P. Diddy," 124
"A Common Word Between Us and
    You," 90–92
communication, 155, 202
Communism, 135
community service, 197
Companionships.org, 207
Compilation of Islamic Law, 172
concubines, 175
"Confronting Islamophobia: Education for
    Tolerance and Understanding," 236
congregational prayer. *See juma*
consensus, 75, 159, 190, 244
conservatives, 47, 66, 227
Constitution of Medina, 82, 242
consumerism, 125
contraception, 174
convivencia, 84
Coptic Orthodox Church, 178
Coulter, Ann, 237
Council on American-Islamic Relations
    (CAIR), 224
courting, 111
cremation, 128–29
Crusades, xiv, 79, 84–85, 87–88, 189
CSID. *See* Center for the Study of Islam
    and Democracy

dancing, 121
dar al-Islam, 175, 242
dating, 111
David (king), 77, 188
dawa, 7, 242
Day of Dignity, 199
Day of Judgment, 28, 45, 56
Day of Resurrection, 28
death penalty, 74, 180
declaration of faith *(shahada)*, 18, 20
deen, 122, 125
democracy, 190, 192
Deutsche Bank, 201
dhimmi, 74, 83, 175, 242
din, 242
al-Din, Salah, 85, 89
discrimination, 224, 227, 235, 238–39
    gender and, 97, 100–101
    against Muslims, xv
divisions within Islam, 42–43

divorce, 116–17, 167–68
    gender discrimination in, 97, 100–101
    guidelines for, 117, 169–70
dogma, 19, 77
dogs, 118–19
Dome of the Rock, 88, 189
domestic violence, 114–16
dress and fashion: beards, 109–10
    burqa, 106, 233–34, 242
    garments for *Hajj*, 22
    hijab, 106–7, 233–34, 243
    skullcaps, 109, 234
    veiling, 101, 105–8
dua, 27, 242
Duncan, Rex, 238

East Timor, 81
education, 41–42, 114, 222
    law schools, 47, 160, 243, 245, 247
    women and, 102–3
egalitarianism, 16
Eid al-Adha, 36, 242
Eid al-Fitr, 22, 36, 242
El Fadl, Khaled Abou, 69
Elijah, 35
El-Shabazz, El Hajj Malik. *See* Malcolm X
ensoulment, 173–74
environmentalism, 129–30
    organizations of, 131–32
equity, 159
Erbakan, Necmettin, 69
ethnic diversity, 4, 221, 224
Eurabia, 232
Europe: Christianity in, 232
    imperialism of, 184
    Muslims of, 228–29, 231–32. *See also*
        colonialism
Eve, 124
Everlast, 124
exclusivism, religious, 75
extremism, 73, 145–46, 185
    appearance and, 110
    groups of, 186
    Islamic, 193
    madrasas and, 42
    terrorism and, 138
    U.S. and, 153
    Wahhabi, 55. *See also* terrorism

Fadlallah, Mohammed Hussein, 177
Fahd (king), 190
FAIR. *See* Forum Against Islamophobia
    and Racism
Falwell, Jerry, 79, 238
Family Code, 172
family law, 66, 160, 167–68, 170

Fard, Wallace D., 57–60
Farm Aid, 122
Farrakhan, Louis, 60–61
fashion. *See* dress and fashion
Fast for the Planet, 132
fasting, 21
Fast of Ramadan, 21
Fatima (daughter of Muhammad), 43,
    49, 105, 242
Fatimid Dynasty, 51
fatwa, 38, 141, 144, 164, 209, 243
    by Fiqh Council of North America,
        149
    by Ibn Taymiyya, 45
    role of, 166
    on Rushdie, 156
Feast of Sacrifice, 36
Feast of the Breaking of the Fast
    (*Eid al-Fitr*), 22
Feed the World, 122
female genital mutilation (FGM), 177–78
Ferdinand (king), 83
fez, 109, 243
FGM. *See* female genital mutilation
Fiasco, Lupe, 124–25
finance, 199–201
Fiqh Council of North America, 149
fitnah, 96
Five Pillars of Islam. *See* Pillars of Islam
Fivers. *See* Zaydis
Five Tips for a Good
    Product, 206
folk dancing, 121
folk music, 123
foreign policy, 213
    of U.S., 153–54
Forum Against Islamophobia and
    Racism (FAIR), 239
Four Rightly Guarded Caliphs, 44. *See*
    also caliphs
FPÖ. *See* Austrian Freedom
    Party
Francis of Assisi, 85
freedom, religious, 91, 188
Freedom Party, 234
free will, 46
The Fugees, 124
Fulani, 62
fundamentalism, 47–48, 55, 64
    Islamic, 63
    rise of, 80
funeral rites, 128–29

Gabriel (angel), 28
galabeya, 106, 243

Gamaa Islamiyya, 80
Garden of Paradise, 29
gender, 95
    afterlife and, 31
    biology and, 99
    discrimination, 97, 100–101
    equality of, 172
    inequalities, 99, 101, 103
    marriage and, 169
    Pillars of Islam and, 97. *See*
        also women
Genghis Khan, 45
Ghoneem, Ibrehiem, 127
Gingrich, Newt, 238
globalization, 66, 90, 134–35
    of communication, 155, 202
Goldman Sachs, 201
Goldstein, Baruch, 142
Gomaa, Sheikh Ali, 75, 177–78
Gospels, xiv, 8, 10
government: religion
    and, 160–61
    unelected, 192
Graham, Franklin, 79
Grand Mosque, 22–24
Grand Mufti, 38
Great Deceiver (al-Dajjal), 28–29
"greater jihad," 61
green faith, 130–31
Green Mosque Project, 132
greetings, 127–28
G-Town, 127
Gulf War, 192–93, 212
Gymnastiar, Abdullah, 203,
    205–6

hadith, 12–13, 98, 104, 129, 243
    on animals, 118
    collections of, 116
    conflict of, 14
    on suicide, 142
    ummah and, 17
    on women, 96
Hagar, 6–7, 78
Hagee, John, 79
hajj, 22, 24, 36, 39, 243
halal, 111, 126, 243
Haleem, M. Abdel, 98
Hamas, 83, 136, 139, 142, 186,
    196
Hanafi law school, 243
Hanbali law school, 243
handshakes, 118
haram, 126, 200, 243
Haram al-Sharif, 89

Hassan, 105
hate crimes, 235
headscarf. *See hijab*
healthcare clinics, 198
heaven, 29–30
Hebrew Bible, 5
hell, 29–30
Henzell-Thomas, Jeremy, 239–40
heresies, 211
Hidden Imam, 52, 141, 243
hijab, 106–7, 233–34, 243
hijacking, 140
hijra, 243
Hill, Lauren, 124
Hinn, Benny, 238
hip-hop, 123–24, 126–27
  themes of, 125. See also
  specific artists
Hizbollah, 136, 143, 186, 196
holidays, 36–37
Holy Sepulchre Church, 189
holy wars, 77, 87, 91, 134–35. *See also jihad*
homosexuality, 173
honor killings, 176–77
horticulture, 216–17
Hossein, Sayyid, 69
hostage taking, 140
houris, 30–31, 143
House of Wisdom, 219
HSBC, 201
hudud, 179–80, 243
Humanitarian Day, 199
human rights, 90, 177, 179
Huntington, Samuel, 212–13
Hussein (grandson of Muhammad), 37,
  49–50, 105, 152, 244
Hussein, Saddam, 147, 192
al-Husseini, Karim, 52

Ibn al-Hajjaj, 13
Ibn al-Khattab, Umar, 105
Ibn al-Mathrun, 215
Ibn Awwam, 216
Ibn Hayyan, Jabir, 217
Ibn Khuldun, 218
Ibn Rushd, 219
Ibn Saud, Abdulaziz, 55
Ibn Saud, Muhammad, 54
Ibn Sina, 216, 219
Ibn Taymiyya, 44–45
Ibrahim, Anwar, 69
Ice Cube, 124
ICNA. *See* Islamic Circle of North
  America
identity, 164, 193, 230–31

Islamic, 16–17, 225–26
  race and, 221
idolatry, 14–15, 32, 53–54
IFEES. *See* Islamic Foundation for
  Ecology and Environmental
  Services
ijarah, 202, 244
ijma, 159, 190, 244
ijtihad, 38, 48, 160, 170, 190, 244
illiteracy, 101
ILM Foundation, 199
images, 14–15
imam, 51, 71, 208, 244
  birthday celebrations of, 37
  Hidden Imam, 52, 141, 243
  in worship service, 36. *See also specific
  individuals*
IMAN. *See* Inner-City Muslim Action
  Network
IMC. *See* International Medical Corps
immigrants, 209, 228–29, 233
imperialism, European, 184
Industrial Revolution, 214
inequality, 98, 101, 103
infanticide, 97
inheritance, 167–68, 170
Inner-City Muslim Action Network
  (IMAN), 198
Inquisition, 84–85
Institute for Global Engagement, 94
integration, 94, 230
intercession, 32
interfaith: dialogue, 90
  relations, 231
International Medical Corps (IMC), 199
International Renewable Energy Agency
  (IRENA), 132
Internet, 207–9
intifada, 142, 244
intolerance, religious, 73
invocation of peace *(salam)*, 27
IRA, 186
Iran-Iraq War, 212
Iraq, 154
IRENA. *See* International Renewable
  Energy Agency
Isabella (queen), 83
Islam (glossary entry), 244
Islam, Yusuf (Cat Stevens), 122
Islamic centers, 40
Islamic Circle of North America (ICNA),
  224
Islamic Foundation for Ecology and
  Environmental Services (IFEES), 131
IslamiCity.com, 208

Islamic Jihad, 44, 80, 146
Islamic Jihad Palestine, 136
Islamic law, 158–59, 182, 200
    on apostasy, 74
    Compilation of, 172
    diversity of opinions and, 46
    family and, 167–68
    schools of, 160
    support for, 162
    terrorism and, 137, 140
    views of, 161
    women and, 98. *See also* Shariah
Islamic Relief USA, 199
Islamic Resistance Movement, 136, 142
Islamic revolution, 50
Islamic Society of North America
    (ISNA), 224
Islamic state, 181, 185
Islamic Youth Movement (ABIM), 69
Islamism, 17, 63–64, 185
Islamization programs, 86
IslamOnline.net, 208
Islamophobia, xv, 3, 234
    fueling of, 237–38
    increase of, 162, 227, 232
    9/11 and, 235–37, 240
    result of, 239
Islamophobia: A Challenge for Us All, 235
Ismail, 6–7
Ismailis (Seveners), 51, 244
ISNA. *See* Islamic Society of North
    America
isnad, 14
Israel, 79
    creation of, 223
    Palestine and, 80
    U.S. and, 155
Israfil (angel), 28
istihsan, 159
Ithna Ashari (Twelvers), 38, 51–52, 244

Jafari law school, 47, 244
Jamaat-i-Islami, 68
Jean, Wyclef, 124
Jerusalem, 82, 87, 188–90
Jesus, 11, 33, 152
    in Quran, 34
    Second Coming of, 28–29
Jews and Judaism, 7–9, 65, 163
    anti-Semitism, 235, 240
    Islam and, 19, 76, 81, 83
    organizations of, 227
    as "People of the Book," 5, 78, 81. *See
        also* Israel;
        Judeo-Christian tradition

jihad, 13, 91, 158, 244
    global, 134–36
    "greater," 61
    madrasas, 42
    martyrdom and, 152–53
    meanings of, 134
    in Quran, 133
jizya, 74, 244
Jobbik, 234
John of Damascus, 84
John Paul II (pope), 148
John the Baptist, 5, 12
Joseph, 12
Joshua, 77
Judaism. *See* Jews and Judaism
Judeo-Christian tradition, xiii, xvi, 225
juma, 35, 245
Junoon, 127
jurisprudence, 46. *See also*
    Islamic law; law
justice, social, 194, 196–97

Kaaba, 7, 20, 22–24, 54, 245
kafir, 126, 245
al-Kamil, al-Malik, 85
Karzai, Hamid, 171
keffiyah, 109, 245
Khadija (wife of Muhammad), 15, 104,
    245
Khaled, Amr, 203–5
kharaja, 44
Kharijites, 43–44, 75, 141, 146,
    245
Khatami, Mohammad, 69
Khomeini, Ruhollah (Ayatollah), 50, 63,
    135, 156
khums, 21
khutba, 36, 207, 245
al-Khwarizmi, Muhammad Ibn Musa,
    217–18, 220
Koran. *See* Quran
kufr, 163
Kulthum, Umm, 123
Kumasi, 125
kutubiya, 215
Kutubya Mosque, 215

language, 187
    Arabic, 9–10, 41, 215
    origins of, 218–20
Laskar Jihad, 80
Last Day. *See* Day of Judgment
law: Bible and, 161
    family, 66, 160, 167–68, 170
    religious, 77

schools, 47
ulama and, 158
Yasa code of, 45. *See also* Islamic law
Lebanese Civil War, 192
lesser pilgrimages. *See umrah*
LeVine, Mark, 126
Lewis, Bernard, 232
Life for Relief and Development, 198
Limbaugh, Rush, 237
literacy, 104
Little, Malcolm. *See* Malcolm X
"living Quran," 11–13. *See also*
    Muhammad
Lloyds TSB, 201
"Love of God, Love of Neighbor," 93
"Loving God and Neighbor Together,"
    93
Lugo, Luis, 224
Lutheran World Federation, 92

Madjid, Nurcholish, 75
madrasa, 40–42
magic, 62
Mahdi, 28, 62, 245
Malcolm X, 58
Maliki law school, 245
Mami, Cheb, 123
mamluk, 175, 245
Management by Conscience, 205
Manat, 156
Maronite Christians, 80
marriage, 97, 167–68
    arranged, 111
    domestic violence and,
        114–16
    gender roles and, 169
    monogamy, 101, 112–13
    polygamy, 100–101, 112–13, 169, 206
    rape in, 171
    sex in, 173. *See also* divorce
Martel, Charles, 84
martyrdom, 143, 151–53
Marxism, 64
Mary, Mother of Jesus, 33–34, 78
masjid, 245
maslaha, 159, 190, 245
materialism, 61, 125
mathematics, 217–18
matn, 14
Mawlawi/Mevlevi order,
    121
Mecca, 8, 245
    pilgrimage to, 22–23
    significance of, 24–25
Mecca2Medina, 124

mechanization, 67
medicine, 216
Medina, 82, 246
MEPA. *See* Meteorology and
    Environmental Protection
    Administration
messengers, 12
Meteorology and Environmental
    Protection Administration (MEPA),
    132
Michael (angel), 28
Middle East, 7
mihrab, 35, 38, 246
millet system, 86–87, 246
Million Man March, 60
minaret, 233–34, 246
minbar, 35, 38, 246
Minhaj-ul-Quran
    International, 204
miracles, 34
Miss Undastood, 125
Mobile Food Pantry, 199
modernity and modernization, 47, 67,
    184, 187, 214
modesty, 96, 106
Mogahed, Dalia, 197
Mongols, 45
monogamy, 101, 112–13
monotheism, 5, 7, 18, 54, 76,
    78, 114
moral conduct, 125
Morgan Stanley, 201
Moriscos, 222–23
mortgages, 201–2
Mos Def, 124
Moses, 5–6, 8, 19, 72
Mosque of the Patriarch, 142
mosques, 38–40, 246
Mount of Mercy, 23
MPAC. *See* Muslim Public
    Affairs Council
M-Team, 124–25
Muawiyyah, 75, 85
mudaraba, 246
muezzin, 246
mufti, 38, 208, 210, 246
    qualifications of, 167
    women as, 96
Mughal Empire, 183
Muhamaddiyya, 69
Muhammad (Prophet), 4, 8, 11, 29, 49,
    72, 82, 246
    birthplace of, 24
    images of, 14–15
    life of, 12–14

Muhammad (Prophet) (*continued*)
  as "living Quran," 11–13
  as "seal of the prophets," 9, 19, 83
  wives of, 15
Muhammad, Elijah, 57–59
Muhammad, Warith Deen. *See* Fard,
    Wallace D.
mujahid, 246
mujahidin, 134–35
mujtahid, 38, 52, 167, 246
multiculturalism, 240
Munkar (angel), 151
al-Muntazar, Muhammad, 52
murahaba, 201
musharakah, 201, 246
music, 122–23. *See also specific genres*
Muslim (glossary entry), 246.
Muslim Brotherhood, 68, 69, 195
MuslimFriends.com, 207
"A Muslim Green Guide," 131
Muslim Public Affairs Council (MPAC),
    224
Muslim Serve, 197–98
Muslim Student Association, 199
muwahhidun, 246
Myrick, Sue, 238
mysticism, 38, 64

Nakir (angel), 151
Napoleonic Penal Code, 176
National Council of
    Churches, 90
nationalism, 17
  black, 58–59
  in Palestine, 139
Nation of Gods and Earths, 124
Nation of Islam (NOI), 57–58, 124, 246
Native Deen, 122
neocolonialism, xiv
neo-traditionalists, 211
New Testament, 5, 8, 92, 181
Night Journey, 188–89
Night of Power, 22
9/11, xiii, xv, 110, 193, 212–13
  condemnation of, 144, 148–50, 204
  fundamentalism and, 63
  influence of, 224–25
  Islamophobia and, 235–37,
    240
  madrasas and, 41–42
  suicide bombing of, 142
niqab, 233–34, 247
Nizari Ismaili, 51, 52, 143, 247. *See also*
    Assassins
Noah, 12

Noble Sanctuary, 89
NOI. *See* Nation of Islam
nushuz, 115
Nyang, Sulayman, 69

Obama, Barack, xv, 41, 197, 223
"occultation," 52
Old Testament, 5–6, 8
Operation Cast Lead, 187
Organization of the Islamic Conference,
    149
Original Sin, 35
orphans, 112–13
orthodoxy, 159
orthopraxy, 159
Osman, Fathi, 69
Ottoman Empire, 17, 86, 90, 183
Outlandish, 127

paganism, 53
Pakistan: Christianity in, 80
  movements in, 68
  U.S. and, 63
  women in, 103
Palestine: conflict in, 80–81, 142–43
  invasion of, 189
  Islamic Jihad, 136
  nationalism in, 139
  occupation of, 89
  Zionism and, 83
Palladius, 217
pan-Africanism, 59
Park51, 236–38
Party of Ali, 49
patriarchy, 98–99, 101–2, 117, 170, 176
pax vobiscum, 77
PBUH ("peace be upon him"), 128
peace greetings, 20, 77
Pentagon, 63, 142, 193, 235
People of the Book, 83, 113, 247
  Christians and Jews as, 5, 78, 81. *See
    also dhimmi*
People's Party, 234
pesantrens, 41, 206
Peters, Francis E., 88
pets, 118–19
Pew Forum on Religion & Public Life,
    224
philosophy, 219
pilgrimage. *See hajj*
Pillars of Islam, 58–59, 195
  gender and, 97
  listed, 18–22
  Sixth, 133
pir, 38, 247

Plato, 219
PLO, 139
pluralism, xvi, 86, 94
    debate on, 73–74
    reform and, 87
    Western, 228
PNA, 139
Poetic Pilgrimage, 124
political Islam, 63–64
politics, 86, 222
    religion and, 182–85
polygamy (polygyny), 100–101, 112–13,
        169, 206
polytheism, 8, 34, 56
Poole, Elijah. *See* Muhammad, Elijah
pop music, 122
pork, 119–20
poverty, 194–95
practice, 77
prayer, 20
    adhan, 19, 123, 241
    functions of, 25
    juma, 35, 245
    movements of, 26
predestination, 46
principalities, 192
procreation, 173
Project Downtown, 199
property rights, 170
prophets, 4
    seal of, 9, 19, 83. See also specific
        prophets
proportionality, 145
prostration, 26–27, 35
Public Enemy, 124
punishment, 28, 178–79
purgatory, 151
purification, 25. *See also zakat*

qadi, 179, 182, 247
Qadri, Muhammad, 150, 167, 204–5
al-Qaradawi, Sheikh Yusuf, 144–45
Qassem Brigade, 142
qibla, 35, 188, 247
qiyas, 159, 247
Queen Latifah, 124
Queen of Sheba, 105
Quran, 5–6, 6, 8, 14, 16, 72, 92, 247
    afterlife in, 29–31
    Jesus in, 34
    jihad in, 133
    "living Quran," 11–13
    loyalty to, 191
    meaning of, 9
    opening discourse of, 26

recitation of, 10–11
    recordings of, 123
    women in, 96
Quran and Woman (Wadud), 69
Quraysh, 24, 82
Qutb, Sayyid, 196

race, 57–58
    identity and, 221
racism, 235, 240
radicalism, xv, 63, 146, 153, 232
Rahman, Sheikh Omar Abdel, 64
rai music, 123
Rais, Amien, 69
raka, 247
Ramadan, 21–22, 39, 247
Ramadan, Tariq, 69
al-Razi, Mohammad Ibn Zakariya,
        216–17
reciprocity, 93
reform, 68–69, 75
    Islamic, 70–71
    obstacles to, 210–11
    opponents of, 211
    pluralism and, 87
religion: conflict of, 80–81
    exclusivism of, 75
    freedom of, 91, 188
    government and, 160–61
    intolerance and, 73
    law and, 77
    politics and, 182–85
    tolerance and, 73–74, 94, 226, 228. *See
        also specific religions*
religious scholars. *See ulama*
repentance, 32–33
Resource Recycle, 132
resurrection, 28–29
revelations, 76
revivalism, 62, 185
riba, 200, 247
Richard the Lion-Hearted, 77, 89
rights: human, 90, 177, 179
    property, 170
    of women, 101–2, 117, 160–61, 168, 172
Robertson, Pat, 79, 237–38
rock music, 122
Roman Catholicism, 93
Rosh Hashanah, 36
Run-DMC, 124
Rushdie, Salman, 155–57

SAAS. *See Salah Allah alayi wa-salam*
Sabbath, 35. *See also* holidays
Sachedina, Abdulaziz, 69

Sadat, Anwar, 44
al-Sadiq, Jafar, 51
Safavid Empire, 183
Saffron Road, 131
Sagol 59, 127
sainthood, 31–32
Saladin. *See* al-Din, Salah
salaf, 55
Salafi Islam, 55–56
Salah al-Din, 189
Salah Allah alayi wa-salam (SAAS), 128
salam, 27, 247
salam alaykum, 77
salat, 19, 247. *See also* prayer
Salat al-Janazah, 129
Sanusi, 62
Sarah, 6, 78
Sasanian Empire, 138
Satan, 45, 76, 119
The Satanic Verses (Rushdie), 155–57
Saudi Arabia, 55, 182. *See also* Mecca
     Medina
Savory, Roger, 89
sayyid, 109, 247
sciences, social, 218–19
seclusion, 95
secularism, 94, 147, 164, 187–88, 232
segregation, 95–96, 101. *See also* gender
Seiple, Chris, 94
Seljuq Dynasty, 141
separation of church and
     state, 180–81
September 11, 2001. *See* 9/11
sermon. *See khutba*
Seveners. *See* Ismailis
Seven Tips for Success, 206
sexuality, 173
Shaffi law school, 247
Shah, Hasan Ali, 52
shahada, 18, 20, 126, 151, 247
shahid (witness), 151, 248
Shah of Iran, 50
Shah of Persia, 27
Shakur, Tupac, 124
shalom aleichem, 77
Shariah, 45, 119, 158, 191, 248
     compliant products, 200
     implementation of, 165
     in West, 162–63
al-Sheikh, Sheikh Abdulaziz, 144, 149
Shifa Clinic, 198
Shii Family Law, 171
Shii Islam, 4, 37, 43–45, 56, 118, 248
     differences from Sunni, 48–50
     divisions of, 51–52

history of, 50
     law schools of, 47
     martyrdom and, 152
shirk, 32, 56, 248
shura, 190, 248
Sikhs, 78, 109
sin, 32–33
SingleMuslim.com, 207
Six Day War, 189
Sixth Pillar of Islam, 133. *See also jihad*
skullcaps, 109, 234
slavery, 175–76
social justice, 194, 196–97
social networking, 207
social sciences, 218–19
socioeconomics, 222
soft terrorism, 232
Soldiers of Allah, 126
Solomon, 8, 76
Spain, 84
Standard Chartered, 201
stem cell research, 174–75
Stevens, Cat. *See* Islam, Yusuf
Sting, 123
stoning, 179
al-Subail, Sheikh Muhammad bin
     Abdullah, 145
Sudan, 80–81
suf, 61
Sufism, 4, 38, 61–62, 64
     chanting, 21
     dancing, 121
     glossary entry, 248
     music and, 123
     sainthood and, 32
suicide bombers, 143, 149–50
     debate over, 144
     hadith on, 142
Sunnah, 11, 61, 71, 110
     followers of, 49
     glossary entry, 248
     Wahhabi and, 54
Sunni Islam, 4, 13, 38, 43–45, 141
     differences from Shii, 48–50
     glossary entry, 248
     Islamic law and, 159
     law schools of, 47
     martyrdom and, 152
     orthodox, 59
superstition, 62
Supreme Council of Islamic Research,
     178
surah, 9, 248
Swiss Re, 201
"sword verses," 138

tafsir, 41
takfir, 45, 248
Taliban, 161, 178, 180
  beards and, 109–10
  idolatry and, 15, 54
  music and, 122–23
  rise of, 42
  women and, 103
Tamil Tigers, 139
T'ang Dynasty, 27
Tantawi, Sheikh Muhammad Sayyid,
  144–45
taqlid, 53, 248
Tauran, Jean-Louis, 93
tawbah, 33
tawhid, 18, 54, 121, 248
taxes, 21, 74
tazir, 179, 248
technology, 136, 190
televangelism, 202–3, 205
Temple Mount of the Noble Sanctuary,
  188
Temple of Solomon, 89
"10 Terms Not to Use with Muslims"
  (Seiple), 94
terrorism, xiii, 56, 63–64, 80
  bin Laden and, 141, 166, 186
  cause of, 137
  condemnation of, 167, 205
  denouncement of, 148
  fears of, 224, 232
  justifying, 140
  madrasas and, 42
  soft, 232. *See also* 9/11; suicide
    bombers; *specific organizations*
theocracy, 162
theology, 77, 159
tolerance, religious, 73–74, 94, 226, 228
Torah, xiv, 5, 8, 10, 72, 92
Total Planning and Development
  Doctrine (TPDD), 132
tradition. *See hadith*
traditionalism, 47
tribalism, 195
trigonometry, 218
Trinity, 34
turban, 109, 234, 248
Turkey, 171–72
  secularism in, 188
  women leaders in, 185–86
Twelvers, 38. *See also* Ithna Ashari
Two Great Commandments, 92

UBS, 201
ulama, 37, 171, 182, 210

  authority of, 41
  birth control and, 174
  glossary entry, 248
  as interpreters of Islam, 70
  law and, 158
  murders of, 141
Umayyad Empire, 44, 46, 183
UMMA Clinic. *See* University Muslim
  Medical Association Community
  Clinic
ummah, 49, 73, 182, 209
  beliefs about, 16–17
  Constitution of Medina and, 82
  glossary entry, 248
  interconnectedness of, 135
  tribalism and, 195
umrah, 22, 40, 248
UNICEF, 178
Unitarians, 54, 246
United Nations Human Development
  Report, 176
United States (U.S.), 163–65
  anti-Americanism, 153,
    212–13
  foreign policy of, 153–54
  Israel and, 155
  Muslims in, 221–22, 224–26
  Pakistan and, 63
  views of, 154, 213
United States Conference of Catholic
  Bishops, 90
United We Serve: Muslim Americans
  Answer the Call, 197
University Muslim Medical Association
  Community Clinic (UMMA Clinic),
  198
Urban II (pope), 87–88
U.S. *See* United States
usury, 200

Vatican, 93
veiling, 101, 105
  criticisms of, 106–8
  support for, 107
violence, xiii, 145–46
  domestic, 114–16
  opposition to, 127. *See also* extremism;
    suicide bombers; terrorism
Virgin Mary. *See* Mary, Mother of Jesus
Vision 2020, 132
voting, 103

Wa-alaykum-as-salam, 127
Wadud, Amina, 69
al-Wahhab, Muhammad Ibn Abd, 53

Wahhabi, 53–55, 139, 249
Wahid, Abdurrahman, 69
wali, 31–32, 249
war, 192
    civil, 80–81, 192
    holy, 77, 87, 91, 134–35
    on terror, 139. *See also specific wars*
wealth, 196
weddings, 10, 121
West, xv
    dependence on, 194
    hypocrisy of, 155
    pluralism of, 228
    Shariah in, 162–63
    values of, 190
Westernization, 66
Whirling Dervishes, 121. *See also* Sufism
White House Advisory Council on
        Faith-Based and Neighborhood
        Partnerships, 197
Wilder, Geert, 234
Williams, Rowan, 165
WIN. *See* Wisdom in Nature
Wisdom in Nature (WIN), 132
witnessing, 26–27
women: adultery and, 180
    clothing of, 105–6, 233
    education of, 102–3
    FGM and, 177–78
    honor killings and, 176–77
    as leaders, 185–86
    literacy of, 104
    modern, 108
    in Quran, 96
    rights of, 101–2, 117, 160–61, 168, 172
    roles of, 102
    segregation of, 95–96, 103, 108
    status of, 97–99, 106, 168
    as witnesses, 99–100
Women's Learning Partnership, 208
World Council of Churches, 90
World Trade Center, 135, 139, 142, 193
World War II, 223, 228
worldwide Muslim community. *See
    ummah*

xenophobia, 235

Yahweh, 18
Yasa code of laws, 45
Yasin, Sheikh Ahmad, 144
Yazid, 49, 50, 152
Yom Kippur, 36
Yusuf, Sami, 127

zakat, 195–96, 249
    collection and distribution of, 39
    as Pillar of Islam, 20–21
Zaman International, 199
Zamzam, 23, 249
al-Zawahiri, Ayman, 65
Zayd *(imam)*, 51
Zaydis (Fivers), 51, 249
Zelenik, Lou Ann, 238
Zionism, 83, 227. *See also* Israel
Zoroastrianism, 7–8